Hebrews

Looking Unto Jesus

by

W. Max Alderman

Printed

November 2007

Copyright ©

For additional copies of this book or

other titles by Dr. Max Alderman, write:

(In United States)

"Strengthen the Things Which Remain"

Ministries

Evangelist W. Max Alderman

406 Myrtle Crossing Lane

Statesboro, Georgia, 30458

912-601-2137

Email Philipministry@gmail.com

(In Canada)

Bethel Baptist Church,

4212 Campbell St. N.,

London, Ont. N6P 1A6

1-866-295-4143 (Toll Free) • 519-652-2619 (voice)
info@bethelbaptist.ca (e-mail)

Printed in Canada by

Bethel Baptist Print Ministry

Table of Contents

    Introduction..4

1. The Doctrine of God 6
2. His Superiority Should Inspire Us 16
3. His Superiority Should Warn Us 28
4. A Lesson on Angels Should Challenge Us 42
5. Who We Are Because of Who He Is 57
6. Christ the Partaker..75
7. Whom Should We Consider 89
8. Do Not Be Hindered by Unbelief 104
9. Rest 118
10. Cure for Unbelief..133
11. A Further Look at the Great High Priest..................147
12. The Order of Melchisedec 161
13. When Truth is Neglected 175
14. Let Us Go On 188
15. The Rain, the Seed, and the Anchor 204
16. Let Melchisedec Show You Jesus............................223
17. Good Math 239
18. The Earthly, the Eternal, and the Enduring Priesthood (Part One) 253
19. The Earthly, the Eternal, and the Enduring Priesthood (Part Two)..266
20. No Pleasure 275
21. Let Us Draw Near With a True Heart.......................284
22. Faith's Hall of Fame 293
23. Looking Unto Jesus..305

24. The Two Mountains..316
25. A Final Challenge To Holy Living 328

Chapter One

THE DOCTRINE OF GOD

Text: Hebrews 1:1-4

1 God, who at sundry times and in divers manners spake in time past unto the fathers by the prophets,
2 Hath in these last days spoken unto us by his Son, whom he hath appointed heir of all things, by whom also he made the worlds;
3 Who being the brightness of his glory, and the express image of his person, and upholding all things by the word of his power, when he had by himself purged our sins, sat down on the right hand of the Majesty on high;
4 Being made so much better than the angels, as he hath by inheritance obtained a more excellent name than they.

I. THE WAY GOD COMMUNICATES. (1:1-2a)

Since the days when Abraham had become the friend of

God, God has been speaking to the chosen race. It was the grace and the kindness of God that let Him communicate to His chosen people. It was a good way in which He spoke, but the better way was reserved for His Son. It was good that He met as a Theophany to reveal Himself to mankind and also that He spoke through His prophets. The prophets were His instruments. But it was a better way when He spoke by His Son. As you study Hebrews, you will find that it is a book of better things. In this study we will consider the way that God revealed Himself. We will begin this study as we consider the way He spoke prophetically.

A. In the Past He Spoke Prophetically. (1:1)

The designation "prophet" is often used to describe one who foretells the future, but not always. W.E. Vine says, "Prophecy is not necessarily, nor even primarily, fore-telling. It is the declaration of that which cannot be known by natural means, Matthew 26:68, it is the forth-telling of the will of God, whether with reference to the past, the present, or the future" (Expository Dictionary, p. 221).

When we refer to the writings of the prophets as found in the canon of Scripture, we refer to them as either the Major Prophets or the Minor Prophets. This does not at all measure the degree to which their writings were inspired; it refers instead to the volume of their writings. Whether it was Isaiah or Jonah, their writings carry the signature of inspiration. Their writings were a means whereby God spake *"in times past unto the fathers."* "By *the prophets"* was the means that God spoke.

The first verse of Hebrews begins with the subject of inspiration. Every word that constitutes the Bible is inspired. We do not have a partially inspired Bible. When considering the Old Testament, it is not inferior in its inspiration. It is only lacking what proved to be a better way, again not in reference to quality, but to convenience. To illustrate this using something that we may all relate to, I will consider the writing of a letter from my wife versus speaking to her face-to-face. The quality of the written letter is not to be questioned. When I was in the military, my wife would write me and thrill me as she did. Yet, as thrilling as that may have been, it was not nearly as thrilling as sitting in her presence. Could I not say that it was more convenient to be physically with her instead of just hearing from her? In the Old Testament, the bridge of truth was connected by the prophets. The formula read something like this: God → the prophets → the fathers.

Before we consider the more convenient way or better way of God revealing Himself, may we first consider how we may be inspired to go on unto perfection by having complete confidence in knowing that the entire Bible beginning with the Old Testament Prophecy is given to us by God. The Bible in its entirety is to be received. Just recently I heard that some churches and their pastors will not allow any study or preaching to take place borrowing from the Old Testament. Yet it is my conviction that one cannot properly mature unless he builds upon the entire foundation of Truth.

B. In the Present, He Speaks Personally. (1:2a)

"Hath in these last days spoken unto us by his Son." It is not so much that Jesus brought a message from the Father; He *is* a message from the Father. God previously spoke to Moses in the burning bush (Exodus 3), to Elijah in a still, small voice (I Kings 19), to Isaiah in a heavenly vision (Isaiah 6), to Hosea in his family crisis (Hosea 1:2), and to Amos in a basket of fruit (Amos 8:1). He now speaks through His Son.

The vivid line of demarcation that sets off the first days from the last days is the age of Christ. *These last days* refer to the age of the Messiah; it is a rather long period, but it is still referred to as the last days. We may refer to these days as being the present days. We are presently living in the last days having God speak to us as God the Son through His Word, the Bible. Can you recognize the agreement in such a statement? Can you not see God the Father revealing Himself through His Word? The first epistle of John so wonderfully conveys what is meant by the Son revealing the Father. *"That which was from the beginning, which we have heard, which we have seen with our eyes, which we have looked upon, and our hands have handled, of the Word of Life; (For the life was manifested, and we have seen it, and bear witness, and shew unto you that eternal life, which was with the Father, and was manifested unto us;)"* (1 John 1:1- 2).

What an honor to have God come to this sin-cursed world and speak. God sent Himself. He now, Himself, as

God the Son speaks to men. The prophetical revelations of old time were incomplete or perhaps better said, a shadow of the things to come. When Christ came, the darkness was lifted and He came as the brightness of His glory (v. 3). Brightness is *apaugasma,* which "denotes the radiance shining forth from the source of light" meaning that, "Jesus is the beam of God's glory; we have never seen the sun, only the rays of its light as it comes to us. Even so, we have never seen the Father, but we have seen Him through the 'rays' of the Son" (Guzik).

The Scriptures refer to Christ as *"being the brightness of His glory."* The word *being* is a very small or tiny Greek word but its importance is infinitely greater. The word implies absolute and timeless existence. The word *being* carries the similar significance of the "I AM" title of Jesus. His glorious effulgence is not connected to a switch to be turned off and on at will. It is the glory of God that has neither beginning nor ending.

How might one describe the glory of God? Books have been written wonderfully, but also in a vain attempt to fully describe His glory. Even the great Oxford dictionary finds it a rather difficult undertaking to fully give the meaning of glory. Here are some of the words and phrases used to describe His glory from which we get our word doxology. It is "exalted renown; honorable fame; resplendence; radiance; majesty; beauty; bliss; magnificence; light; splendor; aureole; exaltation. All these, and more, are necessary to convey to us some little idea of that which is inscrutable. Glory is the out-shining of an intrinsic excellence" (Flanigan).

His glory should render to us a radiant challenge to look unto Jesus while going on unto perfection. Later in Hebrews chapter 12, we are told to look unto Jesus; to consider Him; to look diligently unto Him. There is no greater challenge to go on unto perfection than by keeping our eyes fixed on Jesus as we behold His glory.

II. THE WAY GOD CREATES. (1:2b-3a)

A. He is the Maker in Creation. (1:2b)

Let there be no mistake in one's thinking; the worlds did not just come into existence on their own. Evolution is a lie of Satan. Why such a lie, one might ask? Any method that Satan can employ to keep men from coming to Christ, he will use. It should be obvious that a person cannot go on unto perfection if that person's sins have not been purged (v. 3). Also, men will not come to Christ if they fail to recognize or to acknowledge His awesome power.

The Hebrews had no problem accepting Christ as the Creator; the Greeks did. Paul, when preaching to the Greeks, had to first establish God as the Creator before he could present Christ as the Saviour. Our text describes Christ as not only being *"the express image of his person"* but also as *"upholding all things by the word of his power"* (v. 3). In John 1:1-3, the Scriptures read, *"In the beginning was the Word, and the Word was with God, and the Word was God. The same was in the beginning with God. All things were made by him; and without him was not any thing made that was made."*

The same Word that created everything that is, also sustains His creation. For creation to be sustained it also needs to *be*. It was He *"whom he had appointed heir of all things, by whom also he made the worlds;"* Noticing the word *heir* in the verse, we are reminded of the prodigal or younger son in Luke chapter 15. The younger son said to his father, *"Father, give me the portion of goods that falleth to me. And he divided unto them his living"* (Luke 15:12). The father took the portion that belonged to the younger son and gave it to him in advance of his own death. The word *heir* (kleronomos) as used in our text has its root meaning in the word "lot." The common meaning of the word *lot* meant lots were drawn. The way the land was divided was dependent upon the number of descendants. If there were only one child then he would inherit it all. The uniqueness of the only begotten Son of God is that He is the heir of His own creation. Another consideration is that He did not need to wait for the death of His Father. Though the Father did not and cannot die, His Son, without His death, is the benefactor of all creation. God the Father has turned over the creation to His Son.

Satan, as a liar, discounts and refuses to acknowledge that the creation is under the domain of the Lord. Satan is allowed to reign as a fallen monarch, but his term is limited. In this state he maliciously blinds the minds of men, not just those who are simple minded, but even those who are intellectually endowed. He is able to pervert their minds by his subtle suggestions. Even our little children are being taught by the teachers of Satan, teachers who have been programmed to re-teach the humanistic doctrines that they were once taught. The minds of good men have been retarded by his malicious inventions. The doctrine of evolution is such a means whereby Satan has encroached upon the minds of others. To say that Christ is not the Creator and the Heir of His own creation means that another explanation to our existence must be invented.

Evolution, though commonly taught, makes absolutely no sense. Scientifically the teaching is flawed and cannot be supported by the use of the scientific method. There is no reliability found in the evolution model. No aspect of it can be observed to be happening. The evolutionary event cannot be predicted nor grafted on a chart, yet professors who have been blinded stand as stones of granite in their classrooms teaching that they really believe it to be so. Satan has cunningly invaded their minds. What a tragedy.

B. He is the Manager in Creation. (1:3)

Verse three tells us that the creation is upheld by the *"word of his power."* This statement is very profound. Paul's letter to the Colossians tells us, *"For by him were all things created, that are in heaven, and that are in earth, visible and invisible, whether they be thrones, or dominions, or principalities, or powers: all things were created by him, and for him: And he is before all things, and by him all things consist"* (Colossians 1:16-17).

Christ, the Creator, manages His creation. He sustains His creation by His order and His organizational power. Every microcosm has His signature upon it.

Amazingly, the genetic code that orders everything about us, the color of our eyes, the color of our hair, our personality, etc., is programmed by God. When considering the laws of physics or nature (as we call them, they are actually the laws of God), such as gravity, inertia, combustion, mass, velocity, time, motion, etc.; God programmed it all, and it can be both measured and anticipated.

As Christians, we should find great comfort in knowing that God sustains His creation. The same God that sustains His creation is quite capable of sustaining those of us who are His in His creation.

As he manages His creation within His prescribed laws, He is also able to manage His children. He does this by His Word, the Bible.

III. THE WAY GOD CONQUERS. (1:3b-4)

A. He Alone has Conquered. (1:3b)

"When he had by himself purged our sins, sat down on the right hand of the Majesty on high;" Notice, *"when he had by himself."* He needed no help to do the work of grace on the cross of Calvary. There was only one Man that hung there in our stead. He alone paid the price. In purging our sins, He did the work of purification. J. N. Darley has an interesting statement relating to Jesus doing His great

work. "The Greek verb has here a peculiar form, which gives it a reflective sense, causing the thing done to return unto the doer, throwing back the glory of the thing done upon the one who did it" (Synopsis Vol. 5, p. 182, footnote). Everything that He has done comes back to Him. How wonderfully this further indicates that all glory belongs to Him.

There was no qualified candidate who could take the place of Jesus. It was Jesus Himself who paid it all. In the old economy, the priesthood was constantly changing. When Christ Jesus offered Himself, He did once and for all that which had previously been done in succession.

The priest of the Old Testament, with the possible exception of one, was never seen sitting. Sitting denoted a finished or completed task. God established the priesthood and the office of high priest in the days of Moses (Exodus 28:1). Jesus is the only Priest who is qualified to sit, signifying His task is completed.

In describing the priesthood, it may be understood that the priesthood originated in Israel, who was known as Jacob before his name was changed. Israel, a grandson of Abraham, had twelve sons. All the priests came from his son Levi. God set the tribe of Levi apart to do His service and to be representatives of the entire nation (Exodus 13:2; Numbers 3:40-41).

Levi had three sons, Gershon, Kohath, and Merari who had particular responsibilities. Gershon's family had care of the tabernacle and tent and the covering thereof; the hangings for the door and court, the curtain for the door, and the cords of it for all the service thereof (Numbers 3:25-26). Kohath's family had the care of the ark, the table, the candlestick, the altars, the vessels of the sanctuary, the hanging and all the service thereof (Numbers 3:31:32). Merari's family had the care of the boards, bars, pillars, and sockets of the tabernacle, and all the vessels thereof, and all that serveth thereto, and the pillars of the court, and their sockets, pins, and cords (Numbers 3:36-37). These families were not properly priests, though they were Levites.

It was of Aaron, who was the brother of Moses and of the family of Kohath, that the priests came. The family and descendants of Aaron made up the priests and also the high priest. The high priest was generally the eldest son of Aaron. Nadab and Abihu (Leviticus 10:1-3) would be the exceptions. The regulation for the priesthood was given in Leviticus chapter 21.

The priest had 146 external requirements that he had to meet to retain his qualifications as a priest. Unlike the previous priests, the Lord met all the requirements without chance of disqualification with one major exception. He was not of the Aaronic priesthood. With this being the case, the Hebrews had difficulty accepting Jesus as the High Priest. They could not understand how He was qualified by not being of the lineage of Aaron. Instead, He was of the order of Melchisedec (Hebrews 7:17). Therefore, by right of His unchanging Priesthood, He was able to conquer.

B. He Alone was Crowned. (1:4)

One's name identifies one's personage. Our text describes His character. The two words *"express image"* comes from the one word *charakter* and this is the only time that this word appears in the New Testament. It is to be distinguished from the word *"image"* that appears in II Corinthians 4:4 and Colossians 1:15. The word used there is the word *eikon* which tells us that Christ is the visible *representation* and *manifestation* of God.

The words *"express image"* comes from the word that we get our English words "character and characteristic." An image on a printer's die impresses on the paper exactly what appeared on the die. This carries the thought that the Son is the exact expression of all that God is. We cannot dissect and separate the essence of God the Father from God the Son.

The name of Christ is a name that is greater than all names. Philippians 2:9-10 says, *"Wherefore God also hath highly exalted him, and given him a name which is above every name: That at the name of Jesus every knee should bow, of things in heaven, and things in earth, and things under the earth;"* The crowning superiority of Christ is shown in His name as seen in Revelation 19:16, *"And he hath on his vesture and on his thigh a name written, KING OF KINGS, AND LORD OF LORDS."* And that He is!

This study should give us a greater appreciation of the

way that the Lord revealed Himself to us to do the will of the Father and to bring unto us salvation.

Chapter Two

HIS SUPERIORITY SHOULD INSPIRE US

Text: Hebrews 1:5-14

5 For unto which of the angels said he at any time, Thou art my Son, this day have I begotten thee? And again, I will be to him a Father, and he shall be to me a Son?
6 And again, when he bringeth in the firstbegotten into the world, he saith, And let all the angels of God worship him.
7 And of the angels he saith, Who maketh his angels spirits, and his ministers a flame of fire.
8 But unto the Son he saith, Thy throne, O God, is for ever and ever: a sceptre of righteousness is the sceptre of thy kingdom.
9 Thou hast loved righteousness, and hated iniquity; therefore God, even thy God, hath anointed thee with the oil of gladness above thy fellows.
10 And, Thou, Lord, in the beginning hast laid the foundation of the earth; and the heavens are the works of thine hands:
11 They shall perish; but thou remainest; and they all shall wax old as doth a garment;
12 And as a vesture shalt thou fold them up, and they shall be changed: but thou art the same, and thy years shall not fail.
13 But to which of the angels said he at any time, Sit on my right hand, until I make thine enemies thy footstool?
14 Are they not all ministering spirits, sent forth to minister for them who shall be heirs of salvation?

The first of the Beatitudes says, *"Blessed are the poor in spirit: for theirs is the kingdom of heaven"* (Matt. 5:3). A great indication that one is going on unto perfection is when that one begins to recognize his total dependence upon the Lord. He also recognizes that Christ in His superiority is the One he must absolutely follow. Obviously there is none greater than He. It is Christ's superiority that should inspire each of us. The word inspire means to "cause, move, impel, or influence."

Hebrews 12:2a could very well be the challenging and the inspiring theme of our entire study when it says, *"Looking unto Jesus the author and finisher of our faith;"* The focal point of this study will certainly be Jesus. May He inspire us in ways that He never has before. May we grow in the faith of the One who inspires us. May we also properly understand the true foundation upon which faith rests.

The Word of God is that foundation. It is neither feelings nor impressions that we rest our belief upon, though I have had those who have blatantly said, "I do not care what the Scriptures say, I know what I felt or experienced." Such a statement is foreign to the whole body of Truth as outlined in the Scriptures. George Mueller said, "Impressions have neither one thing nor the other to do with faith. Faith has to do with the Word of God. It is not impressions, strong or weak, which will make the difference. We have to do with the written Word and not ourselves or our impressions."

Any information that we will gather which will serve to inspire us to go on unto perfection will be found only by the application of God's Word. It is not what we must think about Christ, it is what we must know. *"So then faith cometh by hearing, and hearing by the word of God"* (Romans 10:17). Study Him; study Christ; He alone should inspire us to go on unto perfection.

Learn of Him from the Gospels. Learn how He confronted His opposition. Learn how He ministered to the sick and to the dying. Learn what He said about money and what He said about greed. Learn the way He sacrifices and the method He used in helping the faithless conquer their fear. Study and learn all that you can about Him. Ask of Him; He will teach you. For your superior example, ask of none other.

Proceeding in this study, let us note a couple of reasons why His superiority should inspire us. First, He is superior in His majesty; and second, He is superior in His quality.

I. HE IS SUPERIOR IN HIS MAJESTY. (1:5-9)

Majesty! What a word. When I traveled to the island of Grenada, I went to their churches and was always thrilled when their congregations blended their voices together and sang the song "Majesty." I have heard no one sing the song with more feeling and meaning than they. Hebrews declares His majesty quite unlike any other New

Testament book. The theme of Hebrews is "Christ the Superior One." One must note His preeminence radiating throughout the book to rightfully appreciate His majesty.

A. His Majesty as Seen by His Preeminence. (1:5-7)

"For unto which of the angels said he at any time, Thou art my Son, this day have I begotten thee? And again, I will be to him a Father, and he shall be to me a Son?" There are seven quotations that demonstrate the majesty and the quality of Christ's superiority in this section, with verse five being the first. These seven quotations are the means whereby God ties together the complete Old Testament prophecy pertaining to Christ's superiority over the angels. During the writing of Hebrews, there was evidence of a heretical teaching which stated that Jesus was nothing more than an angel.

Such is not true, and the writer of Hebrews builds a case to prove it. The first quotation found in verse five is a verse that bridges the truth that God became man as expressed in this thought, *"Thou art my Son; this day have I begotten thee."* It is a quote from the second Psalm. Just as David was raised up for a nation, it was through the seed of David that Christ was raised up as the Saviour (Acts 13:23), and what a Saviour He is! The second Psalm is known as a royal psalm because the emphasis is upon the Messiah being the Supreme King.

In Psalm two, verse seven, the Messiah as

mentioned is seen as the S*upreme* King. In Acts 13:33-49, He may be recognized as the *Sovereign* Saviour. In Hebrews 5:5, when the second Psalm is again quoted, we will see Him appointed as the *Sure High Priest*. In each of these instances we see Christ as the Superior One who inspires us. This truth is also recognized when we consider how this quotation is used in our text. Christ is presented as the S*ent Son.*

     The second quotation, *"I will be to him a Father, and he shall be to me a Son,"* is restated again in II Samuel 7:14, I Chronicles 17:13, and Psalm 89. Never could this statement describe an angel. Angels may be *collectively* called "sons of God" (Job 1:6), but no angel would ever be given that title *individually.* There is not a more endearing expression that could be used to describe this relationship than, *"I will be to him a Father, and he shall be to me a Son."* In human terms this kind of relationship can be a wonderful thing, but nothing to compare to that which is implied when the Father God refers to God the Son in such a manner. The Old Testament's prophets, under divine inspiration, were given a preview of the truth that is so brilliantly declared in John 3:16, *"For God so loved the world, that he gave his only begotten Son..."* The relationship described is a singular relationship that only the Heavenly Father and Jesus could know which would introduce many sons into the family of God (Hebrews 2:11, 13).

     The third quotation contributes to the argument of Him being preeminent over the angels, when in verse six it says, *"and let all the angels of God worship him."* Satan, or Lucifer, is no exception. It was in Lucifer's rebelling against this command that he was cast down.

Verse seven is in contrast to verse eight with the angels being referred to as servants or ministers whereas Christ is seen in verse eight as God the King. This contrast further exclaims that Christ is the preeminent One, superior to the angels in His kingdom. Verse seven borrows this from a quote that is found in Psalm 104:4.

B. His Majesty as Seen by His Perpetuality. (1:8-9a)

May we examine verse eight in more detail. *"But unto the Son he saith, Thy throne, O God, is for ever and ever: a sceptre of righteousness is the sceptre of thy kingdom."*
Kingly perpetuity is by right and fact Christ's alone. He has an unchanging kingdom as He also has an unchanging Priesthood. Again, this fifth quotation is one of the seven, and is found in Psalm 45:6-7. As one of the Messianic Psalms, there is a human side and a divine side. This psalm is a marriage hymn for a royal wedding. Fused into the very heart of this Psalm is a glimpse of King Jesus and His beloved bride. More than that, there is the statement that can only describe the better, eternal kingdom of the Messiah. This statement of truth says, *"Thy throne, O God, is for ever and ever: the sceptre of thy kingdom is a right sceptre (Psalm 45:6).* Some would interpret this statement as being a royal hyperbole of the king referred to in this psalm. This king very well could have been King Solomon. However, in the mind of God, there is only one that could accurately fit this extravagant exaggeration, and

that would be Jesus Christ. He is the only king who will perpetually rule His kingdom.

This fact should further inspire us to *"go on unto perfection,"* while realizing that the divine order and management of the kingdom will be sustained without any break at all. Verse nine qualifies and gives a description of the kind of kingdom that will be set up. This is certainly important that we consider the kind of kingdom to be expected. Can you imagine how awful a perpetual kingdom would be if it were built on the wickedness of the king? Verse nine tells us that the king spoken of *"loved righteousness, and hated iniquity."* Referring back to verse eight, we are told that *"a sceptre of righteousness is the sceptre of thy kingdom."* How very encouraging it is in knowing that evil will not prevail and rule, but God's righteousness will instead. The order of God's kingdom will be perfectly maintained without compromise "as the ages roll."

Perpetuity could therefore be either a curse or a blessing. The fact that God's righteousness will prevail should challenge us to be righteous. This concept is expressed clearly in II Peter 3:9-13, *"The Lord is not slack concerning his promise, as some men count slackness; but is longsuffering to us-ward, not willing that any should perish, but that all should come to repentance. But the day of the Lord will come as a thief in the night; in the which the heavens shall pass away with a great noise, and the elements shall melt with fervent heat, the earth also and the works that are therein shall be burned up. Seeing then that all these things shall be dissolved, what manner of persons ought ye to be in all holy conversation and godliness, Looking for and hasting unto the coming of the day of God, wherein the heavens being on fire shall be dissolved, and the elements shall melt with fervent heat? Nevertheless we, according to his promise, look for new heavens and a new earth, wherein dwelleth righteousness."* Notice particularly verse 13, *"Nevertheless we, according to his promise, look for new heavens and a new earth, wherein dwelleth righteousness."* The new heavens and new earth will be ruled in such a way that it may be said about them, therein *"dwelleth righteousness."* Our righteous ruling king will rule in this manner for all eternity.

C. His Majesty as Seen by His Privilege. (1:9b)

Once again, a reminder to this effect should be in order. The seven quotations from the Old Testament were mostly in reference to an earthly king, but when transferred to the book of Hebrews, they are obviously Messianic in nature. The way that these Messianic quotes are characterized suggest a greater privilege for Christ Jesus than that which could be attributed to a mere mortal. Mortality belongs only to the human realm. Eternality belongs to the divine. This eternality that describes only Christ Jesus is a special privilege afforded to no other ruler.

Added to this is the fact that His kingdom, which is eternal, is completely void of evil. This constitutes a *"glad anointing"* or being anointed with the *"oil of gladness."* This is a most thrilling concept in that all His subjects may recognize His superiority in every way. The angels are His created beings and their worship and service are in association with the earthly order as signified by being ministers of wind and fire. Wind and fire are both recognized earthly terms in association with a limited time of service, whereas the Lord's throne is forever.

The special privilege belonging only to Jesus is seen by the anointing that must be a superior anointing as signified by the wording of verse 9b, *"therefore God, even thy God, hath anointed thee with the oil of gladness above thy fellows."* The word *"fellows"* likely means more than just the angels. It most likely refers to all those who are companions to Christ in the dispensation of grace. Though we all may be fellow partakers within His kingdom, the special adoration belongs to Him and Him alone. This would be as true as the statement found in verse six that says, *"And let all the angels of God worship him."* J. N. Darley said, "Worship is the honour and adoration rendered to God for what He is in Himself, and for what He means to those who render it." The word "worship" is comprised of two words, *pros* and *kuneś*. The first is a preposition which means "towards." The second means "to kiss." When compounded together the new word for worship means to approach with reverent affection and obeisance.

Therefore, Christ is anointed above all with the special privilege of being the object of a superior worship. Though we may be benefactors of His anointing by its origin, His anointing is still superior. May we be now inspired by His quality.

II. HIS QUALITY SHOULD INSPIRE US. (1:10)

While growing older, I have learned to appreciate more the concept of quality. There could be no qualification without quality. Quality becomes a standard. With Christ, His quality is the standard. The Heavenly Father, remember, was *"well-pleased"* with His Son. If I am more concerned now when I purchase a vehicle or some other earthly possession that there be quality, should I not be much more concerned that there be quality in my belief system? I do not want a lesser quality as I worship, but a greater quality. The very concept of worship involves a "lesser" recognizing a "greater."

When younger, I was not as particular with the idea of something having quality as I am today. One reason is that quality often further insures reliability. "Will the car get me there?" To me, this is important. Again, much more so, do I have a quality or superior belief system? "Will it get me there?"

A. It is an Immeasurable Quality. (1:10)

When introducing the word quality into our consideration, there must be a standard to either qualify or appraise the value of that quality. With the Lord there is an infinite or immeasurable aspect of His quality. There is no way that His quality can be explained nor defined. His quality is the standard. In verse ten we read, *"And, Thou, Lord, in the beginning hast laid the foundation of the earth; and the heavens are the works of thine hands:"* The Lord has laid the foundation of the earth. This speaks of there being a creation standard. The foundation was perfect. Even after the sin curse has invaded the created system there is still a precision and an order that is recognized by any honest scientist. The precise manner in which the earth rotates upon its axis testifies to this. The relationship that the earth has to the moon is detected even in the ocean tides. The thickness of the earth's mantle in relationship to its fiery liquid center is in perfect proportion. The volume of water in comparison to its land mass has measurable significance. The frozen mass in ratio to liquid is recognized to be in perfect proportion. The magnetic attraction on the surface of the earth is within critical bounds. The human body must maintain a proper chemistry for its own survival. The earth has its own proper chemical and ecological balance that could not have been achieved by happenstance. The math of such a happening is simply not there.

The speed of sound in contrast to the speed of light is within God's purpose and design as well. To alter either would bring havoc to the world of physics. All of these are the works of God's hands. There is no way to calculate the full benefits of God's doings. His quality of workmanship is without comparison. It was the sin curse that invaded and destroyed the perfect quality of His workmanship. Yet, His own quality did not suffer change or loss.

The latter part of verse ten says it all when considering the ingredient of an immeasurable quality. It says, *"the heavens are the works of thine hands:"* What kind of hands? Psalm 48:10 tells us that His *"right hand is full of righteousness."* The word *full* when describing God's hands is an immeasurable quality. Isaiah 48:13 says, *"Mine hand also hath laid the foundation of the earth, and my right hand hath spanned the heavens: when I call unto them, they stand up together."* What a magnificent way to illustrate the power of God, yet at the same time, show that no one can calculate His omnipotence, for it is an immeasurable quality.

B. It is an Unchanging Quality. (1:11-12)

Between verses 10 and 11, there is an understood event. It is the sin curse taking place. The curse that befell mankind left its indelible mark on creation. God's perfect creation work has been invaded by sin and bears the scars thereof. Thus, verse 11 must say, *"They shall perish; but thou remainest; and they all shall wax old as doth a garment;"* In the scientific realm, this recognizable condition befalling all matter, when it goes from order to disorder, is referred to as the second law of thermodynamics. This law is just as real as the law of gravity. This law will be in effect until the curse is removed. Romans 8:22 explains this state when it says, *"For we know that the whole creation groaneth and travaileth in pain together until now."* The decay may seem miniscule at times; nevertheless, the constant wearing away because of sin is always in effect. Even when a restoration takes place, it is only for a little while. During a period in my life, I would bring home a car that was old and appeared to have very little hope of being restored. I would tell my wife that it was a "diamond in the rough." After much expense and many tedious hours, the vehicle under consideration began to take on its original qualities. Sadly, this could only be temporary because the wearing down process would only start over again. Given enough time, the diamond would become rough again.

In verse 12 we read, *"And as a vesture shalt thou fold them up, and they shall be changed: but thou art the same, and thy years shall not fail."* The Creator is showing that He is still in control. The consequences and the results of the original curse will play out. Just as the lady of the house takes the soiled sheets off the bed and then puts fresh ones in their place, so shall the Lord do with creation. My wife has told me countless times, "Honey, we will not make up the bed now; I will change the sheets first." In a similar fashion the Lord will make the change necessary to undo the sin curse.

This creation is described in II Peter 3:10-13. *"But the day of the Lord will come as a thief in the night; in the which the heavens shall pass away with a great noise, and the elements shall melt with fervent heat, the earth also and the works that are therein shall be burned up. Seeing then that all these things shall be dissolved, what manner of persons ought ye to be in all holy conversation and godliness, Looking for and hasting unto the coming of the day of God, wherein the heavens being on fire shall be dissolved, and the elements shall melt with fervent heat? Nevertheless we, according to his promise, look for new heavens and a new earth, wherein dwelleth righteousness."* Everything has been affected by the curse, including the heavens. The Lord will, as promised, destroy the old earth and the heavens and replace them with new heavens and a new earth. This truth is further indicated in Revelation 21:1, *"And I saw a new heaven and a new earth: for the first heaven and the first earth were passed away; and there was no more sea."*

When Lucifer rebelled against God (Rev. 12:3-4) along with a third of the angels, they were cast to the earth. The final act of redemption will bring about the replacement of the earth and the heaven that was destroyed by fire because of sin. God's righteous standards will not be compromised. Praise God, the curse will one day be removed!

C. It is an Incomparable Quality. (1:13-14)

When Christ laid the foundation, He did it as the perfect architect and as the perfect builder. This sixth quotation which told us this, originally appeared in Psalm 102:25-27. Who is it that compares to our Creator God? No one. The answer to that must be obvious to the believer. The Father asked questions that demonstrated that there is absolutely no one who compares to Him. Notice the questions asked, *"But to which of the angels said he at any time, Sit on my right hand, until I make thine enemies thy footstool? Are they not all ministering spirits, sent forth to minister for them who shall be heirs of salvation?"* (Hebrews 1:13-14).

As a means of illustrating this truth, could there be a way of making a comparison that would show to some degree how superior He is in reference to all that there is? The first thing that came to my mind would be to let all there is be represented by one single candle. Then let Jesus Christ be represented by our closest star, which we call the sun. The candle light could be seen and felt only a few feet away. The light of the sun can be seen and felt many millions of miles away. There is no comparison when comparing the candle light to the sunlight. Just the same, no one or thing compares to Christ. He is truly the Superior One. His superiority should inspire us to *go on unto perfection*.

The seventh and final quote in this section from Psalm 110:1 is applied to the Lord Jesus' final victory over His enemies. All the devils of hell will be no match for Him. Psalm 110 is a true Messianic Psalm that has no connection to an earthly king; it only has the purpose of describing prophetically the finished work of Christ Jesus. This finished work permits Him by right to be seated at the Father's right hand. No one else has that right. He alone has prevailed!

Chapter Three

HIS SUPERIORITY SHOULD WARN US

Text: Hebrews 2:1-4

1 Therefore we ought to give the more earnest heed to the things which we have heard, lest at any time we should let them slip.
2 For if the word spoken by angels was stedfast, and every transgression and disobedience received a just recompence of reward;
3 How shall we escape, if we neglect so great salvation; which at the first began to be spoken by the Lord, and was confirmed unto us by them that heard him;
4 God also bearing them witness, both with signs and wonders, and with divers miracles, and gifts of the Holy Ghost, according to his own will?

Many years ago, I asked an evangelist what he wished to accomplish when he preached his sermons. His answer went something like this, "I want what I say to be heard; I want what I say to be understood; I want what I say to be remembered; I want what I say never to be forgotten, and I want what I say to be applied." Words are extremely important when transferring intelligence. Words need to be precise and carefully stated within the body of the sentence. Even the punctuation is very important. An added or missing comma could change the entire meaning of a sentence. Not only should words be properly understood for the purpose of receiving information, but also the words should be remembered and not forgotten. This is the primary warning that introduces this second chapter. The gravity of the warning is called attention to by the use of the transitional word *"Therefore."* This word is a strong reminder that everything said in chapter one is to be properly considered when reading chapter two.

"The Lord speaks" is the theme of chapter one (Hebrews 1:2). He is to be heard; *He must be heard*. These four verses under consideration in this second chapter give a warning of the consequences of not being heard. May we analyze this portion of scripture in this manner: I. We have something to think about (V. 1); II. We have something to be careful about (Vv. 2-3a); III. We have something to shout about (Vv. 3b-4).

I. WE HAVE SOMETHING TO THINK ABOUT. (2:1)

A. **Think About the Things Which We Have Heard.**
   (2:1a)

The word *therefore* solemnly used here, is used

almost fifty times in this Hebrew epistle. The word *therefore* may be defined to be read, "For this reason." For this reason (as mentioned in chapter one) we should *"give the more earnest heed to the things which we have heard."* The expression, *"we ought to,"* does not lessen the importance of the request. "You must give the more earnest heed…" would be more demanding, but using the expression *"we ought to"* carries the idea of willfully choosing to do what is asked, by personally recognizing the importance of doing so. Our relationship to the Lord should be more than a demanded relationship; it should be a delightful relationship. Spiritual maturity is marked by one personally acting out of conscience rather than out of command.

The thought should be this, "because God has spoken I will listen, while giving serious heed to His words." The words spoken should be carefully attended to, both by hearing and considering. Meditation is spoken of in the first Psalm. A man is blessed who meditates on the Word. There are so many mental distractions that keep us from meditating upon the things of God. Psalm chapter one tells us about the one who delights in the law of the Lord, and meditates day and night. May we refresh our minds by looking once again at this Psalm. *"Blessed is the man that walketh not in the counsel of the ungodly, nor standeth in the way of sinners, nor sitteth in the seat of the scornful. But his delight is in the law of the LORD; and in his law doth he meditate day and night. And he shall be like a tree planted by the rivers of water, that bringeth forth his fruit in his season; his leaf also shall not wither; and whatsoever he doeth shall prosper. The ungodly are not so: but are like the chaff which the wind driveth away. Therefore the ungodly shall not stand in the judgment, nor sinners in the congregation of the righteous. For the LORD knoweth the way of the righteous: but the way of the ungodly shall perish."*

This Psalm gives attention to the *"godly"* and also to the *"ungodly."* One outstanding aspect of the person who gives the *more earnest heed to* the Word of God, is that he shall prosper in every way. The word of God is given for soul prosperity. It is also given for practical prosperity. When I say practical prosperity, I am not teaching "prosperity theology" or "name it and claim it" theology. Instead, I am saying that the Word of God gives us practical help in directing every facet of our lives.

One who loves the Lord should love the Word and give the more earnest heed to the Word. One cannot go on unto perfection without giving heed to the Word of God. Paul knew the extreme value of this as reflected throughout his epistles. An example of this may be seen when he wrote to the church at Colosse. Notice the way Colossians 1:9-10 illustrates this truth, *"For this cause we also, since the day we heard it, do not cease to pray for you, and to desire that ye might be filled with the knowledge of his will in all wisdom and spiritual understanding; That ye might walk worthy of the Lord unto all pleasing, being fruitful in every good work, and increasing in the knowledge of God."* Notice the phrase, *"ye might be filled with the knowledge of his will in all wisdom and spiritual understanding;"* (V. 9). Verse ten indicates that when the Word of God is doing its job in the life of the believer, he will *"walk worthy of the Lord"* and will be *"fruitful in every good work."* Paul further challenges the believer to *"Let the word of Christ dwell in you richly in all wisdom"* (Colossians 3:16a). The number one danger for the believer is a failure to *hear* the truth. Another danger just as great is a failure to *heed* the truth.

B. Think of Those Things Which We Must Hold. (2:1b)

The last part of this verse indicates how quickly ("at any time") we can let the words spoken and heard *slip*. To properly interpret what is being said, we must understand clearly the meaning of the word *slip*. The definition of the word *slip* means to drift away, to flow past, and to glide by.

Most of us who drive automobiles have experienced more than once driving past the road we intended to turn onto. I confess. Just yesterday, while returning from a hospital visit in a neighboring town, I received a call on my cell phone. While talking, I drove past my exit. In the language of our text, I drifted by. So many things can distract us and cause us to drift on by God's intended purpose. This word gives us that purpose. We must give earnest heed to it.

There are some interesting word pictures that show the meaning of the word *slip*. My favorite is the illustration of the ship that is piloted by a drunkard sailor. He, in his intoxicated state, drifts by the inlet that will let him set anchor and go ashore. He intended to do just that, but the alcohol inhibited his thinking, causing him to drift back into open sea. There was nothing wrong with his original thinking and purpose. He certainly intended to go ashore. Likewise, when we do not guard our minds and our thoughts we can let the truth of God's word just slip away.

Another picture is that of a ring on one's finger that loosens. Perhaps the wearer of the ring begins to lose weight. The weight loss was so gradual, hardly noticeable, as the ring became looser on the finger. The one wearing the ring knew that he needed to resize the ring, but put it off until it slipped off the finger. His intentions were good, but he waited too late. This reminds me of the saying "The road to Hell is paved with good intentions." Giving heed to the things that we have heard requires that we diligently receive and apply the Word to our lives. To put off doing that which is right, like the resizing of the ring, results in our losing that which is very precious.

A final pictorial of the way that the word *slip* may be used and applied is in this fashion. In the olden days barrels were commonly made of wooden slats that were banded together with steel rings or bands. Before liquid could be stored in these barrels, there needed to be a time of soaking, allowing the wood to swell, which in turn would contain the liquid. When the wooden barrels were thought to be ready for use, the liquid was poured in and checked for leakage. Sometimes there was leakage but it was not always obvious. This required that future checking of the barrels be done. If this was neglected, the contents could slowly leak out and be lost forever.

Has there ever been a truth that one has received only to be lost with the passing of time? Certainly this makes it imperative that we reinforce truth by constantly calling it back to our remembrance. Peter certainly understood this concept as shown in his second epistle. II Peter 1:12 says, *"Wherefore I will not be negligent to put you always in remembrance of these things, though ye know them, and be established in the present truth."* Peter went further to say that even after his death he wanted the truth to be remembered and not forgotten, spoken in this way, *"to have these things always in remembrance"* (II Peter 1:15b). He was saying, just as in the language of the Hebrew epistle, that he did not want the truth to *slip* away, but to always be remembered.

The wording of this first verse reminds us of the attitude that we should have towards the Word of God. It should be contained and preserved, and at the same time, we should be mindful of the Word's extreme value as we go on unto perfection. Now, may we consider that we have something to be careful about.

II. WE HAVE SOMETHING TO BE CAREFUL ABOUT. (2:2-3a)

A. Because of the Integrity of the Word. (2:2a)

God's message is too important to be ignored. This is the writer's intention when giving this first warning in Hebrews. *"For if the word spoken by angels was stedfast, and every transgression and disobedience received a just recompence of reward;"* (V. 2). This verse serves the purpose of reminding the reader of how superior the Word of Christ was to the *"word spoken by angels."* The superiority in this case lies not just in the truthfulness of the spoken word, but in the superiority of the One speaking the truth.

At Sinai, according to Galatians 3:19, the law was given by the angels and Moses to Israel. Stephen, while indicting the Jews in Acts 7:53 said, *"Who have received the law by the disposition of angels, and have not kept it."* In our study we will learn the consequences of Israel not keeping the law, but our interest at this point is to contrast the truth spoken by the angels to the truth that is spoken by the Lord. If the word spoken by the angels was stedfast, then certainly what Christ speaks is also forever settled in Heaven. Thus, we must be careful as we handle the Word. Sadly, a proper respect of the Word of God is missing in our pulpits as well as in the pews.

For one to go on unto perfection, or unto maturity, one must give the more earnest heed of the integrity of the Word. Satan, in the same spirit that caused him to ask, *"Hath God said?"* is capable of influencing the modernistic theologian and liberal Bible professor in the same way. The Bible doubter and corrector have become nothing more than puppets of Satan. When such a theologian or professor becomes satanically cloned in his thinking, he develops a prideful, superior attitude toward those who have elected to embrace the Word of God without question.

The truth that absolutely must not be refused is the truth pertaining to a *"so great salvation."* This truth is the truth that is to portray the superiority of the workings of grace, as contrasted with law. John the Baptist knew the meaning of this passage in Hebrews when he stated in John 1:15-17 these words, *"John bare witness of him, and cried, saying, This was he of whom I spake, He that cometh after me is preferred before me: for he was before me. And of his fullness have all we received, and grace for grace. For the law was given by Moses, but grace and truth came by Jesus Christ."* John stated clearly that the law was given by Moses, but grace and truth came by Jesus Christ. The Hebrew epistle is developing the theme that, *in every way Christ is better.* Again, He does this by the integrity of His Word.

B. Because of the Severity of the Word. *(2:2b-3a)*

Though we are writing that which pertains to the grace age, that does not discard the fact that when one despises the Word and *"hath done despite unto the Spirit of grace,"* that he can expect *"a certain fearful looking for of judgment and fiery indignation, which shall devour the adversaries"* (Hebrews 10:27, 29).

The earthly king who exercises his power and sovereignty from his own realm may have the powers of life and death according to his own word. One may determine such a king's range of power according to the severity of his word. Such is the case in regards to the words of the Lord Jesus Christ.

Notice verse three, *"How shall we escape, if we neglect so great salvation; which at the first began to be spoken by the Lord, and was confirmed unto us by them that heard him;"* Notice that verses two through four all make up one sentence. This sentence is an interrogative comprised of over seventy-five words. Another consideration is that this sentence is not recognized as a question until the beginning of the twenty-first word. This is a great question about a great quality. The thing that makes this question so great is its subject. It deals with salvation. Salvation, in the way that Hebrews describes it, is foreign to the Hebrew mindset.

Salvation as it involves the Word of God and Christ Jesus will be proven superior to the old economy of law or Judaism. While showing the severity of the words, this question is employed to show to what extent Christ and His words are to be reckoned.

We will notice first how straight the question is, and second how serious the question is. To observe how *straight* the question is, we will first *ponder* the question. Did you ever stop to consider how many questions there are in the Bible? Listen to how God used questions. God asked Adam, *"where art thou, Adam?"* or *"For what doth it profit a man if he should gain the whole world and lose his own soul?"* Another question, *"What is your life, it is even a vapour that appeareth for a little time and then vanisheth away?"* Paul asked, *"Lord, what wilt thou have me to do?"* These are only a few of the ways that questions are used in the Bible.

As this particular question is pondered, give thought to the words, *"How shall."* This part of the question may be referred to as the attention getter. The question *How shall* is not worded or asked by the Lord for information, but for inspiration. God knows that there can be absolutely no escape for neglecting so great salvation (which will be considered further) by refusing His words.

When looking at the way this question begins, the

question is pondered. Notice now that the question is pointed, *"How shall we."* The word *we,* as used in this question, is the same as the second word of the first verse. It is the pronoun "we" that refers to all who have heard or who shall hear the glad tidings of the great salvation which is in Christ Jesus. The pronoun *we* used this way, and correctly, is used in a general sense. It does, however, have a use which signifies that the writer is speaking to the Jews. It was to the Jews that the Messiah came first (Romans 1:16). The Jews rejected the Messiah and this warning section is for the Jews who chose to disregard the teachings of grace and remain under the teachings of law. This truth will be further developed in this study. May we keep in mind, however, that this book is not to be ignored as being a book for the Jew only, as some hyper-dispensationalists have done, but know as we have already said that it is a book for us now.

This great question has been *pondered*; it is a question that is *pointed*; now notice the question's *purpose*. The purpose of this question is to cause us to *think*. The emphasis of this question is to cause us to think as stated in verse number one, *"Therefore, we ought to give the more earnest heed to the things which we have heard, lest at any time we should let them slip."* Thinking is quickly becoming a lost art. A negative aspect of much of our television programming is that it thinks for us. Many of the high-tech games are designed for reflexive action rather than to make us think. The wording of this great question is to make us think. Think in these simple terms, *"How shall we escape, if we neglect so great salvation;"*

Another purpose of this question is, not only for us to think, but for us to *turn* or to repent. If we find ourselves neglecting God's Word, we should repent of it, knowing the severity of His words, and thereby go on unto perfection.

The question is asked, *"How shall we escape, if we neglect so great salvation;"* May we examine what it means to *neglect* so great salvation. Neglect as used here means: to do absolutely nothing. You are aware of the truth that has been delivered to you, but you do not at all give heed or attention to it. You let the truth "slip." Using the example of the leaking vessel, it would be like knowing that the vessel is leaking, but you ignore it until the precious fluid has completely been wasted. It would be like a person knowing that the grass has grown tall and needs cutting, but by neglect the grass grows and the weeds come and the yard is taken over by the weeds of neglect. How tragic for us to have such a great salvation, but only neglect its greatness.

III. WE HAVE SOMETHING TO SHOUT ABOUT. (2:3b-4)

A. We Can Shout About Our Great Salvation. (2:3b)

May we notice these three words, *"so great salvation."* The *noun* "salvation" is what we are talking about. The *adjective* "great" describes and says something about the salvation. Then, the *adverb* "so" intensifies the greatness of the salvation. Salvation considered alone has an inherent greatness about it, in and of itself. Our text magnifies the salvation by calling it a great and then, *so great* salvation.

The greatness of salvation is declared by the prophets. Isaiah 9:6 says, *"For unto us a child is born, unto us a son is given: and the government shall be upon his shoulder: and his name shall be called Wonderful, Counsellor, The mighty God, The everlasting Father, The Prince of Peace."* In this and many other prophecies, the prophets declared the greatness of the salvation of the Lord.

In our dispensation the great salvation message is delivered by the preachers. Preaching has such an important part in the dispensing of the grace of God as well as the greatness of salvation. God ordained preaching giving it purpose. Originally, preaching was called a gospel talk, or literally, a talk about the Gospel. The Greeks were skilled at just talking, taking much delight as they did. The act of preaching takes "talking" to a spiritual plane for the purpose of carryng out God's sacred purposes. There is a *primary* purpose found in preaching. The primary purpose of preaching a *so great salvation* is that the lost might be saved. (Romans 1:16-17; Ephesians 1:13) and that the saved might be *sure* (Hebrews 10:22-24). Within the design of carrying out God's purpose the Word of God must be heeded (V. 1). There is no way that we can de-emphasize this truth. A person will have no comprehension of the greatness of salvation if he neglects to give heed to the Word of God. A person will have no assurance of the greatness of salvation if he fails to take heed to the Word.

Not only is there a primary purpose of preaching, there is the *pastoral* purpose of preaching. The *pastoral* purpose of preaching is to grow the sheep and to guard the sheep. The growth of the sheep, or the church, is in direct proportion to the way it receives the *words* of God. God-ordained preaching should in every aspect magnify the greatness of God's salvation. It is a salvation not to be neglected.

The Bible says in Mark 3:14, *"And he ordained twelve, that they should be with him, and that he might send them forth to preach."* The word *preach* here means "to be a herald; to proclaim; to publish; to preach." The word *preach* is the picture of the minister standing before people in all the dignity and authority of God Himself. It is the word that was used of the ambassador who was sent forth by the king to proclaim his message in all the authority and dignity of the king himself.

The word *preach* carries with it the idea of intense feeling, gravity, and authority, so much so that it MUST be listened to and heeded. The person who preaches is the herald of Jesus Christ, not of someone else. The herald does not share his own opinions and views; he proclaims the truth of Jesus Christ (Practical Word Studies in the New Testament, Volume 2).

The Greek scholar, Kenneth Wuest, has one of the most challenging descriptions of the word *preach* ever penned by man: "The word *preach* is a command to be obeyed at once. It is a sharp command as in military language. The preacher must present, not book reviews, not politics, not economics, not current topics of the day, not a philosophy of life denying the Bible and based upon unproven theories of science, but the Word. The preacher as a herald cannot choose his message. He is given a message to proclaim by his Sovereign. If he will not proclaim that, let him step down from his exalted position." (p. 154).

The greatness of God is: I. Declared by the prophets; II. Delivered by the preachers; and III. Defined by his people. As witnesses, when we take heed to the Word, people will know it. The Word of God leaves its imprint upon the receiving of it. I am discovering that the more time I spend in the Word, the more I want to proclaim or shout the good news to others. Not only can we shout in knowing that we have a great salvation, we can shout in knowing that we have a great Saviour. May we conclude this study with this thought, "we can shout about our great Saviour."

B. We Can Shout About Our Great Saviour. (2:3c-4)

"...which at the first began to be spoken by the Lord, and was confirmed unto us by them that heard him; God also bearing them witness, both with signs and wonders, and with divers miracles, and gifts of the Holy Ghost, according to his own will?" These verses show the triune work of the Godhead. In respect to humanity, the focus is upon Christ the Saviour. It was God's purpose to reveal Christ to us. The work of and the approval of Christ is shown by God bearing witness with both *"signs and wonders, and with divers miracles, and gifts of the Holy Ghost, according to his own will."*

These three words, "signs, wonders, and miracles"

form a trilogy in several instances as found in the New Testament. W. E. Vine, in his *Expository Dictionary*, defines them as follows.

> 1. Signs (*sçmeion*): A sign or mark or token attesting authenticity or authority.
>
> 2. Wonders (*teras*): Something strange, causing the beholder to marvel. It is always used in the plural.
>
> 3. Miracles (*dunamis*): Power, inherent ability, works of supernatural origin and character, such as could not be produced by natural agents and means.

Vine continues, "A sign is intended to appeal to the understanding; a wonder appeals to the imagination; a power indicated the source as supernatural."

J. M. Flanigan, in *What the Bible Teaches: Hebrews*, says on page 44, "Apart from the intrinsic value and inherent greatness of the message itself, there are now three reasons adduced as to why it ought not to be neglected. First, that it was initially introduced by the Lord Himself. Second, that it has been reliably and firmly brought to us by those who actually heard Him. And third, that there has been the added witness of heaven in the miraculous events of those early days. As Marcus Dods so beautifully remarked, "The salvation was at first proclaimed not by angels sent out to minister, not by servants or delegates...but by the Lord Himself, the Supreme. The source then is unquestionably one link between the Lord and you, they that heard Him delivered the message to you, and God by witnessing with them certifies its truth. What a message is this that has come to us by the witness of men, by the witness of God, and by the witness of a Man who was God. We must not neglect such a gospel."

The Acts of the Apostles reveal the truth pertaining to the signs, wonders, and miracles. The healing of the lame man at the gate called Beautiful (Acts 3:1-11); the deaths of Ananias and Sapphira (Acts 5:1-12); the healing of the sick in Jerusalem (Acts 5;16); the opening of prison doors (Acts 5:19); the curing of the man with palsy (Acts 9:32-34); the raising of Dorcas (Acts 9:36-41); the opening of the prison gates the second time (Acts 12:5-10); the fearful death of Herod (Acts 12:21-23); and the blindness of Elymas the sorcerer (Acts 13:8-12).

Each of these miracles was done to authenticate the gospel and demonstrate the greatness of salvation. These are added reasons why one should never at all neglect "so great salvation"!

Chapter Four

A LESSON ON ANGELS SHOULD CHALLENGE US

Text: Hebrews 2:5-9

5 For unto the angels hath he not put in subjection the world to come, whereof we speak.
6 But one in a certain place testified, saying, What is man, that thou art mindful of him? or the son of man, that thou visitest him?
7 Thou madest him a little lower than the angels; thou crownedst him with glory and honour, and didst set him over the works of thy hands:
8 Thou hast put all things in subjection under his feet. For in that he put all in subjection under him, he left nothing that is not put under him. But now we see not yet all things put under him.
9 But we see Jesus, who was made a little lower than the angels for the suffering of death, crowned with glory and honour; that he by the grace of God should taste death for every man.

Satan does not at all want believers to understand correctly the doctrine of angels. However, he does not mind the perverted perception that most people have concerning angels. What is commonly believed about angels borders on the absurd. To many, an angel is nothing more than a "pet rock" or some kind of superstitious good luck charm to be called upon when needed. Satan does not at all mind one having an improper understanding of angels such as this. He just does not want you to know who he really is.

To properly understand angelology is to understand that Satan or Lucifer was a fallen angel. Satan would rather people not know the truth about him. Another false, wicked teaching says that Satan and Jesus Christ were both angels. This teaching says that Satan and Jesus were brothers. Such teaching is a blatant attack on the deity of Christ.

In recognizing that Christ is superior to the angels, may we learn just who they are. We will consider three thoughts in this brief but important study. Notice: I. The responsibilities of the angels (V. 5); II. The ranking of the angels (Vv. 6-7); III. The replacement for the angels (Vv. 8-9).

I. THE RESPONSIBILITIES OF THE ANGELS (2:5)

A. What Was Their Responsibility in the Past? (2:5)

How did the angels come into existence? In answering this question, there is no room for speculation. To speculate at this very foundational point in our consideration would make us no different than those who have a superstitious belief in angels. We complement the question "how did the angels come into existence with this question, "What truth do we have for obtaining our answer?" The only truth that we find available is the Word of God.

What does the Bible say regarding angels? In answering this question, the Bible plainly tells us that God created all things that are on the earth including man, as shown in Genesis chapter one. Psalm 148:5 tells us of the origin of angels. They were created by God.

Since they were created by God, He had a definite purpose for their creation. They were not created just to exist. Psalm 148:5 refers to the angels that were created and also to the way that they were created. The verse says, *"Let them praise the name of the LORD: for he commanded, and they were created."* They were created to glorify God; to worship, and to serve Him. Their existence is taught in at least 34 books of the Bible. The word *angel* appears about 275 times in the scriptures. The New Testament book of Colossians (1:16) tells us that all things, including the angels, were created by Him and for Him. *"For by him were all things created, that are in heaven, and that are in earth, visible and invisible, whether they be thrones, or dominions, or principalities, or powers: all things were created by him, and for him:"*

Jesus Christ spoke very tenderly about angels in Matthew 18:10, *"Take heed that ye despise not one of these little ones; for I say unto you, That in heaven their angels do always behold the face of my Father which is in heaven."* This verse shows the special ministry that the angels have which allows us to refer to them as guardian angels (Psalm 91:11; Acts 12:15). More will be later said about this facet of their ministry.

Out of respect to the volume of time required in completing our Hebrew study we will abbreviate the time spent on the study of angels. We will, however, give enough in-depth material to help us understand the way the angels work within the context of our Hebrew study. We must first understand the beginning or the past work of the angels.

One does not need to read very much in the Bible before he sees the part that the angels play in worship. This part of their ministry is clearly defined in Isaiah chapter six. The Seraphim (used here to describe the heavenly angels) were present when Isaiah saw in a vision the throne of the Lord. The Seraphim are seen functioning for the purpose of ascribing to the Lord the perfect holiness of God. They were also attending to Isaiah upon his confession of sin, followed by the purging of his sin (Isaiah 6:6-7), that he might be fit for worship.

The word *angel* means "messenger" in both the Hebrew and the Greek. Angels are seen performing in this capacity as illustrated in Psalm 103:20, *"Bless the LORD, ye his angels, that excel in strength, that do his commandments, hearkening unto the voice of his word."* David is the writer of this Psalm which shows the gratitude that he personally had for angels. He both recognized their place of service and thanked the Lord for such.

Gabriel, along with Michael, was one of the angels

that were named in the Bible. The only other was Lucifer. C. Fred Dickason, on page 72 in his book *Angels Elect and Evil*, says this about Michael and Gabriel; "Whereas Michael is God's special champion for Israel in her warfare, Gabriel seems to be God's special messenger of His kingdom program in each of the four times he appears in the Bible record. He stands in the presence of God ready to do His bidding (Luke 1:19) and quickly obeys to accomplish His purpose (Daniel 9:21). He reveals and interprets God's purpose and program concerning the Messiah and His kingdom to the prophets and people of Israel."

Gabriel was used for the purpose of bringing prophetic truth to Daniel. It was Gabriel who revealed Daniel's interpretation of the vision of the ram and the rough goat. He was shown that the two-horned ram represented the Medo-Persian Empire, and the great horned goat represented the Grecian Empire under Alexander. Gabriel was also the messenger of interpretation who accurately predicted the first coming date of the Messiah.

Gabriel appeared to Zacharias and Mary for the purpose of announcing the birth of John the Baptist and of Jesus. It appears that Gabriel has the special privilege of announcing the major events that are associated with the Messiah. Gabriel's name means "mighty one of God," and all the scriptural references to him indicate this to be so.

Michael's name means "Who is like God?" This name is a testimony to the truth that God is superior to the angels. His name is by meaning an ongoing testimony to this truth. Michael, the archangel, had a special ministry to

Israel (Daniel 10:13, 20). He also was the leader of an army of angels who battles Satan (Revelation 12:7). Even during the tribulation Michael will have the special honor of guarding Israel during the time of Jacob's troubles or distress (Jeremiah 30:7).

The past work of the angels included the comforting of Hagar by the angel of Jehovah (Genesis 16, 21). Abraham communed with the angels; two angels delivered Lot and his family from Sodom before the fire fell (Genesis 18, 19). Moses was commissioned by the Angel of Jehovah to deliver Israel from Egypt (Exodus 3:2). An angel led Moses and the nation of Israel through the wilderness (Exodus 14:19; 23:20). While considering the past work of angels, it would be profitable to study the many references to angels in the New Testament. The gospels tell of the work and the activity of the angels. Much of what Matthew and Luke records is connected with the birth of Christ and the predictions relating to His birth.

Acts records much angelic activity. When Christ ascended, there were two angels who announced His second coming (Acts 1:10-11). Angels were used to open the doors after the apostles were cast into prison. It was an angel that led Philip the Evangelist from Samaria to the Gaza strip so that he could preach Christ to the Ethiopian eunuch. Peter also was delivered from prison by an angel of the Lord (Acts 12:5-11).

The Epistles have many teachings regarding the ministry of the angels. There are also warnings against the worship of angels as promoted by false religion (Colossians 2:15, 18). The book of Revelation has about 70 references to angels, with much of their work involving the future.

It may be noted that all the angelic activity of the past was under the government of "He who is greater than the angels." Every event and act involving the angels was orchestrated by God Himself. The more that one is permitted to study the role of angels, the more one should be convinced that Christ is the Superior One. This, however, does not and should not take away from the great work that the angels do presently.

B. What is Their Responsibility in the Present? (2:5)

Realizing that the fallen angels have a present activity, we must consider their work as well. This consideration is not for the purpose of the glorification of them, but instead for the identification of them. They need to be identified that they may be recognized.

Regarding the present work of the angels, the Scriptures do not reveal very much. It may be inferred that angels are still very much involved in our lives in ways that we do not recognize. Angels may be used to keep evil in check, as was the case at Lot's rescue (Genesis 18:22; 19:1,10-11) and as was the case when Balaam was kept from doing what he maliciously intended against Israel

(Numbers 22:22-35).

From the examples in the Scriptures, it appears that angels may still be used of God to execute human government. Sickness and death may be a tool held by the angels to punish God's enemies and to even chastise God's own children. Angels may have a purpose in influencing the climatic events upon the earth. Scripture indicates that they will do just that during the tribulation (Revelation 7:1). Regardless of how much and to what degree angels are involved, their involvement is under the direct hand of God. There have been several events in my life that may be attributed to angelic intervention. I am careful not to sensationalize for fear of being caught up in the modern day charismatic system that puts so much stock in what they feel or experience. Please bear with me if you feel that this illustration deserves a different interpretation than what I give. While a student at Tabernacle Bible College in Greenville, South Carolina, I received a call from my wife telling me that a snow and ice storm was coming through the area and that I needed to pick up our children from school. I picked them up and began what was normally a 30-minute trip home. Before I could get them home, the weather had made the roads almost undriveable. (The trip ended up taking me much longer than 30 minutes.) I approached a bridge with great caution thinking that it may have frozen over. Sure enough, it had, and I immediately met a semi-truck loaded with steel. My truck would slide within inches of hitting the traveling truck, and before hitting it, I would slide back towards the side of the bridge. Again, just before my vehicle would hit the bridge, I would slide back toward the truck. Within the space of several seconds my truck went from side to side several times without hitting anything. I immediately felt, upon getting to the other side and off of the bridge, that God or His guardian angels had protected me!

I continued to drive home and when I got in sight of my house, I saw that the snow and ice had brought down a large tree. I looked where my new car was parked and thought that it was completely covered by the tree. I expected the worse. Yet, when I pulled into the drive, I saw that the tree had fallen and draped itself around the car in such a way that the car was not even brushed by the tree. It was as though the branches were cut out as a pattern around the car.

Upon looking at this scene and remembering the supernatural way that I was spared from hitting the truck or the bridge, I felt that the angels of Heaven were at work; to God be the glory, the praise and the honor! Much of what takes place in this life, which may never be clearly explained nor understood down here, may prove to be the work of angels. Again, if that be so, we must remember that they do the biddings of the Lord.

The fallen angels that we referred to earlier also have a present day activity that we should consider. Though not already considered, they too had a past activity beginning with their fall from glory. The highest representative of this group would be Satan. Satan, though created by God, was not created in the state that he presently exhibits. Ezekiel 28:14-15 sheds light on who he is, *"Thou art the anointed cherub that covereth; and I have set thee so: thou wast upon the holy mountain of God; thou hast walked up and down in the midst of the stones of fire. Thou wast perfect in thy ways from the day that thou wast created, till iniquity was found in thee."*

Satan was cast out of his original position in Heaven (Ezekiel 28:16). His judgment or doom was pronounced in Eden (Genesis 3:14-15). Satan will eventually be cast into the lake of fire at the end of the millennium (Revelation 20:10). As a creature, Satan has the same limitations as do the rest of the fallen angels.

Satan lifted up himself in pride against God and authority. The spirit of his rebellion still fuels his anger and hatred toward the believers and toward Christ. He presently organizes the activity of the fallen angels (Matthew 25:41; Revelation 12:9). These fallen angels work under him to carry out his diabolical schemes. Apart from the Lord, there is nothing under the sun that can escape his influence. His influence has affected the wicked to become more wicked, the believer to become objects of his purpose, and the nations to be ruled with a deception causing them to have a bias against Christ. He has counterfeited religion and religious activities to steer mankind away from the truth. There is so much that can be said about the present work of Satan, but due to the nature of our study we can only hint at those things.

The fallen angels are presently working under the leadership of Satan, and have been commonly referred to as demons or devils. They are antagonistic to the people and things of God. Their fiery darts blaze into the minds of willing subjects. They obviously affect the proponents of the pornographic industry; they guide the wicked carnal directors in Hollywood as they make their vulgar movies. They suggest their poison and bias to the minds of the perverted professors as they stand in their classrooms. They are to be reckoned with as they tempt believers to do wicked (Ephesians 2:2-3; I Thessalonians 4:3-5; I John 2:16). Demons are permitted to inflict disease upon people. The Bible lists some of the possibilities: dumbness (Matthew 9:32-33), blindness (Matthew 12:22), seizures (Matthew 17:15-18). Demons are doing all that they can *presently* to disrupt the order and the ordering of God's purpose. We will now consider briefly the future activities of the fallen angels.

C. What Will Be Their Responsibility in the Prophetical? (2:5)

To conclude this section regarding the future of the demons, I wish to quote C. Fred Dickason; "Satan and the demons are no match for Christ, the God-man. In the face of Satanic opposition, the cross accomplished God's self-glorification, released the devil's prisoners, publicly routed evil spirits, and sealed their judgment. Though judged, Satan and his angels are actively promoting apostasy and occultism. Their increasing activity will reach a high point during the Tribulation, when God's restraining is removed so that the human antichrist may become a world ruler, and demons will, under Satan, persecute and kill men and battle with God's angels. Righteousness characterized the kingdom when Satan and demons are bound, but upon their release they find rebels ready to join them in one final rebellion against God. Some demons are bound now in the abyss, some in the River Euphrates, and some in Tartarus; but all will be bound forever in the lake of fire." Amen!

II. THE RANKING OF THE ANGELS. (2:6-7)

A. Their Ranking in Relationship to Man. (cf. 2:5; 2:6)

Verse five reads, *"For unto the angels hath he not put in subjection the world to come, whereof we speak."* While understanding the role of the angels a little more clearly in their relationship to man, may we further notice the way the angels are ranked. Verse five is in reference to the millennium. Man will be removed from the effects of the curse and will be restored to the privileges similar to that which was enjoyed by Adam in the Garden of Eden. Creation will be placed back under the rule of man and Christ. Revelation 1:5-6 speaks of this state that will be enjoyed by the redeemed. *"And from Jesus Christ, who is the faithful witness, and the first begotten of the dead, and the prince of the kings of the earth. Unto him that loved us, and washed us from our sins in his own blood. And hath made us kings and priests unto God and his Father; to him be glory and dominion for ever and ever. Amen."* Revelation 5:10 says that the redeemed are made kings and priests. This is not said of the angels. Notice this verse, *"And hast made us unto our God kings and priests: and we shall reign on the earth."*

While considering the ranking of the angels, it is profitable to our study to consider them numerically. Hebrews 12:22 speaks of *"an innumerable company of angels."* Obviously, that is from man's standpoint. The Lord knows how many he created. When one considers a number that cannot be numbered or counted, it certainly is a very large number. John describes the number of angels this way in Revelation 5:11, *"ten thousand times ten thousand, and thousands of thousands;"* Using scientific notation, depending if the two groups of numbers are added or multiplied, you have these possibilities: $1 \times 10^8 + 1 \times 10^6 = 101{,}000{,}000$, or $1 \times 10^8 \times 1 \times 10^6 = 100{,}000{,}000{,}000$ with the latter being a number that man could not count. With such a large number of angels there must have been a system for governing them. One could only imagine an army of soldiers having no rank or order and the chaos that would exist. Such would be true with the angels. If one related to the angels from a military perspective, they would recognize Michael as being the archangel or the general of the angelic army. In Revelation 12:7, we read, *"And there was war in heaven: Michael and his angels fought against the dragon; and the dragon fought and his angels,"* This verse speaks of *"Michael and his angels"* and *"the dragon fought and his angels."* The indication is that both the good angels and the fallen angels are operating within a system.

In I Corinthians 6:3, Paul tells the church at Corinth, *"Know ye not that we shall judge angels? how much more things that pertain to this life?"* This indicates that after we are brought into His glory, we will share in the exercising of His dominion. The angels ranking in relationship to man is emphasized in Hebrews 2:6, *"But one in a certain place testified, saying, What is man, that thou art mindful of him? Or the son of man, that thou visitest him?"* This consideration is given to man, not to the angels. There is no way to comprehend the fullness of such a statement. It is mind boggling just to think that God is mindful of man. God's grace is certainly on display when the full ramification of such a statement is put into effect.

The Lord has chosen to deliver to man the mystery of God's grace (Ephesians 3:1-5). He also chose to reveal the mystery of the church to the angels through the ministry of the church. Ephesians 3:10 speaks of this, *"To the intent that now unto the principalities and powers in heavenly places might be known by the church the manifold wisdom of God."* May we now consider the ranking of the angels in relationship to the Maker (Creator).

B. Their Ranking in Relationship to the Maker. (2:7)

Verse seven, *"Thou madest him a little lower than the angels; thou crownedst him with glory and honour, and didst set him over the works of thy hands:"* Notice how this verse begins, *"Thou madest."* Who is the maker here? Every aspect of God's creation is with purpose. The Bible shows this, yet so many are blinded to this concept or truth. I was speaking to a college student just yesterday who had faced ridicule for quoting from the Bible. The college professor who ridiculed the student was unwilling to let the Bible be used as evidence in regards to the origin of man. Very likely, this professor has only been told by someone else that the Bible was a book that had no credibility. When considering the ongoing demonic activity, this is not hard to believe. Christ Jesus who is superior to the angels by right of creation has the right to rank them as He pleases. No wonder the Psalmist exclaimed, *"What is man, that thou art mindful of him?"* As undeserving as we are, He still graciously bestows His love upon us.

For us to properly accept what is being taught in Hebrews, and somewhat understand what is being taught, we must accept what the writer said about creation. Hebrews uses creation as a means of establishing Christ's right to rule, reign, and designate as He pleases. He is sovereign, and in His sovereignty He chose to elevate man to the place of glory that excels that of the angels; He has this right as the Creator God. Another thing that is clear is that the angels are not to be worshipped. In Colossians 2:18, Paul warns against the worship of angels, *"Let no man beguile you of your reward in a voluntary humility and worshipping of angels, intruding into those things which he hath not seen, vainly puffed up by his fleshly mind,"* Also, in Revelation 22:8-9 and Revelation 19:10, the warning is against angel worship. Christ Jesus is superior to the angels; all of them, including Satan.

III. The Replacement For The Angels. (2:8-9)

A. This Replacement Will Demonstrate God's Grace Towards Man. (2:8)

To refresh us in our thinking, may we look at verse eight again, *"Thou has put all things in subjection under his feet. For in that he put all in subjection under him, he left nothing that is not put under him. But now we see not yet all things put under him."* The writer of Hebrews, while writing under the inspiration of God, makes several statements that both describe the way things are presently, and the way things are to be prophetically. The curse took away from man the ruler-ship that was previously his. Verse eight is referring to man, instead of Christ, who was given dominion over the creation (Genesis 1:28) but who lost it when he sinned (Romans 8:20) and who will regain it in the future millennial kingdom because of Christ's death for sin (v.100 (Ryrie).

It is so very thrilling to see the way the Lord is going to regain that which was lost by the sin curse. The Lord is not just resurrecting Eden only for man to reclaim. Instead, He is putting all things under the rule of mankind. At the present everything in God's creation is in a state where it *"groaneth and travaileth in pain together until now"* (Romans 8:22). Yet, according to Jesus, as recorded in John's gospel, all shall be raised at that last day. *"And this is the Father's will which hath sent me, that of all which he hath given me I should lose nothing, but should raise it up again at the last day. And this is the will of him that sent me, that every one which seeth the Son, and believeth on him, may have everlasting life: and I will raise him up at the last day."* (John 6:38-39). This will grant man the privilege according to God's grace to rule and reign with Him.

B. **This Replacement Will Define God's Judgment.**

(2:9)

"But we see Jesus, who was made a little lower than the angels for the suffering of death, crowned with glory and honour; that he by the grace of God should taste death for every man." This verse shows the relationship that Jesus took to the angels, when it says that He *"was made a little lower than the angels."* He did this for the purpose of suffering death that He might be crowned with glory and honour. This glory and honour came when he tasted death for every man. Verse ten in Hebrews chapter two shows us that this was the method that Christ Jesus chose to bring *"many sons unto glory."*

This was accomplished by the *kenosis* (emptying) of Christ during His incarnation. By Him making "himself of no reputation: (Philippians 2:5-11) it did not at all mean that He surrendered any attributes of deity, but that He instead took on the limitations of humanity" (Ryrie). Notice this passage of scripture in Philippians and you will see the steps that Jesus took in His kenosis. *"Let this mind be in you, which was also in Christ Jesus: Who, being in the form of God, thought it not robbery to be equal with God: But made himself of no reputation, and took upon him the form of a servant, and was made in the likeness of men: And being found in fashion as a man, he humbled himself, and became obedient unto death, even the death of the cross. Wherefore God also hath highly exalted him, and given him a name which is above every name: That at the name of Jesus every knee should bow, of things in heaven, and things in earth, and things under the earth; And that every tongue should confess that Jesus Christ is Lord, to the glory of God the Father."*

He was first described as being in the form of God. Second, He made Himself of no reputation, and took upon Him the form of a servant. Third, He was made in the likeness of men. Fourth, He became obedient unto death, "even the death of the cross."

This describes the tasting of death for every man that we read of in verse nine of our text. The crowning with glory and honour speaks of the quality of His government, being mindful that He who hates iniquity and loves righteousness (Hebrews 1:9) will rule with a scepter of righteousness. Topping it off, we will have the privilege of ruling and reigning with Him in this manner, above the angels. To God be the glory!

Chapter Five

WHO WE ARE BECAUSE OF WHO HE IS

Text: Hebrews 2:10-13

10 For it became him, for whom are all things, and by whom are all things, in bringing many sons unto glory, to make the captain of their salvation perfect through sufferings.

11 For both he that sanctifieth and they who are sanctified are all of one: for which cause he is not ashamed to call them brethren,

12 Saying, I will declare thy name unto my brethren, in the midst of the church will I sing praise unto thee.

13 And again, I will put my trust in him. And again, Behold I and the children which God hath given me.

The writer of Hebrews has magnified the person of Christ by showing His superiority over the prophets, over His creation, and over the angels. With just a few words written in a classical manner, His superiority and His majesty have been absolutely declared. As we consider this section we will learn who *we* are because of *who* He is. How thrilling it is to learn that so much of what He did by coming into the world, He did for us. Scripture clearly shows His condescending love to us *"while we were yet sinners."* How wonderful do these words speak to our hearts showing the way that He came to us. *"But God commendeth his love toward us, in that, while we were yet sinners, Christ died for us"* (Romans 5:8). *"For God so loved the world, that he gave his only begotten Son, that whosoever believeth in him should not perish, but have everlasting life"* (John 3:16). *"But God, who is rich in mercy, for his great love wherewith he loved us, Even when we were dead in sins, hath quickened us together with Christ, (by grace ye are saved;) And hath raised us up together, and made us sit together in heavenly places in Christ Jesus: That in the ages to come he might shew the exceeding riches of his grace in his kindness toward us through Christ Jesus"* (Ephesians 2:4-7).

As wicked and depraved as man is, Christ still came. He gave up His splendor in glory to do what only He was capable of doing by bringing *"many sons unto glory"* (V. 10). It is only in His greatness that we can achieve greatness.

May we consider three thoughts that show "who we are because of Him." Consider: I. The Wonderful Redemption from Him (V. 10); II. The Wonderful Relationship with Him (V. 11); III. The Wonderful Revelation by Him (Vv. 12-13).

I. THE WONDERFUL REDEMPTION FROM HIM.

(2:10)

The word *redemption* does not appear in this study, but to arrive at this word, we do so by applying a hermeneutical principle given to us in Isaiah 28:9-10 in this study. *"Whom shall he teach knowledge? and whom shall he make to understand doctrine? them that are weaned from the milk, and drawn from the breasts. For precept must be upon precept, precept upon precept; line upon line, line upon line; here a little, and there a little:"* Notice, *"line upon line, here a little, and there a little."* Our study in Hebrews permits us to use this method of study and interpretation. While reading and interpreting our text line by line, we must be conscious of the need of comparative study. While considering a precept or truth, we develop this truth further by looking at related passages in the Bible. Though the word *redemption* is not mentioned in this verse, the activity of redemption is certainly hinted at. Everything that this verse stands upon must be understood relative to the truth of redemption. May we notice:

A.   By His Humiliation He Redeems Us. (2:10a)

The first phrase begins in this manner, *"For it became him."* As foreign as the suffering Messiah is to Jewish thinking, that is exactly what this phrase signifies. Peter could not even comprehend that Christ could or would suffer, when he said in a rebuking manner to the Lord, *"Be it far from thee, Lord: this shall not be unto thee"* (Matthew 16:22). We must remind ourselves that the prophets had predicted that Christ would suffer as a *"root out of a dry ground:"* (Isaiah 53:2). The prophet Isaiah spoke that which was revealed to him, but yet asked three questions showing his concern for the way his words would be received. He asked, *"Who hath believed our report? and to whom is the arm of the Lord revealed?"* and *"who shall declare his generation?"*

The prophets who predicted the humiliation of Jesus, even as Isaiah did in the 52nd and 53rd chapters of Isaiah, wondered how any of their readers and especially the Jews would be able to understand what they were prophesying. They preferred to let the *"root out of a dry ground"* be most anyone other than the suffering Messiah. The Jews, as they study passages pertaining to the predicted Messiah, break some very basic laws of Bible interpretation as they wrestle with the scriptures in an effort to formulate their own biased interpretation. For example, they do this when they say that the servant is Israel in Isaiah chapter 53. While comparing scripture with scripture this interpretation could not be so, because Israel is referred to in the feminine gender, not in the masculine as seen in the 53rd chapter of Isaiah. In the first chapter of Isaiah, Israel is seen as *"the daughter of Zion"* (V. 8).

To the Jew, Isaiah 53, while describing the humiliation of Christ, is referred to as "the chamber of tragedy" and as "the synagogue of punishment" (C.L. Roach). The feeling of contempt for this chapter was so strong that their children were punished if found reading it. Even some Gentiles (liberals and modernists) despise this chapter because of how accurately it predicts the crucifixion of Christ.

The phrase, *"For it became him"* is the written way of communicating that the humiliation of Christ was such that it befitted Him. This was shown in a most expressive way, when Jesus endured the cross. This is what is being portrayed by the phrase, *"who for the joy that was set before him endured the cross."* The humiliation of Christ, even as it related to the crucifixion, was desired by Him knowing that it would take this to accomplish the wonderful purpose of *"bringing many sons unto glory."*

The way His humiliation pertains unto redemption is understood in this manner. To serve as our redeemer, there must be several requirements met. There had to be someone qualified to serve as the redeemer; there had to be someone who was willing to serve as the redeemer; there had to be someone who was of close kin; and there had to be someone who could pay the price of redemption. *"For it became him,"* in His humiliation He came to the world to serve as Redeemer, meeting all the requirements willingly.

B.   By His Creation He Redeems Us. (2:10b)

"...for whom are all things, and by whom are all things." When recognizing Christ's ability and His right to redeem, we must not drift away from nor neglect the truth that He is the Creator God. Creation originated in the mind of the Father and was accomplished through the Son. *"for whom,"* describes the originating purpose of creation being of God the Father and the performing of it being of the Son. It is expressed in this way, *"by whom are all things."*

J. M. Flanigan in his Hebrews studies used a phrase that is worthy of repeating, when describing the work of the Father and the Son; "Notice the holy interchange of glories between divine Persons." The "holy interchange of glories" describes how the will of the Father was perfectly performed by the Son in a *most* holy manner.

Creation must be carefully considered when observing the workings of Christ. Everything has its origin in the creation work of the Father-Son. When we understand this, it should give us some capacity to understand also that salvation is a creation work. II Corinthians 5:17 conveys this when it says, *"Therefore if any man be in Christ, he is a new creature: old things are passed away; behold, all things are become new." "A new creature"* may also be expressed this way; a new *creation*. For when one is born again, God uses creation power, just as He did when He spake the worlds into existence. When the worlds were brought into existence, it was by the use of a creation miracle. He took *nothing* and then made *something*. Likewise, regarding the miracle of salvation, God can take a lost hell-bound nobody and make him into a son. He has brought *"many sons unto glory"* in this fashion.

C. By His Identification He Redeems Us. (2:10c)

"...in bringing many sons unto glory." Again, how thrilling to be birthed into the family of God. The beloved John, the apostle, recognized this truth when he wrote, under the

inspiration of God, the Epistle of I John. I John 3:1-3 says, *"Behold, what manner of love the Father hath bestowed upon us, that we should be called the sons of God: therefore the world knoweth us not, because it knew him not. Beloved, now are we the sons of God, and it doth not yet appear what we shall be: but we know that, when he shall appear, we shall be like him; for we shall see him as he is. And every man that hath this hope in him purifieth himself, even as he is pure."*

To properly understand the meaning of the statement that pertains to many sons being brought unto glory requires going back to Isaiah chapter 53. In Isaiah 53:8a, we read, *"He was taken from prison and from judgment: and who shall declare his generation?"*

The question, *"Who shall declare his generation?"* is based upon the Jewish legal system. Before this statement is explained, it would be helpful to give some background while borrowing from the Jewish culture. To the Jew, marriage was a sacred part of their religious heritage. Each marriage was given in hopes of continuing the lineage of Abraham with the greater hope of either laying claim to the throne of David or giving birth to the Messiah. To lay claim to this hope, it was expected that marriage would take place by age 18 and that one would be a father by age 19 and a grandfather by age 38. To the Jew, for Jesus to not be married and to have no children was a shame. He was despised for this, and even when He was being tried He was thought to be *less than a man*. In His unmarried and childless state the question was asked with great concern, *"and who shall declare his generation?"*

According to the Jewish legal system, when a capital crime had been committed, the guilty man had 40 days of grace in which to call upon his family to travel throughout the land *declaring his generation* with the hopes that this opportunity would provide for the discovery of evidence to prove the accused innocent. When the prophet Isaiah saw that the Messiah in His humiliation would be put to death, knowing that He was innocent, he wondered who would *declare His generation*.

The Jewish and the Roman legal system broke at least nine different laws when they condemned and crucified Christ. He had no opportunity to prove His innocence. Yet through His humiliation and then His resurrection, He was able to bring many sons unto glory. After His resurrection, it is of interest, but certainly no accident, that Jesus had 40 days before His ascension. During these 40 days the believers were able to witness not only His innocence but also His truthfulness in regards to that which He spoke concerning His own death, burial, and resurrection. The many sons born into His family, even until the day in which we now live, also declare His generation. This answers Isaiah's sober question, *"and who shall declare his generation?"*

The word *son* is used with signification, rather than the word *children*. Sons of God! It is the word *huios,* "sons," not "children." This designation seems to be for the purpose of creating a closer tie back to Jesus who is the unique, only begotten Son of God.

In verse 14 the word *children* is given in answer to the Jewish criticism that Christ was less than a man and incapable of having children. Also there is indication that *"flesh and blood"* children were given to Him and that they became *huios* or sons of God (V. 14). This all took place because of the crucifixion.

D. By His Crucifixion He Redeems Us. (2:10d)

"...to make the captain of their salvation perfect through sufferings." This statement says much about the *kenosis* (self-limiting) of Christ. Christ, as the leader-captain may lead by divine right. He personally suffered. The word *teleioo* is defined in W. E. Vine's *Expository Dictionary* in this manner, "*Teleioo*, to bring to an end by completing or perfecting, is used 1. of accomplishing; 2. of bringing to completeness;… of Christ's assured completion of His earthly cause, in the accomplishment of the Father's will, the successive stages culminating in His death (Luke 13:32; Hebrews 2:10) to make Him perfect, legally and officially for all that He would be to His people on the ground of His sacrifice." Through those things that He faced while upon earth, and the way that He faced them qualifies Him to be our Leader. To know how to properly face and deal with our daily encounters in life we must remind ourselves to look to Jesus. He certainly is our Captain.

Hebrews 12:2, when it says *"Looking unto Jesus the author and finisher of our faith…,"* uses the word author in a similar fashion as the word *captain* used here. The word also means pioneer. If you take the three meanings of the word *captain* as used in our text, they are as follows: I. Leader; II. Author; and III. Pioneer.

Viewing Christ Jesus as Leader, we may make these remarks. He was introduced to the human family by His kenosis. Already, we have discussed the reason that He limited Himself in His incarnation by coming to the earth as the God-man. One aspect of His coming to the earth involved testimony. Normally, when something is put to the test it is for the purpose of assuring the item's quality. There are testing laboratories in major industry for the purpose of quality control or quality assurance. There is always the question on the part of the tester, "Is this product exactly what it is supposed to be?" The testing is for the purpose of determining the credibility of the product.

The testing of Christ was very different. There was no possibility of Him being found with any flaws. He was to be tested for the purpose of public declaration. The declaration was to determine that He was everything that the prophets had declared Him to be. His suffering was a public display of His full identity with mankind, showing by example how He handled His suffering. This gave credibility to Him being our Leader. For this reason we should willingly follow Him as Leader. In Luke 9:23 we read, *"And he said to them all, If any man will come after me, let him deny himself, and take up his cross daily, and follow me."* Here the use of the word *follow* comes from the Greek word *akoloutheo*, translated "follow, or followed" which appears 88 times in the New Testament. The prefix "a" indicates a likeness, and "koloutheo" is the word for road, or way. Thus, the term suggests going down the same road, or going in the same way. In this sense, a follower of Christ is one who is going to the same place, the same way, and going just like Christ. When Christ as the Captain or Leader says, "Follow me" He has already been there and He certainly knows the way.

As Captain He is also the Author. One who authors something does so with words. He creates with words. The name of Jesus that indicates this is, *"The Word"* (John 1:1). He not only spoke into existence all of creation, He continues to speak to us as our Captain by the written Word, the Bible. The Captain's strategy or plan of action is the Bible, and He is the Author of it.

By usage the word *pioneer* also defines the meaning of the word *captain*. The word *pioneer* is one of my favorite words describing Him as the Captain. The word *pioneer* speaks of doing that which no one else has done. Charles Lindberg was an aviation pioneer when referring to the history of the airplane. John Glynn was a space pioneer when describing space travel.

Regarding salvation, Christ Jesus was a pioneer as He journeyed to the cross. His was not the first crucifixion, but His was the first crucifixion followed by a resurrection. His death, burial, and resurrection were uniquely His. He alone pioneered our redemption through His sufferings as Isaiah chapter 53 records. For a greater appreciation of His pioneering work, carefully notice theses verses in Isaiah 53:3-7. *"He is despised and rejected of men; a man of sorrows, and acquainted with grief: and we hid as it were our faces from him; he was despised, and we esteemed him not. Surely he hath borne our griefs, and carried our sorrows: yet we did esteem him stricken, smitten of God, and afflicted. But he was wounded for our transgressions, he was bruised for our iniquities: the chastisement of our peace was upon him; and with his stripes we are healed. All we like sheep have gone astray; we have turned every one to his own way; and the LORD hath laid on him the iniquity of us all. He was oppressed, and he was afflicted, yet he opened not his mouth: he is brought as a lamb to the slaughter, and as a sheep before her shearers is dumb, so he openeth not his mouth."*

II. THE WONDERFUL RELATIONSHIP WITH HIM. (2:11)

A. Look at the Sanctifier's Purpose. (2:11a)

"For both he that sanctifieth and they who are sanctified are all of one." Can any statement be more honorable and gracious than this statement? What makes it so very honorable is that God's power and purpose are welded together in such a way that the two cannot be divided. It was God's powerful purpose that the One sanctified would be one with the Sanctifier. God had the power or the strength to fulfill His purpose. The word *sanctified* as used here and also in chapters 9:13; 10:10, 14, 29; 13:12, needs to be precisely understood. To bring about such an understanding may we look at the meaning of the word

sanctify and how it is used. It means to be set apart for special service. The Bible speaks of things other than people being set apart for special purpose. The tabernacle furniture (Exodus 40:10-11, 13) was set apart, as was a mountain (Exodus 19:20), and food (I Timothy 4:5). In following Christ as captain, He sets us apart by being our Leader, Author, and our Pioneer. For us to follow Him by faith, we may enter positionally into a state of sanctification whereas we are no different than He. The entire book of Ephesians wonderfully demonstrates this truth. Consider these verses relative to our discussion. *"But God, who is rich in mercy, for his great love wherewith he loved us, Even when we were dead in sins, hath quickened us together with Christ, (by grace ye are saved;) And hath raised us up together, and made us sit together in heavenly places in Christ Jesus:"* (Ephesians 2:4-6). Notice the word "together". This word shows how we are bonded together in Him. We are seated together. We may sanctify or consecrate our own bodies to Him as indicated in Romans 12:1. *"I beseech you therefore, brethren, by the mercies of God, that ye present your bodies a living sacrifice, holy, acceptable unto God, which is your reasonable service."*

We are as sons, the offspring of God, enjoying a sanctified state. This gives us our ability to function with the bestowed honor of being called His brethren. Acts 17:28 tells of this relationship. *"For in him we live, and move, and have our being; as certain also of your own poets have said, For we are also his offspring."*

J. N. Darby gives detailed truth concerning the Sanctifier and the sanctified that is worthy of our consideration. "This shews us Christ standing in the midst of those who are saved, whom God brings to glory.... Observe that it is only of sanctified persons that this is said. Christ and the sanctified ones are all one company, men together in the same position before God. But the idea goes a little farther. It is not of one and the same Father; had it been so, it could not have been said, 'He is not ashamed to call them brethren.' He could not then do otherwise than call them brethren.

"If we say, 'of the same mass' the expression may be pushed too far, as though He and the others were of the same nature as children of Adam, sinners together. In this case He would have to call every man His brother; whereas it is only the children whom God has given Him, 'sanctified' ones that He so calls. But He and the sanctified ones are all as men in the same nature and position together before God. When I say 'the same,' it is not in the same state of sin, but the contrary, for they are the Sanctifier and the Sanctified, but in the same truth of human position as it is before God, as sanctified to Him; the same as for man when He, as the sanctified One, is before God."

B. Look at the Sanctified Position. (2:11b)

"Not ashamed to call them brethren." Being sons should determine our actions so that Christ Jesus would not be ashamed to call us brethren. Our staff evangelist, Ray Brown, preached a tremendous sermon on sanctification and consecration in the church that I pastor. I asked him to

summarize his points in written form for our study here. May what he has to say bless you.

"Before considering our subject, may we look at the definitions of sanctification and consecration?

Sanctification:

The act of making holy (Noah Webster 1828). In an evangelical sense, the act of God's grace by which the affections of men are purified or alienated from sin and the world, and exalted to a supreme love of God. God hath from the beginning chosen you to salvation, through sanctification of the Spirit and belief of the truth (II Thessalonians 2, I Peter 1).

The act of consecrating or of setting apart for a special purpose;

Consecration:

Making sacred; appropriating to a sacred use; dedicating to the service of God; devoting; rendering vulnerable (Noah Webster 1828).

Consecration is the act or ceremony of separating from a common to a sacred use, or of devoting and dedicating a person or thing to the service and worship of God, by certain rites or solemnities. Consecration does not make a person or thing really holy, but declares it to be sacred, that is, devoted to God or divine service; as the consecration of priests among the Israelites; the consecration of the vessels used in the temple.

When a person is saved by the grace of God there is something supernatural that takes place. At that very moment the Holy Spirit moves on the inside of that person and begins to dwell. We call this being saved, but we also call it being justified. Someone has said, 'justification means the act of being made just and that means just as if we had never sinned.' However, it means much more than this because as God looks at us justified, He looks through the blood of His Son Jesus Christ and sees us just as if we never *could* have sinned. All of this takes place when we by faith trust Jesus Christ as our personal Saviour (Romans 3:30, Romans 8:33). We do not have to wait on justification; it is a present fact according to Romans 5:1 and Galatians 2:16. Being justified is our *position* in Christ (how we stand or how He sees us). This means that because we have placed our faith and trust in the Lord Jesus Christ we now have given up *our rights* and freely given them to Him. In other words, He purchased us with His own blood. We *were not* holy in and of ourselves; Christ Jesus has made us holy. As we have already mentioned by definition from Noah Webster 1828 the words *consecration* and *sanctification* are very similar. In the Old Testament temple or tabernacle the vessels were sanctified (set apart) for the use of the holy only. These vessels were objects made with the same materials that any other objects were made, such as the gold that one would have in one's wedding band. So the materials used in the vessels were of the same material that would be commonly found with the difference being, these materials were sanctified. A preacher is made of the same material God makes everyone else except that God sanctifies him (sets apart) for a specific purpose. We have vessels in our churches today such as offering plates, communion tables, pianos and organs. We would not think of using the offering plates for soup and sandwiches, or think of using the piano in a bar, because they have been sanctified for the use of the holy. We would not dream of holding a dance or setting up a bazaar in the church, because the church building has been sanctified for the use of the holy (only). Holiness does not come from being sanctified or consecrated, but rather the consecration to God of that which has already been made holy by God. We can do anything with our life and body that anyone else could do with theirs, but we have given up these rights to the rights of the One who has purchased us with His own blood. God is a jealous God and has *declared* us holy. This is the reason we should not do what the world is doing. Not because we do not have the ability to do so, but because we have been set apart and declared to be holy as He is holy (1 Peter 1:16). Jesus Christ died so that we could live. The more that we die to self, the more that we can live to Him. The Christian life is not "more doing" but "more dying." Dying to self means less of me is seen and more of Him is seen. God help us to empty ourselves and be filled with Him!"

When we consider Romans 12:1, Paul's epistle to the Christians in the city of Rome, we notice that He begins with the words "*I beseech.*" In the Old Testament it would have probably read, "I command." The reason being is because by grace we have been made partakers of the mercies of God. In light of the mercies of God, Paul felt like there should be no need for this being a command because of our blessings and benefits coming from His mercies. In the earlier chapter of Romans all the way to chapter 11, he describes the mercies of God. We find ourselves condemned as sinners, then justified as saints, and glorified in the days to come. He felt that we should present ourselves with delight instead of just duty. It is like this, "I don't have to read my Bible, I get to read it. I don't have to pray, I get to pray. I don't have to preach, I get to preach." Because of what He has done for me, what a privilege and what a blessing it is to serve Him.

III. THE WONDERFUL REVELATION BY HIM.

(2:12)

"Saying, I will declare thy name unto my brethren, in the midst of the church will I sing praise unto thee."

A. The Exaltation of the Sovereign. (2:12a)

Because of the work of sanctification many good things happen for the believer. The believer who is yoked up with Christ has with that union the benefits of the church. In Psalm 22 the first part deals with the humiliation of Christ; the last part deals with the glorification of Christ. This Hebrews passage is a quote from Psalm 22:22, 25. The word *congregation* in verse 25 is changed to *church* in verse 12 of Hebrews chapter two. The reason for this could be because the Hebrew Epistle is directed primarily to a Gentile audience. Many commentators do not accept this, believing instead that the book is only for the Jews during the Tribulation. Yet, the Bible teaches that the church will not be around during the Tribulation. It goes up in the Rapture; praise God!

This passage is showing the benefits of those who are in the church, which are one in Christ. Christ says in verse 12, *"I will declare thy name unto my brethren, in the midst of the church will I sing praise unto thee."* Instead of this being a bodily manifestation of Christ in the midst of the church, it is the Spirit of Christ that is at work. Many wonderful services have taken place because Christ was there. However, there is nothing more dead than when Christ does not show up. The absolute presence of Christ is what makes the services alive. May I illustrate how this is so with a passage of scripture that is found in Matthew 18:20, *"For where two or three are gathered together in my name, there am I in the midst of them."* This is a clear passage indicating the omniscience of Christ as well as His omnipresence. He is all knowing and all present by His Spirit. The Holy Spirit is God the Father as well as God the Son; you cannot dissect God's Spirit. Romans 8:9-11 shows this statement to be absolutely true. *"But ye are not in the flesh, but in the Spirit, if so be that the Spirit of God dwell in you. Now if any man have not the Spirit of Christ, he is none of his. And if Christ be in you, the body is dead because of sin; but the Spirit is life because of righteousness. But if the Spirit of him that raised up Jesus from the dead dwell in you, he that raised up Christ from the dead shall also quicken your mortal bodies by his Spirit that dwelleth in you."* Notice the phrase in verse nine, *"the Spirit of God dwell in you."* Whose Spirit? God's Spirit. Notice also in verse nine, *the Spirit of Christ"*; again, whose Spirit? The Spirit of Christ.

In Matthew 18:20 when Jesus Christ says that He is in the midst of those who were involved in church discipline, it is by His Spirit. Likewise, noticing our text in Hebrews, for Christ says that He was in their midst, and it certainly also was by His Spirit that He could say this. If He were describing just a bodily appearance then such an appearance would be with great limitations; He could only be at one place at a time, but by His Holy Spirit He may elect to be in any congregation that He pleases.

B. The Jubilation by the Son. (2:12b)

"...in the midst of the church will I sing praise unto thee." Again, the same truth of Christ's presence being manifested by His Spirit is meant here. Practically, Christ sings through His saints. May we all have a song; may we all sing. When one is filled with the Spirit and sings, then Christ by the believer also sings. How else could Christ sing in the midst of the church except it be by His Spirit? Ephesians 5:18-19 says, *"And be not drunk with wine, wherein is excess; but be filled with the Spirit; Speaking to yourselves in psalms and hymns and spiritual songs, singing and making melody in your heart to the Lord";* the imperative *"be filled with the Spirit"* is a command that allows for Christ to express Himself through the believer. The Spirit-filled life is the only way that there can be a spiritual manifestation. For Christ to be revealed, Christ must be within. He is released in one's service. When one is operating in the energy of the flesh, it is with no spiritual results. When one is filled with the Spirit then there will be spiritual results.

The Spirit-filled life is not for the purpose of putting one's spirituality on display. Spiritually, that would be just as absurd as putting a sign on one's car saying that it is full of gas and parking it at a busy intersection for people to see. The practical purpose of putting gasoline into a car is so that the car can be used. The practical significance of being filled with the Spirit is so that in spiritual service one might empty Christ whenever he serves, only to be filled again so that he might continue to serve.

When Christ is in the midst of the church, three major things take place. There is a work of declaration, a work of adoration, and a work of continuation. Verse 12 shows how the work of *declaration* is ongoing by saying *"I will declare thy name unto my brethren."* Every Gospel sermon should be a declaration plainly given with the thought being, no matter who speaks, it really must be Christ speaking through us. Also, when *adoration* is going on, Christ should be so real that even our praising God should reveal Christ praising God through us. The *continuation* that goes on, because of Christ Jesus, should cause people who observe the Spirit-filled Christian to remark, "That person reminds me of Christ!"

Chapter Six

CHRIST THE PARTAKER

Text: Hebrews 2:14-18

14 Forasmuch then as the children are partakers of flesh and blood, he also himself likewise took part of the same; that through death he might destroy him that had the power of death, that is, the devil;

15 And deliver them who through fear of death were all their lifetime subject to bondage.

16 For verily he took not on him the nature of angels; but he took on him the seed of Abraham.

17 Wherefore in all things it behoved him to be made like unto his brethren, that he might be a merciful and faithful high priest in things pertaining to God, to make reconciliation for the sins of the people.

18 For in that he himself hath suffered being tempted, he is able to succor them that are tempted.

"*Forasmuch then as the children are partakers of flesh and blood, he also himself likewise took part of the same…*" This verse as it begins is so wonderfully worded. My heart is touched even as I consider this opening thought. How marvelous that God Almighty loved His fallen, sinful creation enough to come to this world as man and to hang in open shame upon the cross of Calvary. He did this becoming a partaker of flesh and blood. In biblical days, His becoming a partaker of flesh and blood was an expression that was used to describe His taking on a human frame.

This expression is not a pretty expression but a very graphic expression that accurately portrays sin-weakened humanity. Humanity is not described as "iron and steel". We think of ourselves as having that kind of invulnerability. But the troubles of life show us otherwise. We are certainly of few days and many troubles. The daily encounters with failing health and our troubles of all kinds are sober reminders that we are only *flesh and blood*. We can dream, but just for a little while; for we are *only* flesh and blood. We can build, but only for a little while, as we are *only* flesh and blood.

God in His infinite wisdom chose not to make us as iron and steel to complement and make easier our pilgrimage upon this earth, but instead did something far greater. He came to us as a partaker of flesh and blood, thus identifying with us as we truly are. He walked as a man so that He could be touched by our infirmities. He came also, as we have learned, that He *"should taste death for every man"* (Hebrews 2:9). In this study, may we look at three reasons for Him being a partaker of flesh and blood: I. He Became a Partaker of Flesh and Blood to Destroy the Devil (V. 14); II. He Became a Partaker of Flesh and Blood to Deliver the Defiled (Vv. 15-17); III. He Became a Partaker of Flesh and Blood to Defend the Discouraged (V. 18).

I. CHRIST BECAME A PARTAKER OF FLESH AND

BLOOD TO DESTROY THE DEVIL. (2:14)

A. The Devil Described. (2:14a)

Just who *really* is the devil? To answer this within the context of our study, we remind ourselves that the devil is a fallen angel. Even though God became flesh and blood, He still is God, and can prove as Paul said, that *"the foolishness of God is wiser than men; and the weakness of God is stronger than men"* (I Corinthians 1:25). Even though He took on the form that required in theological terms a *kenosis*, He still was and still is God. God has taken the route of identifying with "flesh and blood," which is, to the worldly wise man, a very humiliating and degrading way to accomplish this. To the world this appears to be a rather foolish way to bring destruction to the devil. Our text tells us that, *"he also himself likewise took part of the same; that through death he might destroy him that had the power of death, that is, the devil;"* (V. 14).

Previously in our study, we looked at Satan, or the Devil. May we identify further just who this creature is. We may begin this study by tracing his diabolical origin. He was not created by God in an evil state, for God cannot create evil. His holiness would not permit such. Satan chose to fall from his original lofty state. His choosing to do evil is the first recorded instance of rebellion taking place. It showed up originally as a sin of pride, giving us understanding as to why God hates pride so much and instructs us to do the same (Proverbs 8:13). Satan's pride is described in this manner in Ezekiel 28:17, *"Thine heart was lifted up because of thy beauty, thou hast corrupted thy wisdom by reason of thy brightness: I will cast thee to the ground, I will lay thee before kings, that they may behold thee."*

Satan was the anointed one of the cherub class of angelic beings, being described as *"full of wisdom"* and *"perfect in beauty"* (Ezekiel 28:12). Before his rebellion he was also described as being perfect in his ways from the day that he was created, until iniquity was found in him (V. 15).

In Isaiah 14:13-14, we notice five statements that characterized the haughtiness of Satan which led to him being cast out of heaven.

(1) *"I will ascend into heaven."* Satan as the exalted cherub could have gone freely into the presence of God as indicated by Ezekiel 28:14 where we see that he *"walked up and down in the midst of the stones of fire."* Yet, being motivated by pride and ambition, he was no longer content with who he was. This pictures how we may become discontented and selfishly demand more than God wishes us to have, and in the process fall from God's favor. God still hates pride.

(2) *"I will exalt my throne above the stars of God."* By this statement it seems that Satan has a desire to be further elevated above the angels. Angels are referred to as *"stars."* Again, this is a very graphic picture of how Satan became prideful and aggressive above that which God intended.

(3) "I will sit also upon the mount of the congregation, in the sides of the north." Isaiah 2:2 says, *"And it shall come to pass in the last days, that the mountain of the LORD'S house shall be established in the top of the mountains, and shall be exalted above the hills; and all nations shall flow unto it."* This verse as seen in the context, describes the Millennial

Kingdom. This statement by Satan could very well have expressed his desire to not only rule the heavens but rule all else that there is.

(4) "I will ascend above the heights of the clouds." Symbolism is being used in these several verses. The stars picture the angels; the mountains speak of rulership, and the clouds seem to refer to Satan's desire to have more glory bestowed upon him. Very profitable studies may be made by observing the way clouds appear in the Scriptures. The Lord led Israel *"by day in a pillar of a cloud"* (Exodus 13:21). This cloud was the assurance of God's presence. In Exodus 40:34, the Scriptures tell us that, *"a cloud covered the tent of the congregation, and the glory of the LORD filled the tabernacle."* Verse 35 says, *"And Moses was not able to enter into the tent of the congregation, because the cloud abode thereon, and the glory of the LORD filled the tabernacle."*

(5) "I will be like the most High." This statement clearly indicates the desire of Satan. He acknowledged that he wanted to be like the most High. This desire was nothing more than a satanic lust for power.

Isaiah chapter 14 reveals information to us pertaining to Satan's fall. Satan said that he will *"be like the most High,"* but verse 15 answers the true future state of Satan when it says, *"Yet thou shalt be brought down to hell, to the sides of the pit."* As I was writing this, it was just like the Holy Spirit had said, "Notice where Satan is going to find himself in hell...," *"to the sides of the pit"* meaning that he will not even be the *center* of attention in Hell. Praise God!

Satan is a liar and a murderer (John 8:44). He is an accuser (Revelations 12:10); he is a confirmed sinner (I John 3:8), and the adversary (I Peter 5:8). He is known scripturally by a number of names; he is known as Satan (adversary), as the Devil (slanderer), and as Lucifer (son of the morning). He also is known as Beelzebub (Matthew 12:24) and Belial (II Corinthians 6:15). Just as the Scriptures tell us who Satan is, the Scriptures also tell us where he is going. The word "destroy" is used when describing Satan's fate (V. 14). May we learn more of his fate.

B. The Devil Destroyed. (2:14b)

"...that through death he might destroy him that had the power of death, that is, the devil;" Way back in the Garden of Eden, after man had sinned, Satan was sentenced and cursed. He had taken the form of a serpent. We can only imagine what the serpent was like before the curse. Undoubtedly, he was the most attractive and the most alluring creature on the face of the earth. Knowing the scheming ways of Satan, it could have been no other way. Genesis 3:1 says that *"the serpent was more subtil than any beast of the field which the LORD God had made..."* This verse begins by showing the encounter which results in the fall of man. This also is the first recorded instance of Satan tempting mankind. The Bible is silent as to when Satan rebelled against God. As food for thought, the temptation of Eve could have been the manner by which Satan originally sinned. This could have been Satan's attempt to begin his own rulership by trying to take control of the human race. We have already discovered his desire to be like God, to rule over the angels, and to govern humanity, while at the same

time having the glory of God.

I have never heard what I am going to suggest as being taught, because the way that Satan originally sinned is thought to be a mystery. Yet Satan's fall and the fall of man *could have* coincided together. For it is after the fall of man that the curse and the sentence fell directly on Satan, the serpent. Notice the reading of Genesis 3:14, *"And the LORD God said unto the serpent, Because thou hast done this, thou art cursed above all cattle, and above every beast of the field; upon thy belly shalt thou go, and dust shalt thou eat all the days of thy life:"*

It is then immediately after this curse that the sentence was pronounced upon Satan as recorded in Genesis 3:15. *"And I will put enmity between thee and the woman, and between thy seed and her seed; it shall bruise thy head, and thou shalt bruise his heel."* In Ryrie's footnotes he words very well the interpretation of this verse, when he says, *"between thy seed"* (the spiritual descendants of Satan; cf. John 8:44; Ephesians 2:2) *"and her seed"* (those who are in the family of God). *"It,"* an individual from among the woman's seed, namely Christ, will deal a death blow to Satan's *head* and the cross, while Satan (*thou*) will *bruise* Christ's *heel* (cause Him to suffer).

Another argument that I wish to give for consideration is found in the way that God originally created. He gives us the quality of His creation in verse 31 of Genesis chapter one. *"And God saw every thing that he had made, and, behold, it was very good. And the evening and the morning were the sixth day."* Though God does not spell out everything that He had created, we do know from the Scriptures that the angels are created beings. At least on the sixth day of creation everything was still good.

Sometimes, after Adam and Eve were created, Eve was confronted by Satan the serpent and she was deceived. Revelation chapter 12 describes war in Heaven initiated by Michael and his angels. Notice carefully the reading and how Satan is described. *"And there was war in heaven: Michael and his angels fought against the dragon; and the dragon fought and his angels, And prevailed not; neither was their place found any more in heaven. And the great dragon was cast out, that old serpent, called the Devil, and Satan, which deceiveth the whole world: he was cast out into the earth, and his angels were cast out with him."* Satan is called the great dragon and the old serpent… "which deceiveth the whole world." The serpent title refers back to the original sin. Revelation 20:10 says, *"And the devil that deceived them was cast into the lake of fire and brimstone, where the beast and the false prophet are, and shall be tormented day and night for ever and ever."* Here in this verse he is the *"devil that deceived them."*

With all the emphasis in the Scriptures that pertain to his judgment referring to Satan as the *serpent* and as the *devil that deceived them,* and also in Genesis with his sentence being immediately placed upon him (Genesis 3:14-15), it seems that Satan initiated his rebellion in Eden, and thereby fell from his exalted position as a result of the temptation of Eve. Then, Revelation 20:10 clearly shows how Satan is finally destroyed. This bruising of his head took place on Calvary when Jesus was nailed to the cross. It was predicted in Genesis 3:15.

II. CHRIST BECAME A PARTAKER OF FLESH AND BLOOD TO DELIVER THE DEFILED. (2:15-16)

A. His Purpose—To Make a Relationship With Man. (2:15-16).

We have looked at how the Devil was dealt with; now may we see how death is dealt with. Before doing so, death needs to be defined in theological terms. The medical doctor may have a clinical definition for death, whereas the poet may have a literary description of death.

The Scriptures give us three kinds of death. The first, we will call *physical death*. Physical death takes place when the heart stops beating and the soul of man, along with his spirit, is separated from his body. The second kind of death is *spiritual death*. This death or separation is when man, because of sin, is separated from God. Some have described this death as emptiness or a vacuum that only God can fill. The third kind of death is *eternal death*. It occurs when the unbeliever is separated from God for all eternity in the Lake of Fire.

Romans 5:12 tells us how sin came into the world, *"Wherefore, as by one man sin entered into the world, and death by sin; and so death passed upon all men, for that all have sinned:"* Therefore sin causes death, and death causes fear. Death is said to have a sting, and certainly it does. *"The sting of death is sin…"* (1 Corinthians 15:56). Death brings fear because of all that is associated with it. When one learns that he has an incurable disease, there is a fear that normally sweeps over that person. Humanly speaking, there are enormous pressures and concerns that grip the heart of the person that has such a death sentence weighing upon him.

People often go through stages of anger and denial, before reaching that final point of acceptance. Sometimes family members must give their loved one permission to die, for seemingly they cling to and hold on to life out of a sense of guilt for leaving their loved ones behind. There are so many emotions that must be dealt with. Our text shows that God by His grace can, *"deliver them who through fear of death were all their lifetime subject to bondage."* After hearing Dr. Harold Sightler preach, Evangelist Tom Hayes wrote a song entitled "New Grace." The song says that there is a grace "we've not needed before," but when that time comes, it will be available. Praise God! It is true; I have lost three very close family members to death. In each instance not only was there grace for them, but also for their survivors.

Pertaining to death, our Captain has led the way for each of His brethren. Remember, as Captain, He is the Leader. He tasted death for all men (Hebrews 2:9). He is the Author. By this, He has written by His own life here upon earth, what it means to live as "flesh and blood," but also what it means to die and then be raised from the dead. Revelation 1:8 tells us that Christ is the "Alpha and Omega." This is the first and last letters of the Greek alphabet. There is no ending to the words that can be written and expressed when using the alphabet. He has all the answers in regards to death by being the "Alpha and Omega." Our Captain is not only the Leader, and the Author when it pertains to death, He also is the Pioneer. Revelation 1:5 says that Christ is *"the first begotten of the dead."*

For Christ to accomplish that which was necessary to finally conquer Satan and death, He took *"not on him the nature of angels; but he took on him the seed of Abraham"* (V.16). Christ did not come to save fallen angels, but instead He came to save fallen man! The Hebrew is being shown by this expression, *"seed of Abraham"* which is the way Christ (the Messiah) is identified with the descendants of Abraham. However, this connection is not only a physical connection back to Abraham, but a spiritual connection as well. May we look at the expression, *"he took on him..."* (V. 16).

This expression is wonderfully expounded by Arthur W. Pink, "An Exposition of Hebrews" (page 139), and is worthy of our quoting it in its entirety, "The Greek verb here translated 'He took on' or 'laid hold' is found elsewhere in some very striking connections. It is used of Christ's stretching out His hand and rescuing sinking Peter, Matthew 14:31, then rendered 'caught.' It is used of Christ when He 'took' the blind man by the hand (Mark 8:23). So of the man sick of the dropsy, He 'took' and healed him (Luke 14:4). Here in Hebrews 2:16 the reference is to the almighty power and invincible grace of the captain of our salvation. It receives illustration in those words of the apostles where, referring to his own conversion, he said, 'for which also I am (was) *apprehended* (laid hold) of Christ Jesus' (Philippians 3:12). Thus it was and still is with each of God's elect. In themselves, lost, rushing headlong to destruction; when Christ stretches forth His hand and delivers, so that of each it may be said, 'Is not this a brand *plucked* from the burning' (Zechariah 3:2). 'Laid hold of so securely that none can pluck out of His hand!'" (A. W. Pink).

Primarily, this statement is a statement that our Sovereign God had every right to make. It was His decision as to how He chose, and if He chose to redeem sinful man. Galatians 3:6-9 shows how the Gentile (heathen) would be saved and this was a clear indication that the Abrahamic Covenant was given for the benefit of "all nations" (V. 8). Verse 16 further sheds light when it tells us, *"Now to Abraham and his seed were the promises made. He saith not, And to seeds, as of many; but as of one, And to thy seed, which is Christ."* Reading on in verse 29, *"And if ye be Christ's, then are ye Abraham's seed, and heirs according to the promise."*

How wonderful knowing that the redeemed are also benefactors of the Abrahamic Covenant. This means that there are spiritual descendants who receive blessings as well as the natural descendants.

B. His Plan—To Make Reconciliation for Man. (2:17)

"Wherefore in all things it behoved him to be made like unto his brethren, that he might be a merciful and faithful high priest in things pertaining to God, to make reconciliation for the sins of the people." This verse and the next will end the section which demonstrates Christ's superiority over angels. We have learned that God by purpose identified with man through the seed of Abraham so that Satan could be destroyed. His being destroyed does not signify his annihilation, but means to make null and render powerless. The way this was done was through the seed of the woman. The significance of this is that the woman Eve was the one that Satan approached when he wanted to take control of the human race. Believing this to be the time that Satan initiated his plan to be equal with God, and with him directing his attack on woman, God brings punishment to Satan through the seed of the woman. This shows God to be judicially correct when dealing with the pride and the sin of Satan in reference to the woman.

To bring about this judgment upon Satan and the deliverance of man, it *"behoved him to be made like unto his brethren."* To be made like His brethren is with qualifications. He was made like man in a non-sinning capacity. He compromised neither His holiness nor His deity. To be made like unto his brethren was only to the degree that He could serve as *"a merciful and faithful high priest."* He was merciful to man and faithful to God. This is the reason that Jesus chose to serve as a Priest (from the Latin -"pontifex"). The word *priest* means bridge builder. Man required a priest to close the enormous gulf that sin had opened. He elected to do this by becoming a man.

This had to be done so that reconciliation could take place. Christ Jesus in this capacity knew the holy and just requirements of God, but He also knew the enormous needs of man. The two; the requirements of God, and the needs of man, were met at Calvary.

Jesus Christ being introduced as a merciful and a faithful priest will continue as a dominant theme throughout the remainder of Hebrews. Here His priestly work is introduced showing that reconciliation will take place. This reconciliation happens when our High Priest satisfies God's anger with the offering up of Himself. This reconciliatory work emphasizes the removal of sin by the only sacrifice that satisfies God. This work of propitiation removes sin and restores the relationship. One meaning of reconciliation "is to become friends again." With this thought in mind, "What a friend we have in Jesus."

III. HE BECAME A PARTAKER OF FLESH AND BLOOD TO DEFEND THE DISCOURAGED.

(2:18)

A. Christ Suffered Being Tempted. (2:18a)

"For in that he himself hath suffered being tempted," Matthew chapter four records the temptation that came from Satan. Satan was attempting to disqualify the Saviour so as to thwart God's plan for man's redemption. The Spirit led Jesus to this temptation to publicly prove that His Son was qualified and worthy of being the Saviour.

Our text, Hebrews 2:18 says, *"For in that he himself hath suffered being tempted, he is able to succour them that are tempted."* Think of this verse when reading the account of Christ's temptation. *"Then was Jesus led up of the Spirit into the wilderness to be tempted of the devil. And when he had fasted forty days and forty nights, he was afterward an hungred. And when the tempter came to him, he said, If thou be the Son of God, command that these stones be made bread. But he answered and said, It is written, Man shall not live by bread alone, but by every word that proceedeth out of the mouth of God. Then the devil taketh him up into the holy city, and setteth him on a pinnacle of the temple, And saith unto him, If thou be the Son of God, cast thyself down: for it is written, He shall give his angels charge concerning thee: and in their hands they shall bear thee up, lest at any time thou dash thy foot against a stone. Jesus said unto him, It is written again, Thou shalt not tempt the Lord thy God. Again, the devil taketh him up into an exceeding high mountain, and sheweth him all the kingdoms of the world, and the glory of them; And saith unto him, All these things will I give thee, if thou wilt fall down and worship me. Then saith Jesus unto him, Get thee hence, Satan: for it is written, Thou shalt worship the Lord thy God, and him only shalt thou serve.*

Then the devil leaveth him, and, behold, angels came and ministered unto him." These three temptations that Christ faced involved the temptations that man faces constantly when dealing with "the world," "the flesh," and "the devil."

B. Christ Succours Those Tempted. (2:18)

Because Christ suffered temptations as "flesh and blood," He can therefore succor those who are similarly suffering. He rushes to "succor" them that are tempted. The word *succor* means just that—a rushing to one's side even as a mother will rush to her crying baby's side. The verb *boetheo* is a compounding of two simple words: *boe*, "a shout," and *theo* "to run." Our faithful High Priest runs to help those who call. We shall find the word again in the well known verse 16 in Hebrews chapter four, where there is grace to "help in time of need (Flanigan).

Hebrews 4:14-16 summarizes the truth pertaining to the work of Christ as He "succors" those who need Him. Carefully notice the wording in these verses. *"Seeing then that we have a great high priest, that is passed into the heavens, Jesus the Son of God, let us hold fast our profession. For we have not an high priest which cannot be touched with the feeling of our infirmities; but was in all points tempted like as we are, yet without sin. Let us therefore come boldly unto the throne of grace, that we may obtain mercy, and find grace to help in time of need."* Christ Jesus, our High Priest, feels what we are experiencing because He came as a "flesh and blood" high priest.

Therefore, we can know that He is deeply sensitive to our

concerns. The next chapter will challenge us to consider the Apostle and High Priest of our profession, Christ Jesus. Even as the theme of Hebrews suggests, "Looking unto Jesus." When one looks unto Jesus and sees through the eye of faith, he should be challenged to go on to perfection. This second chapter has richly given us many reasons why we should go on to spiritual maturity. The greatest reason for motivating us is Christ Jesus, Himself.

Chapter 7

WHOM SHOULD WE CONSIDER?

Text: Hebrews 3:1-6

1 Wherefore, holy brethren, partakers of the heavenly calling, consider the Apostle and High Priest of our profession, Christ Jesus;
2 Who was faithful to him that appointed him, as also Moses was faithful in all his house.
3 For this man was counted worthy of more glory than Moses, inasmuch as he who hath builded the house hath more honour than the house.
4 For every house is builded by some man; but he that built all things is God.
5 And Moses verily was faithful in all his house, as a servant, for a testimony of those things which were to be spoken after;
6 But Christ as a son over his own house; whose house are we, if we hold fast the confidence and the rejoicing of the hope firm unto the end.

This third chapter in the development of the argument that Christ is the Superior One, begins with the word, "wherefore." The subject matter relating to His superiority proved that Christ is superior to the prophets; it was then further stated that Christ is superior to the angels. Developing this argument, Christ will be shown to be greater than Moses. This speaks volumes when considering that Moses was greatly honored and respected by the Jew, and should have been. We will look at him more closely later.

This first verse indicates to whom this letter is being addressed. *"Wherefore, holy brethren, partakers of the heavenly calling…"* We have learned that "brethren" is a name that was given as a result of the Sanctifier doing His work of sanctification. Once sanctification has taken place and sons have been brought unto glory (His glory), (Hebrews 2:10) *He then," is not ashamed to call them brethren."* The word *partaker* is now being used in the beginning of chapter three. We who as children are now partakers of flesh and blood have the right to be addressed as *"partakers of the heavenly calling."* The phrase, *"partakers of the heavenly calling"* ties back to the fact that He is not ashamed to call the *"sons unto glory,"* brethren. When Christ calls *"them brethren,"* that calling is certainly to be recognized as a heavenly calling.

Certain requirements must be met for men to be called brethren. Men are not born into the earthly family as sons of God. They are born into the human family of flesh as partakers of flesh and blood and called children. They are referred to as sons only when they are placed into the family of God. Before this takes place they have not in any way been made *"partakers of the heavenly calling."*

To be a partaker of the heavenly calling requires that there be first the call of the gospel. Then, there must be the believing of the truth followed by the sanctifying of the Spirit. II Thessalonians 2:13-14 teaches clearly this truth. Notice these verses, *"But we are bound to give thanks alway to God for you, brethren beloved of the Lord, because God hath from the beginning chosen you to salvation through sanctification of the Spirit and belief of the truth: Whereunto he called you by our gospel, to the obtaining of the glory of our Lord Jesus Christ."* This thirteenth verse teaches us that the work of sanctification is a work of the Spirit. The Spirit of Christ births one into the family of God. Thus, it is absolutely necessary that one be birthed before that one becomes a son and can then be spiritually called a brother.

Recognizing that this third chapter is being addressed to *"holy brethren,"* may we consider three thoughts: I. Whom Should We Consider (V. 1); II. Why Should We Consider (Vv. 2-5); III. The Way We Should Consider (V. 6).

I. WHOM SHOULD WE CONSIDER? (3:1)

A. Consider Christ the Apostle of Our Profession. (3:1)

The word *consider* must first be considered. Look at its meaning. As used here, the Greek verb *katanoeo* is used to challenge the brethren to direct their minds carefully toward Him. For the Jew, this seems to be especially necessary because just a casual glance will not adequately reveal Christ to them. The prophet Isaiah certainly wondered who would believe the prophetic report pertaining to Christ. This was because of the humble way in which Christ was presented. In Hebrews, there seems to be awareness on the part of the writer that Christ must be looked at very carefully and closely to be clearly seen. The writer of Hebrews knows that the Jew will not readily accept the truth pertaining to Christ. By way of application, Christ also is not commonly received today by the masses. For the Jew, there was a judicial blindness; for the unbeliever today there is an intentional blindness. Romans 1:28 says, *"And even as they did not like to retain God in their knowledge, God gave them over to a reprobate mind, to do those things which are not convenient;"*

The admonition from our text is, *"Consider."* This is a probing command. It is a consideration that does not involve just a casual glance. It calls for one to consider in the sense that there is something definitely to be examined and a lesson to be learned by doing so. Luke 12:24 uses this verb *consider*, *"Consider the ravens"* which means there is a lesson that may be learned by the one who intently considers the ravens. Yet the plea here is to *"consider the Apostle."* To consider the Apostle, one should understand why Christ is called an Apostle and be shown what the word *apostle* means.

"In general Biblical usage the word means, to send out. An apostle is a representative; a messenger, an ambassador, a person who is sent out into one country to represent another country. The word "apostle" has both a narrow and a broad usage in the New Testament. Three things are true of the apostle: I. He belongs to the one who has sent him out; II. He is commissioned to be sent out; III. He possesses all the authority and power of the One who sends him out" (Practical Word Studies in the New Testament; Vol. 1). The words *ambassador*, *messenger*, *minister*, and *servant* have been used to clarify the practical use of the word apostle. Jesus was all these things as He was sent or commissioned by the Father.

An apostle must have been chosen by the Lord or by the Holy Spirit having been an eyewitness or a companion of the Lord Jesus. This meant that the choosing had to be done by the Lord Jesus Christ, or in the case of Paul the Holy Spirit. Some scriptures that prove this are: Matthew 10:1-2; Mark 3:13-14; Luke 6:13; Acts 9:6, 15; Acts 13:2; Acts 22:10, 14- 15; and Romans 1:1. Today no one can refer to themselves as an apostle and be scriptural when doing so.

Jesus is called an Apostle of our profession, meaning that He was sent to do a particular work in regards to salvation. We should consider Him relative to that special work that required that He be sent. We also should understand the time in which He came as being of great significance. We are to consider Him as having been sent forth *"in these last days,"* as having *"made the worlds," "who being the brightness of his glory, and the express image of his person,"* who upholds all things *"by the word of his power."* We are to also consider Him as having been *"made so much better than the angels."* We must also consider that He was sent, to *"destroy him that had the power of death, that is the devil."*

The first two chapters give us plenty of reason to consider why he was sent. He, who is the *"Altogether Lovely One,"* is worthy of our constant consideration. By constantly studying and meditating on the Word, we may always be considering Him. Practically, we should consider Him as we make our decisions, as we have our relationships, and as we plan our days. Consider Him by always asking, "What would Jesus do?" Or, maybe better, "Jesus, what would you have me to do?" To consider Him means to be considerate of Him.

B. Consider Christ the High Priest of Our Profession.

(3:16)

It is commonly understood that as "Apostle, Christ Jesus came to earth to represent God to man. When Christ Jesus is referred to as "the Word" (John 1:1), that is what is meant; He is the Word of God. In Hebrews 1:3 we learned that Jesus is the "express image of his person." God the Father sent Jesus to express Himself fully. For believers today, the written Word is still doing just that.

Continuing in verse one of our text, the plea is made to consider Jesus also as the "High Priest of our profession." How may we properly do this? First, this is an idea that the writer to the Hebrews refers to again and again. The idea of Jesus being the High Priest is given as a common concept to the Jew. The entire Jewish system, beginning with Moses appointing Aaron, had served the purpose of educating the people to the workings of the priestly office. The books of Moses lay the foundation for properly understanding the priesthood. A key to understanding the function of the priesthood is by reminding ourselves that the word *priest* in the Latin is *pontifex* which means, *bridge builder.* Christ Jesus is the one who builds the bridge between man and God. For this to be accomplished, He must have a relationship with both man and God. He must know both man and God intimately. On a personal basis, He knows me. He knows all about me. With this being true, He knows what to tell the Father about me. He does this though in a most caring and understanding way (Hebrews 4:15).

He also, as Hebrews 3:2 will tell us, is *"faithful to him that appointed him."* Surely, we must be encouraged by this. Consider this. He is the faithful High Priest always busy about His Father's business as demonstrated when He walked upon the earth. We have been told by the writer of Hebrews to consider Him. Now, may we ask why we should consider him.

II. WHY SHOULD WE CONSIDER HIM? (3:2-6a)

A. Because of the Honor Belonging to Christ Only.

  (3:2-3)

"Who was faithful to him that appointed him, as also

Moses was faithful in all his house. For this man was counted worthy of more glory than Moses, inasmuch as he who hath builded the house hath more honour than the house." Moses was *"faithful in all his house"* but *"this man was counted worthy of more glory than Moses."*

We now will look at Moses to properly understand how we should consider Christ. In the consideration of Christ, Adolph Saphir, D.D. (1831-1891) has proven most helpful in the way he viewed Moses. Dr. Saphir was a Jewish convert to Christianity and has special insight. Some of the thoughts pertaining to Moses are being borrowed from Saphir.

"It is difficult for the Gentile to understand the veneration and the affection that the Jews had for Moses. It was Moses who was sent to them to deliver them out of their bondage. Moses was their apostle. He was the mediator of the old covenant. In Acts the Jews were never ashamed, but proud to say that "we are the disciples of Moses." They recalled how Moses was lifted up out of the bulrushes and taken into the very court of Pharaoh. They knew that Moses was given the training and the luxury that only Pharaoh could have provided. They also knew that Moses forsook all those things to condescend to them and be their leader. We may remind ourselves that Jesus condescended leaving much more than even Moses.

Moses removed himself to the backside of the desert after killing the abusive soldier and burying him in the sand. Yet God was not through with Moses. He was to be resurrected from the desert to lead a mighty nation. He led this nation with great vigor and with great determination.

Through Moses the entire Levitical dispensation was instituted. The learned Benal says, "While two chapters in Genesis are given to tell us how the world was created, there are 16 chapters to tell us how the tabernacle was to be built. For the world was made for the sake of the church; and the great object of all creation is to glorify God in the redemption and sanctification of His people" (Epistle to the Hebrews; Adolph Saphir, page 176).

Moses was introduced as he appealed to Pharaoh in requesting that his people be freed. Miracle after miracle took place demonstrating that Moses was a person unlike any other. He had been given a special honor and a special commission to do the work of the One who sent him. Just as God commissioned Moses, He on a greater plane commissioned His Son Jesus.

Moses accomplished many great things. Through him God led Israel out of Egypt and through the Red Sea. It was by Moses that the Ten Commandments and the law were given. It was also by Moses that the entire national life of Israel was established. The theocracy enjoyed by Israel had its birth in Moses. Moses was said to be faithful *"in all his house,"* and that he was. Without faith it is impossible to please God, but Moses was faithful.

Everything that Moses did in regards to Israel was a part of *"his house."* Moses was used of God to structure its legal system, giving Israel a moral code. He was able to endure as he led them through the wilderness. For forty years he led his people until he came to Mount Nebo to die. They and all that were involved made up his house. Yet his house, as great as it might have been, was inferior to the house of Jesus.

The house of Moses may be called the house that law built; the house of Jesus may be called the house that grace built. John 1:17 says, *"For the law was given by Moses, but grace and truth came by Jesus Christ."* The writer of Hebrews after carefully giving honor to Moses is now moving to show that Christ Jesus is worthy of more honor. It should be understood that Moses is a type of Christ. The type is always only a *shadow*. Christ is the substance. Both Moses and Jesus were threatened by death because of the cruel rulers of their day. Moses was *willing* to die for Israel; Jesus *did* die for humanity. Moses brought the law on tables of stone; The Lord Jesus writes the law on our hearts. As great as Moses was, consider this: Christ is greater!

B. Because of the House Belonging to Christ Only.

(3:4, 6a)

The House of Christ is different than the house of Moses. The writer of Hebrews is encouraging in a very delicate manner for those who were still occupying the old house of law to vacate it and move into the house of Grace. Certainly the old house had served a very noble purpose, but that original purpose had expired. The old house was of another dispensation. The time period that the book of Hebrews was being written was a transitional period. One only needs to study the book of Acts to see this truth amplified. In the book of Romans, Paul stated that the Israelites had *"a zeal of God, but not according to knowledge"* (Romans 10:2). Paul said that they were ignorant of God's righteousness and were going about to establish their own righteousness. In verse three of Romans ten, we are told that they *"have not submitted themselves unto the righteousness of God."* Verse five says that *"Moses describeth the righteousness which is of the law;"* Verse four says, *"For Christ is the end of the law for righteousness to every one that believeth."*

Paul was dealing with the Jews who wanted to stay in the old house. Paul had to leave the old house admitting later that he had stayed in it out of ignorance. Lydia was worshiping God in the old house, but God opened up her heart of unbelief, which allowed her to move into the new house. The Ethiopian eunuch is another example. The Spirit of God directed Philip to the Gaza strip to confront the eunuch with the Gospel of Christ. When the eunuch asked, *"what doth hinder me to be baptized?"* (Acts 8:36), he was ready to move from the old house to the new house. Philip answered the eunuch, *"If thou believest with all thine heart, thou mayest.* And the eunuch said, *"I believe that Jesus Christ is the Son of God"* (V. 37). This is when the Ethiopian moved from the old house to the new house. The new house has much greater honor.

It has greater honor because it is the house that Jesus built. In a greater sense, the house that Jesus built is the Church. He is the Chief Corner Stone, and we are built together as *"lively stones."* The Lord Jesus takes up His abode in us, and we in Him. We are brought together as the Church. As the Church we are framed together. The

Church as described in the New Testament could not have existed in the Old Testament. The requirements of the Law knew nothing of the Spirit of Ephesians when it described the Church. Let the Word itself speak in the following verses found in Ephesians 2:11-22. *"Wherefore remember, that ye being in time past Gentiles in the flesh, who are called Uncircumcision by that which is called the Circumcision in the flesh made by hands; That at that time ye were without Christ, being aliens from the commonwealth of Israel, and strangers from the covenants of promise, having no hope, and without God in the world: But now in Christ Jesus ye who sometimes were far off are made nigh by the blood of Christ. For he is our peace, who hath made both one, and hath broken down the middle wall of partition between us; Having abolished in his flesh the enmity, even the law of commandments contained in ordinances; for to make in himself of twain one new man, so making peace; And that he might reconcile both unto God in one body by the cross, having slain the enmity thereby: And came and preached peace to you which were afar off, and to them that were nigh. For through him we both have access by one Spirit unto the Father. Now therefore ye are no more strangers and foreigners, but fellowcitizens with the saints, and of the household of God; And are built upon the foundation of the apostles and prophets, Jesus Christ himself being the chief corner stone; In whom all the building fitly framed together growth unto an holy temple in the Lord: In whom ye also are builded together for an habitation of God through the Spirit."*

Another major consideration is that Moses was a servant over his house, but in a much more superior way

Christ is a Son over His house. The argument of the superiority of Christ forges on.

III. THE WAY WE SHOULD CONSIDER HIM. (3:6b)

A. By Holding Fast the Confidence. (3:6b)

"But Christ as a son over his own house; whose house are we, if we hold fast the confidence and the rejoicing of the hope firm unto the end." The grace way is also the faith way. One does not satisfy God by working first; one satisfies God by believing first. Once belief has been established then there must be works. God wants us to move from the house of law to the house of grace. Abel worked in offering his bloody sacrifice, but he believed first. Cain worked, but there was no belief. Had there been belief it would have been made evident by Cain's works. This Cain-like spirit is what still separates mere religion from living faith and worship.

The ongoing theme of Hebrews that insures one going on to perfection is keeping our eyes upon Jesus. There is no way that the church collectively, and the church individually, can be strong when it does not operate by faith. So much that we do is calculated without any element of faith. To be ruled by faith, is to walk freely in His grace. Faith must govern the believer. To worship God without faith is not acceptable. Later in this chapter a warning is given, *"Take heed brethren, lest there be in any of you an evil heart of unbelief, in departing from the living God"* (V. 12).

An outstanding mark that characterizes the believer is his love and obedience to the Word of God. To obey the Word of God, one must believe the Word of God to be so. The late Charles Haddon Spurgeon believed the Bible to be perfect. Here is his testimony to the Bible's perfection: "This volume is the writing of the living God: Each letter was penned with an almighty finger; each word in it dropped from the everlasting lips; each sentence was dictated by the Holy Spirit. Albeit, that Moses was employed to write the histories with his fiery pen, God guided that pen. It may be that David touched his harp and let sweet Psalms of melody drop from his fingers, but God moved his hands over the living strings of his golden harp. It may be that Solomon sang canticles of love, or gave forth words of consummate wisdom, but God directed his lips and made the preacher eloquent. If I follow the thundering Nahum, when his horses plough the waters, or Habakkuk, when he sees the tents of Cushan in affliction; if I read Malachi, when the earth is burning like an oven, if I turn to the smooth pages of John, who tells of love, or the rugged, fiery chapter of Peter, who speaks of fire devouring God's enemies; if I turn to Jude, who launches forth anathemas upon the face of God-everywhere I find God speaking. It is God's voice, not man's; the words are God's words, the words of the Eternal, the Invisible, the Almighty, the Jehovah of this earth" (Charles Hadden Spurgeon).

One of the dangers that prevail today is the on-going attack on the King James Bible. The lie that is being perpetrated says that the King James Bible should be replaced. It does not fit in today's English. When one moves like this from truth, he is moving toward a lie. It then becomes impossible to exercise confidence. If one's confidence is being exercised this way, then it is being placed in the wrong thing. We need to "hold fast the confidence" by being steadfast. I Corinthians 15:58 tells us this, *"Therefore, my beloved brethren, be ye stedfast, unmoveable, always abounding in the work of the Lord, forasmuch as ye know that your labour is not in vain in the Lord."* To be stedfast to the work of the Lord, one must be steadfast to the Word of God.

B. By Holding Firm the Rejoicing of the Hope Unto the End. (3:6b)

We certainly have reason to shout and rejoice right unto the end. The book of Hebrews is a very challenging book of the Bible. I was talking to Dr. Charles Keene recently. He said that the book of Hebrews is his favorite book. Dr. Keene has been extremely involved in getting the Scriptures out for several decades. We will look at several verses pertaining mostly to Christ as we close out this section. Verses like this may be the reason Dr. Keene and so many others love the book of Hebrews. These verses will be given greater consideration later, but now may they whet our appetites proving that we have so much to shout about.

Powerful Word—*"For the word of God is quick, and powerful, and sharper than any twoedged sword, piercing even to the dividing asunder of soul and spirit, and of the joints and marrow, and is a discerner of the thoughts and intents of the heart"* (Hebrews 4:12). This verse is a cure for unbelief. It shows us that we should place our confidence and trust in Christ because His Word *"is quick, and powerful and sharper than any twoedged sword."* The Word of God is our weapon as we go on to perfection. It will help us cut through many difficulties along the way.

Great High Priest—*"Seeing then that we have a great high priest, that is passed into the heavens, Jesus the Son of God, let us hold fast our profession. For we have not an high priest which cannot be touched with the feeling of our infirmities; but was in all points tempted like as we are, yet without sin"* (Hebrews 4:14-15). These verses tell us that we can hold fast our profession because our High Priest has victoriously passed into the heavens. He also knows what we are going through day by day.

Saved forever—*"And being made perfect, he became the author of eternal salvation unto all them that obey him;"* (Hebrews 5:9). This verse describes our Saviour being made perfect as the Author of eternal salvation. This truth should put one on shouting ground.

A hope as an anchor—*"Which hope we have as an anchor of the soul, both sure and stedfast, and which entereth into that within the veil;"* (Hebrews 6:19). Christ is our anchor. He is an anchor of the soul; He is sure, and He is steadfast. Many storms may come, but you need not be tossed to and fro, for the Anchor still holds.

An unchangeable priesthood—*"But this man, because he continueth ever, hath an unchangeable priesthood"* (Hebrews 7:24). How wonderful knowing that we have a Priest who is available, and that He will always be available. It is never necessary to call back because of a wrong number, and our High Priest does not put us on hold. The Old Testament priest could not continue by reason of death or defilement. This is not so with our High Priest; He ever lives to make intercession.

He can save to the uttermost—*"Wherefore he is able also to save them to the uttermost that come unto God by him, seeing he ever liveth to make intercession for them"* (Hebrews 7:25). Years ago I heard a message on this text entitled "Saved from the Gutter-most to the Uttermost." His salvation is complete and permanent. He saves to the uttermost. When Jesus saves, it matters not how sinful you are; He can save you completely.

He is higher than the Heavens—*"For such an high priest became us, who is holy, harmless, undefiled, separate from sinners, and made higher than the heavens;"* (Hebrews 7:26). Our High Priest comes to sinners, but sinners do not contaminate Him. He also is holy, harmless, and undefiled.

He obtained eternal redemption for us—*"Neither by the blood of goats and calves, but by his own blood he entered in once into the holy place, having obtained eternal redemption for us"* (Hebrews 9:12). His Priestly work, including His sacrifice, does not have to be repeated. He only needed to go once into the holy place to obtain eternal redemption for us.

He goes into the presence of God for us—*"For Christ is not entered into the holy places made with hands, which are the figures of the true; but into heaven itself, now to appear in the presence of God for us:"* (Hebrews 9:24). Christ Jesus is now in Heaven appearing in the presence of God, on our behalf. He intercedes for His own.

He will make you perfect—*"Now the God of peace, that brought again from the dead our Lord Jesus, that great shepherd of the sheep, through the blood of the everlasting covenant, Make you perfect in every good work to do his will, working in you that which is wellpleasing in his sight, through Jesus Christ; to whom be glory for ever and ever. Amen"* (Hebrews 13:20-21). These two verses are wonderfully given, and show the ongoing work of the Lord to bring about our perfection. It is God's purpose that we are like Him. To be like Him we must keep our eyes upon Him. This is only done when we learn of Him from the Word of God. I can only see His face when I see His face by the Word of God. I can only see His hands when I see His hands by the Word of God. Likewise, I can only see His feet, when I see His feet by His Word. All that I know of Him, He shows me in His Word. May we always *consider Him* this way.

Chapter Eight

DO NOT BE HINDERED BY UNBELIEF

Text: Hebrews 3:7-19

7 Wherefore (as the Holy Ghost saith, To day if ye will hear his voice,
8 Harden not your hearts, as in the provocation, in the day of temptation in the wilderness:
9 When your fathers tempted me, proved me, and saw my works forty years.
10 Wherefore I was grieved with that generation, and said, They do alway err in their heart; and they have not known my ways.
11 So I sware in my wrath, They shall not enter into my rest.)
12 Take heed, brethren, lest there be in any of you an evil heart of unbelief, in departing from the living God.
13 But exhort one another daily, while it is called To day; lest any of you be hardened through the deceitfulness of sin.
14 For we are made partakers of Christ, if we hold the beginning of our confidence stedfast unto the end;
15 While it is said, To day if ye will hear his voice, harden not your hearts, as in the provocation.
16 For some, when they had heard, did provoke: howbeit not all that came out of Egypt by Moses.

17 But with whom was he grieved forty years? was it not with them that had sinned, whose carcases fell in the wilderness?
18 And to whom sware he that they should not enter into his rest, but to them that believed not?
19 So we see that they could not enter in because of unbelief.

While introducing this section may we carefully examine verse seven, *"Wherefore (as the Holy Ghost saith, To day if ye will hear his voice..."* Notice first who is speaking. It is the Holy Ghost. This alone should show us how serious this section is. When the Holy Ghost speaks it is always in the language of the Bible. If one says the Holy Ghost has spoken and there is no connection to the Bible, then He has not spoken! A statement like this should not even need to be said; it should be understood. Yet today there are different authorities that are being religiously accepted. Here are some examples how these authorities are being exercised. Papal authority says that truth and dogma belongs to the Pope and the Catholic Church alone. Creedal authority rests upon the church creeds, whereas charismatic authority accepts feelings and experiences. Yet there are still those of us who have the same battle cry as did those of the Reformation Period when they cried: "*Sola Scriptura*", which means the Scriptures alone. For those of us who embrace the Word of God, the Bible is our only and final authority.

The next word that we may consider is the word *"To day"*. Though spoken to the Hebrews, the urgency is the same to us now. Human nature wants us to put off; we procrastinate even when we hear the Word of God telling us to do otherwise. Anytime truth is delivered it should be received. When instructional truth is given, it should be obeyed immediately. Delayed obedience, is the same as disobedience.

The next phrase, *"if ye will hear his voice"* is a phrase that I want to focus on as we continue to introduce our study. The Holy Ghost says, *"if ye will hear his voice."* Obedience is an act of the will. One obeys when one chooses to obey. There can be no consecration without obedience. When one is not consecrated, he is also not surrendered. Another aspect of obedience is submission. Charles G. Finney said that there are several things implied by true submission. He said there must first be the forsaking of all known sin. He went on to say, "It is absurd to say that an individual is utterly submitted to God if he still indulges in any known sin. To suppose that true submission is consistent with any degree of known sin is to overlook the very nature of submission. Submission belongs to the will and consists of the total devotion of the heart to the whole known will of God" (Principles of Consecration; Charles G. Finney; page 16).

Finny also said that submission implies recognition of the universal providence of God. By this he meant that God is concerned with all events. Many times the providence of God is at work while showing us the will of God. Often I have reminded myself "God opens doors that no man can close, and closes doors that no man can open." Over 25 years ago, God opened the door for me to pastor the Bible Baptist Church. I was called with a 51% vote. I recalled at the time of my accepting the church how Dr. Russell Rice, my college professor at Tabernacle Baptist Bible College had told his class, "Generally you do not take a church unless you have at least 80% of the people calling you." Had it not been for some obvious open doors that God had placed before me, I would not have accepted the pastorate of the Bible Baptist Church. Thanks be unto God, I am enjoying the greatest years of my ministry over 25 years later.

The third thing that Finney said that should mark the act of true submission is an "honest, earnest and diligent inquiry to know the will of God" (ibid; page 17). Man should run towards truth in seeking to know and do the will of God, not away from it. Again, the personal will is critically involved when doing the will of God. One should desire it. The intensity of that desire marks how far one goes into the will of God. Finding the will of God should be as a journey into the heart of God. One cannot know the heart and the mind of God without learning Him, and knowing Him by His Word. We will consider this further later in this study.

This seventh verse is a call to fidelity; it is a very intense verse. For without hearing His voice there will be no response. One of the concerns shown by this Hebrew letter is that the readers were dull of hearing. For instructions to be clearly understood they must be precisely heard. God's Word, the Bible, is clearly given. Each word is God-breathed. True evidence of words really being heard is that the words are being obeyed.

As we are being warned of the calamity of unbelief, may

we observe two things that warns us of the perils of unbelief: I. The Provocation was For Our Example (Vv. 7-12); II. The Exhortation is For Our Escape (Vv. 13-19).

I. THE PROVOCATION WAS FOR OUR EXAMPLE. (3:7-12)

A. Be Warned By the Provocation. (3:7-8)

Verse seven, as already discussed, should remind us that we have a serious choice to either hear or not to hear the Lord's voice. The warning, *"Harden not your hearts, as in the provocation, in the day of temptation in the wilderness"* (V. 8), is a warning that has an example of the consequences of that which happens when your heart is hardened. The verb rendered "harden" means to dry up, to become hard or stiff. Nothing dries a person up like not hearing the Word.

One of the pastoral concerns that I experience when people either do not faithfully attend the church services or do not hear what is being taught is that they are soon to dry up with their hearts being hardened. This is certainly a tragedy and answers the reason they cannot *"enter into his rest"* (V. 18). People like this have no sensitivity to the things of the Lord. The word *provocation* means rebellion and describes the nation of Israel when they hardened their hearts. Rebellion also describes those today who refuse to hear the Word of God.

To properly understand verse eight, verse nine must be read as an explanation. Verse eight refers to the day of temptation. The word *day* here likely does not refer to just one single day but to a period of time that has a common element of similar ongoing activity. This period of time here may be described as a time of rebellion. Verse nine tells how long that *"day"* was; *"when your fathers tempted me, proved me, and saw my works forty years."* Numbers 14:22 speaks of there being ten specific times that rebellion took place. Notice the verse, *"Because all those men which have seen my glory, and my miracles, which I did in Egypt and in the wilderness, and have tempted me now these ten times, and have not hearkened to my voice;"*

May we summarize these ten provocations (times of rebellion), understanding while we do that we should be warned lest we be guilty of hardening our hearts in a similar manner.

(1) At the Red Sea (Exodus 14:11-12). *"And they said unto Moses, Because there were no graves in Egypt, hast thou taken us away to die in the wilderness? wherefore hast thou dealt thus with us, to carry us forth out of Egypt? Is not this the word that we did tell thee in Egypt, saying, Let us alone, that we may serve the Egyptians? For it had been better for us to serve the Egyptians, than that we should die in the wilderness."* The only way that Moses knew how to respond to the Israelites when "their backs were up against the wall" was by saying, *"stand still, and* *see the salvation of the LORD"* (Exodus 14:13). The Israelites speaking to Moses the way they did was attributed to their unbelief. They thought God was going to let them come to the water's edge only for them to be destroyed. God proved Himself otherwise at the Red Sea.

(2) At Marah (Exodus 15:23-24). *"And when they came to Marah, they could not drink of the waters of Marah, for they were bitter: therefore the name of it was called Marah. And the people murmured against Moses, saying, What shall we drink?"* The murmuring of the people, against Moses, was again attributed to their unbelief. As Christians we too will often face bitter waters. We must challenge ourselves to believe that the Lord will deliver us in spite of the bitter waters. In the instance of Moses, he cried to the Lord and the Lord then showed Moses a tree. In our economy the Lord has shown us more than a tree; He showed us the Person on the tree. It was on Calvary's tree that our waters were sweetened.

(3) In the Wilderness of Sin (Exodus 16:2-4). *"And the whole congregation of the children of Israel murmured against Moses and Aaron in the wilderness: And the children of Israel said unto them, Would to God we had died by the hand of the LORD in the land of Egypt, when we sat by the flesh pots, and when we did eat bread to the full; for ye have brought us forth into this wilderness, to kill this whole assembly with hunger. Then said the LORD unto Moses, Behold, I will rain bread from heaven for you;*

and the people shall go out and gather a certain rate every day, that I may prove them, whether they will walk in my law, or no." This time hunger pains caused the children of Israel to murmur. Instead of God destroying Israel, He graciously rained down bread from Heaven. This pictures the grace of God in the similar way that He sent His darling Son, the Bread of Life from Heaven to us.

(4) Pertaining to Manna (Exodus 16:19-20). *"And Moses said, Let no man leave of it till the morning. Notwithstanding they hearkened not unto Moses; but some of them left of it until the morning, and it bred worms, and stank: and Moses was wroth with them."* The people of Israel were greedy. They showed their unbelief and their greed. We should learn from this to trust the Lord for our provisions while being thankful for all that He provides without being greedy.

(5) Again in Connection with Manna (Exodus 16:26-28). *"Six days ye shall gather it; but on the seventh day, which is the sabbath, in it there shall be none. And it came to pass, that there went out some of the people on the seventh day for to gather, and they found none. And the LORD said unto Moses, How long refuse ye to keep my commandments and my laws?"* The unbelief here is demonstrated as the people of Israel disobeyed the Lord pertaining to the Sabbath. Greed is the underlying cause of their rebellion. How much like Israel are we if we walk in disobedience.

(6) At Rephidim (Exodus 17:1-3). *"And all the congregation of the children of Israel journeyed from the wilderness of Sin, after their journeys, according to the commandment of the LORD, and pitched in Rephidim: and there was no water for the people to drink. Wherefore the people did chide with Moses, and said, Give us water that we may drink. And Moses said unto them, Why chide ye with me? wherefore do ye tempt the LORD? And the people thirsted there for water; and the people murmured against Moses, and said, Wherefore is this that thou hast brought us up out of Egypt, to kill us and our children and our cattle with thirst?"* This was where the people *"did chide with Moses"*. They failed to trust the Lord with patience. It was here that God instructed Moses to smite the Rock of Horeb. Then the water came forth after he struck the rock. This very graphically pictures Jesus who is our Rock being smitten on the cross.

(7) At Horeb (Exodus 32:7-8). *"And the LORD said unto Moses, Go, get thee down; for thy people, which thou broughtest out of the land of Egypt, have corrupted themselves: They have turned aside quickly out of the way which I commanded them: they have made them a molten calf, and have worshipped it, and have sacrificed thereunto, and said, These be thy gods, O Israel, which have brought thee up out of the land of Egypt."* This is where the people demonstrated gross wickedness in reverting back to an Egyptian lifestyle. Egypt pictures the world. God's wrath was hot against them for reverting back to the world (Exodus 32:10). Worldliness involves both disobedience and unbelief.

(8) Taberah (Numbers 11:1). *"And when the people complained, it displeased the LORD: and the LORD heard it; and his anger was kindled; and the fire of the LORD burnt among them, and consumed them that were in the uttermost parts of the camp."* The Spirit-filled life is marked by gratitude. When people, as Israel, are void of a thankful heart and have instead a complaining heart it certainly must anger the Lord just as it did against Israel. This illustration pictures the very opposite of the Spirit-filled life.

(9) The Mixed Multitude (Numbers 11:4). *"And the mixt multitude that was among them fell a lusting: and the children of Israel also wept again, and said, Who shall give us flesh to eat?"* This illustration shows the dissatisfaction that comes about when unbelief is going on. This unbelief may be traced back to there being a mixed multitude. The mixed multitude is a type of present day people who are unequally yoked in their relationship to each other and the world.

(10) Kadesh-Barnea (Numbers 14:22-24). *"Because all those men which have seen my glory, and my miracles, which I did in Egypt and in the wilderness, and have tempted me now these ten times, and have not hearkened to my voice; Surely they shall not see the land which I sware unto their fathers, neither shall any of them that provoked me see it: But my servant Caleb, because he had another* *spirit with him, and hath followed me fully, him will I bring into the land whereinto he went; and his seed shall possess it."* This is the grand finale of unbelief. Only Joshua and Caleb exercised faith. The entire fourteenth chapter of Numbers tells the sordid story of *not conquering through unbelief.* This chapter shows the awful consequences of their unbelief, along with the death of millions predicted; *"sin, when it is finished, bringeth forth death"* (James 1:15b).

These ten provocations clearly show how unbelief brings its consequences along with its heartbreaks. May we be warned?

B. Beware of the Temptations. (3:9)

"When your fathers tempted me, proved me, and saw my works forty years." Normally when we think about temptation it is as applied and taught in James 1:2-3. The word *temptation* is used in James to describe one who undergoes trials or testing. The word *tempted* is used in our text in a very negative way. It is questioning God's ability, His power, and His might. Actually it is a total lack of trust towards the Lord. Trust must be one hundred percent. You either trust God or you do not trust Him. The nation of Israel failed to trust God, yet God graciously proved Himself over and over again to be trustworthy.

When the nation of Israel tempted God they were doing so with both their attitudes and their actions. Their tempting God was done in rebellion instead of out of a desire to just see God work. The children of Israel were resisting God and God's man every step of the way. One sure way of recognizing that the temptations were wrong was that the temptations brought forth the Lord's anger. In one case we are told that the Lord's anger was *"kindled"*. In another place the Lord's anger *"waxed hot."*

There are times that it is appropriate to put God to the test. An example of this is in Malachi when the Lord was rebuking the people for robbing God. He challenged them to, *"Bring ye all the tithes into the storehouse, that there may be meat in mine house, and prove me now herewith, saith the Lord of hosts, if I will not open you the windows of heaven, and pour you out a blessing, that there shall not be room enough to receive it"* (Malachi 3:10).

The Lord does not mind us putting Him to the test when our attitudes are right. God is constantly involved in maturing the saints by showing Himself faithful. One wonderful aspect of growing older in the faith is having the ability to categorize the faithful acts of God along the way. My courage is greater simply because I have without fail found God to always be faithful.

Rebellion is a heart thing; it is an attitude that forges or forms one's actions. One cannot boast to be consecrated to the Lord if his attitude is wrong. The warning given in this section is to protect us who have confessed this, lest we be like that *"church in the wilderness"* (Acts 7:38). The Hebrew word for "provocation" is *Meribah*, which means strife. The word for *"temptation"* is *Massah*. For 40 years the people in the wilderness constantly *"tempted"* God, by *"proving"* Him. They simply refused to trust the Lord. Even as the Lord repeatedly proved Himself, they would not believe. We, many times as did Israel, fail to recognize God's power when He does something wonderful for us in the church to then only to be followed by our further discontent and rebellion. God help us to learn, lest our life be only a wilderness experience as was Israel's.

C. Be Wise in Your Generation. (3:10-12)

Verse ten starts, *"Wherefore I was grieved with that generation, and said, They do alway err in their heart; and they have not known my ways."* The Lord was grieved with that generation, and the Lord just as easily can be grieved with this present generation. Analyzing this verse, we notice the two reasons for the Lord being grieved: I. *"They do alway err in their heart."* II. *"they have not known my ways."* Verse 12 says that they had an evil heart of unbelief. This was not an occasional slippage, but something that they always did. They did this because their hearts were hardened. They were impervious to God's ways, because they were impervious to God's words. When people of any generation become hardened to God's words, they will also be hardened to God's ways.

In a practical sense, we should carefully guard our hearts lest we become desensitized to God's whisper. When the Lord whispers we must listen. Now, referring back to the people who were called *"that generation,"* this could be said about them. They were blatantly ignorant of knowing the ways of the Lord. They were guilty of refusing to hear God's man, or to follow God's law. God's law was their standard of righteousness and they failed to measure up to it. In Romans, another generation of Israel was struggling with ignorance. They were, according to Romans 10:3, *"ignorant of God's righteousness."*

They had *"a zeal of God, but not according to knowledge"* (Romans 10:2). This could not be said about Israel in the wilderness; they certainly were lacking the knowledge of God's way, but they also had no zeal of God. They were in blatant rebellion. The writer of Hebrews is strongly warning his readers to be careful, *"Take heed, brethren, lest there be in any of you an evil heart of unbelief, in departing from the living God"* (Hebrews 3:12). The writer is trying to impress upon his readers that the same thing can happen all over again. Never should we think that we are immune to this happening. It can happen to us as well as others. For this reason the next part of our study will consider the value of exhortation.

II. THE EXHORTATION IS FOR OUR ESCAPE. (3:13-19)

A. Exhort One Another While You Can. (3:13-14)

Verse seven says, *"Wherefore (as the Holy Ghost saith, To day if ye will hear his voice..."*. This is the beginning of a quote from Psalm 95:7-11 where the children of Israel were challenging God's authority over them by their rebellion in the wilderness. Notice the words *"To day."* As we have already learned, there is an urgent plea to obey the Lord. That urgency is seen once again in verse 13 in regards to exhortation. Exhortation is something that should be done with urgency. It is critical not to wait too late. This certainly is true in our child rearing. As parents we wake up to realize that our "To day" of opportunity has passed. I recall reading the story of a distraught lady asking her counselor, "What can I do with my rebellious 17 year old son?" He answered, "Shrink him back down to a two year old and start over again." His point obviously was that the lady had waited too late.

A lost person in his hardness can sin away his day of grace and never come to the Lord. I witnessed just this week to a 46 year old man dying with an alcohol-related disease. He had no desire to hear the things of God. Just hours before he died, he told his concerned brother that he did not want to hear him even talk about the Lord. In his sin-hardened state he told his brother to be quiet while at the same time he was using profanity. Very likely he is now burning in Hell, while his sin cursed body lies in the grave.

Not only do unbelievers let their hearts become hardened through the deceitfulness of sin, but believers do as well. It is a dangerous thing for believers to let this happen. Hebrews chapter 12 tells us that the Lord will chasten us to get us to put our eyes and ears back on Jesus. Not having your eyes upon Jesus means that you are not in submission to Him. If you are not in submission to Christ then you cannot be consecrated. People do not mind being in submission when everything seems to be going their way. When one is enjoying prosperity, good health, and is not facing any kind of conflict, it is rather easy to be in submission. There may be a lengthy passing of time before one has the symptoms of not being in submission to the Lord. With the gradual passing of time hardness is setting in. From our text, it is obvious that the Israelites had gradually fallen prey to unbelief, so their successors, the Christians, must watch out that they do not fall prey to the very same trap. We should exhort one another (V. 13) lest we put on or even let someone else put on the same cloak of deceit, as did the children of Israel.

B. Exhort One Another Without Callousness. (3:15-17)

The subject and the plea are still, *"harden not your hearts."* We should constantly remind ourselves that while we exhort others to do right, we must also be doing right. Paul knew the meaning of this concept when in Acts 20:28 he said *"Take heed therefore unto yourselves, and to all the flock..."* The first requirement given by Paul was that the elders or the preacher, first take care of themselves before pretending to be taking care of others. There will be many preachers and religious leaders who will stand in judgment only to hear, *"Depart from me."* They will be cast into the Lake of Fire after having stood in their own pulpits preaching to others and warning others of eternal punishment.

Preaching can be like a medicine that dulls the conscience, even while the preacher preaches to others. The preacher is deceived when thinking that if he is preaching to others, then all must be well. Nothing may be further from the truth. Likewise, a person can be doing good and wonderful things while placing their confidence in what they are *doing*. This shows how deceitful sin can be. It shows how good people can be deceived by their act of doing good, whereas evil people are deceived by their doing evil.

Even when people do good things they can become proud. They can become prideful even as Cain did when he made his offering. Cain surely must have felt *good* when offering *his very best*. God did not want Cain's very best only. God wanted submission. He wanted Cain to submit or to consecrate himself to the Lord. Abel submitted, but Cain did not.

The seventeenth verse tells us that God was grieved with those who sinned. It was their carcasses which fell in the wilderness, reminding us as James tells us, *"sin, when it is finished, bringeth forth death."* Most of the forty years that was spent in the wilderness was an ongoing object lesson on the consequences of sin. May we NOW learn obedience and submission to keep us from grieving the Holy Spirit (Ephesians 4:30). Ephesians 5:15-17 is a warning that complements our text. Notice carefully, *"See then that ye walk circumspectly, not as fools, but as wise, Redeeming the time, because the days are evil. Wherefore be ye not unwise, but understanding what the will of the Lord is."* The key to spiritual growth and maturity is understanding what the will of the Lord is. Our prayer and desire should always be, "Lord what would thou have me to do?"

C. **Exhort One Another With Consideration. (3:18-19)**

"And to whom sware he that they should not enter into his rest, but to them that believed not? So we see that they could not enter in because of unbelief." Verse 19 says, *"So we see that they could not enter in because of unbelief." "So we see,"* meaning that we should also see and consider carefully lest the same things happen to us. God gives rest and refreshment that comes only through belief. As the old song reminds us, "Faith is the key that unlocks the door." May we step through and enjoy all the benefits of grace.

Chapter Nine

REST

Text: Hebrews 4:1-10

1 Let us therefore fear, lest, a promise being left us of entering into his rest, any of you should seem to come short of it.
2 For unto us was the gospel preached, as well as unto them: but the word preached did not profit them, not being mixed with faith in them that heard it.
3 For we which have believed do enter into rest, as he said, As I have sworn in my wrath, if they shall enter into my rest: although the works were finished from the foundation of the world.
4 For he spake in a certain place of the seventh day on this wise, And God did rest the seventh day from all his works.
5 And in this place again, If they shall enter into my rest.
6 Seeing therefore it remaineth that some must enter therein, and they to whom it was first preached entered not in because of unbelief:
7 Again, he limiteth a certain day, saying in David, To day, after so long a time; as it is said, To day if ye will hear his voice, harden not your hearts.
8 For if Jesus had given them rest, then would he not afterward have spoken of another day.
9 There remaineth therefore a rest to the people of God.

10 For he that is entered into his rest, he also hath ceased from his own works, as God did from his.

Because the nation of Israel had erred in their hearts and had not known the ways of the Lord they were prohibited from entering into the rest that God had intended for them. The rest could have been theirs, but they refused to claim it. It was with great tragedy that this was so. They could have experienced the wonderful benefits and the privileges of going into Canaan Land, or Beulah Land as Isaiah called it. Canaan Land would more appropriately be a type of the Spirit-filled life rather than a type of Heaven because of the conflict and the wars that Israel faced when going into Canaan Land. Yet, in a lesser sense it could be a type of Heaven when viewed as a place of rest. As with all types, there are no perfect types. The types are only shadows of the truth.

However, the rest that could have been enjoyed by Israel, had they exercised faith and had they known the ways of the Lord, were forfeited because of unbelief. Even though it was only an earthly rest, it would have permitted them the privileges and blessings that the wilderness could not afford. For the wilderness was just that—a wilderness. Looking at the word *wilderness*, one cannot help but see the root world *wild* in it. A person who presently fails to exercise faith has a wildness about him that can only be tamed by faith. That was the way the nation of Israel could be described while in the wilderness. Their unbelief gave them an untamed spirit that caused them, Moses, and the Lord, much sorrow.

To not be Spirit-filled means that someone other than the Lord is in control. It really means out of control. Our lives should be directed by the Holy Spirit according to the Word of God in order to enjoy God's rest. Where the nation of Israel was only able to secure an earthly rest, we who are in Christ Jesus may obtain a spiritual rest both on earth and in Heaven. This is the truth that is being conveyed in our study of Hebrews. It is very important that we give this section careful consideration. There are many benefits and blessings that we must forfeit both here and in Heaven if we fail to believe. Could it be that we are not considering the seriousness of unbelief, both down here and in Heaven?

May God illuminate us in this study, that we may be absolutely challenged to go on unto perfection. May we be illuminated to the extent that God may make His truth clearly seen and clearly understood? There are three major thoughts that we wish to put under the *microscope of consideration*. these are: I. You Can Receive the Rest (Vv. 1-5); II. Some Have Refused the Rest (Vv. 6-7); III. There Now Remaineth a Rest (Vv. 8-10).

I. YOU CAN RECEIVE THE REST. (4:1-5)

A. A Fear That is Proper For Obtaining Rest. (4:1)

"Let us therefore fear...." Once again the severity of one not entering into rest is to be considered. It is to be considered as a fearful thing not to claim the rest that is

there for us. There are several aspects pertaining to rest that our text will reveal, but I wish to liken this rest to the Spirit-filled life. When one is Spirit-filled, he has ceased from his own labors or works (V. 10) as God did from His. When we attempt to do God's work in the flesh, there is certainly no rest involved. Rest comes only from having the power of God at work in our lives.

The most critical aspect of not being Spirit-filled is that one is occupying his place in the family of God without being obedient. It is certainly commanded that we be Spirit-filled. Another failure that is inexcusable is that one is not exhibiting faith. Faith and obedience are couplets that must appear together for God to be pleased. God swore in His wrath against Israel that because of their disobedience and their unbelief they could not enter into His rest (Hebrews 3:11). God's wrath against unbelief should certainly generate a healthy fear, causing us to be careful not to forfeit His promise of rest.

We should fear so strongly the possibility of not being Spirit-filled that we would not even "seem to come short of it." In other words, it should be obvious to all that we are operating in the Spirit instead of in the flesh. It should also be obvious to all that we are resting in His promises. If I am personally carrying the load, then God is not, and I have not entered into His rest! Matthew 11:28-30 teaches us this truth, *"Come unto me, all ye that labour and are heavy laden, and I will give you rest. Take my yoke upon you, and learn of me; for I am meek and lowly in heart: and ye shall find rest unto your souls. For my yoke is easy, and my burden is light."*

Another passage that shows the state of rest that should mark the believer is found in Psalm 37:3-7. *"Trust in the LORD, and do good; so shalt thou dwell in the land, and verily thou shalt be fed. Delight thyself also in the LORD; and he shall give thee the desires of thine heart. Commit thy way unto the LORD; trust also in him; and he shall bring it to pass. And he shall bring forth thy righteousness as the light, and thy judgment as the noonday.* **Rest in the LORD, and wait patiently for him:** *fret not thyself because of him who prospereth in his way, because of the man who bringeth wicked devices to pass."* To rest in the Lord one must enter by faithful obedience into that rest.

Rest does not mean doing nothing; may this study not leave that impression. Such an impression would be fatal to the truth intended. The way the word *rest* is used here is *in repose*, or *to enter a place of confidence*. Israel, because of unbelief would not enter into a place or state of confidence. Therefore they were not resting at all. Rest and trust must be fused together. If there is no trusting then there is no resting, and if there is no resting then there certainly is no trusting.

When one is Spirit-filled, it must also be said that the Word of Christ is dwelling in that person richly (Colossians 3:16). The Word of Christ is what gives the necessary confidence. Confidence comes from having a kind of trust that would let you confide in someone. Rest can be both a place of confidence, and a place of confiding. If one has confidence in someone, he will also confide in that one. For one to have confidence in the Word of God, that one must believe the Word to be absolutely true. Believing the Word of God to be true, one may rest upon its promises.

A proper fear is a very wonderful benefit in helping to insure one's spiritual maturity. The word fear in Hebrews 4:1 could be analyzed from two different positions. First, there should be a fear that something valuable could be forfeited through neglect. This truth was first presented in the second chapter. We remind ourselves of this truth as we look again at the word *slip*. *"Therefore we ought to give the more earnest heed to the things which we have heard, lest at anytime we shall let them slip"* (Hebrews 2:1). The word *slip* is a word that is similar to the word *harden* in that it implies an almost *unnoticed* and also a very *gradual* movement. The fear should insure that we guard against carelessly neglecting to receive the promise of God's rest.

Then there should be a fear that causes us to guard that which we have in Christ Jesus so that we will not even "seem" to come short of God's blessings and lose His rest. I find myself needing to guard the rest that is found in Christ Jesus, because that rest is exceedingly precious. The formulas for guarding that rest are the same as remaining Spirit-filled. One must avoid sinning while letting the Word of God help us to not sin. It is no different than it was with David. He hid the Word of God in his heart that he might not sin against God. Sin will certainly rob one of having God's rest. That is exactly what was meant when Israel erred in their hearts not knowing the way of the Lord. Their sin kept them from entering God's rest.

The teachings of humanism have as their objective to discount God, or as I have heard it said, "Humanism attempts to deify man and to humanize God." Their efforts may go further in that they desire to deify man and to mortify God. I remember a liberal Bible professor years ago that blatantly declared, "God is dead." I will answer as I did then, "God is not dead; I just talked to Him today!"

B. **A Faith That is Profitable for Obtaining Rest.**

(4:2-5)

"For unto us was the gospel preached, as well as unto them: but the word preached did not profit them, not being mixed with faith in them that heard it. For we which have believed do enter into rest, as he said, As I have sworn in my wrath, if they shall enter into my rest: although the works were finished from the foundation of the world." The preached Word does not profit one unless the Word preached is mixed with faith. The meaning of the word *mixed* as used in our text is crude but very graphic and very instructional. The word *mix* is used when describing food that enters into the stomach. No matter the potential that the food has for being nutritional to the one who eats it, it must also be digested. The food must mix with the digestive juices for the food to have any value. Likewise, the Word preached must be mixed with faith for it to be of any value.

The rest described was available but never claimed because of the total absence of faith. Many of our churches are plagued with cold orthodoxy, or dead services because the messages preached never come to life because there is no faith or trust. Belief with only a mental acceptance of a sterile fact will not bring rest to a soul. Even the acknowledging that Jesus Christ is the Son of God and the Saviour of the world does not give rest. Trusting in Christ, who is greater than the prophets, the angels, Moses and Joshua, brings rest. Alexander Maclaren said, "Trust brings rest, because it sweeps away as the north wind does the banded clouds on the horizon, all the deepest causes of unrest."

A journey must have a starting point if it is to have a completion. If there is no beginning, there is no ending. Such is true with the journey of faith. It must begin when one places his trust in the truth of the Gospel. The Gospel is the good news pertaining to the death, burial, and the resurrection of Christ Jesus. If the journey of faith does not begin at Calvary it will not end in Heaven.

The nation of Israel heard the good news from Joshua and Caleb, but did not mix it with faith. They were afraid to go into Kadesh-Barnea because their faith was lacking. The other ten tribes had facts about the land (Numbers 13:27-29), but did not have faith. The Lord in Numbers 13:2 had given the land to the nation of Israel; they only needed to claim it. Instead of claiming what God had promised them, the majority report of the 12 spies was an evil report. Verse 32 calls their report just that because they had no faith. *"And they brought up an evil report of the land which they had searched unto the children of Israel, saying, The land, through which we have gone to search it, is a land that eateth up the inhabitants thereof; and all the people that we saw in it are men of a great stature. And there we saw the giants, the sons of Anak, which come of the giants: and we were in our own sight as grasshoppers, and so we were in their sight"* (Numbers 13:32-33).

Only two of the 12 spies gave a good report. The minority report was mixed with faith. In Numbers 13:30 it says, *"And Caleb stilled the people before Moses, and said, Let us go up at once, and possess it; for we are well able to overcome it."* Joshua and Caleb exercised great faith and courage as shown in the following verses: *"And Joshua the son of Nun, and Caleb the son of Jephunneh, which were of them that searched the land, rent their clothes: And they spake unto all the company of the children of Israel, saying, The land, which we passed through to search it, is an exceeding good land. If the LORD delight in us, then he will bring us into this land, and give it us; a land which floweth with milk and honey. Only rebel not ye against the LORD, neither fear ye the people of the land; for they are bread for us: their defence is departed from them, and the LORD is with us: fear them not"* (Numbers 14:6-9).

Except for Joshua, Caleb, and all under 20 years of age, the rest had to die in the wilderness. The time of forty years of wandering was assigned with one year for each of the 40 days that the spies were in Kadesh-Barnea. They, who fell in the wilderness, had been told the good news that the land could have been theirs. This reminds us clearly that there is a sin unto death.

Believers have the promise of a yet future rest. It is a salvation rest, which is likened to the rest that God entered into when He finished His work of Creation. This is a rest that is without interruption. I believe that this pictures Heaven. It is alluded to in verse nine and will be addressed further.

II. SOME HAVE REFUSED THE REST. (4:6-7)

A. The Tragedy of Refusing the Rest. (4:6)

"Seeing therefore it remaineth that some must enter therein, and they to whom it was first preached entered not in because of unbelief:" Once again the tragedy of not entering into the rest is pronounced. They who first had the benefit offered let it remain unused. Later in this study we will find that the rest remains and we now can have that rest by receiving it by faith. Just because they first refused it does not mean that the *rest* was destroyed. Though the unbelievers met destruction, the *rest* has not at all suffered loss.

While looking at the practical significance of this study our verse under consideration tells us this, *"Seeing therefore it remaineth…"* This part of the verse does not take into consideration that the second generation did not exercise the kind of faith for which the Lord is looking. They were obedient only after having witnessed for up to 40 years the deaths of an entire generation of rebels. There could have been more fear than faith. From our reading, this could be the thought being conveyed, "There is yet a promise available, because Israel neglected to receive it; take it, it is yours." Then, this instead may be the true meaning of this verse: "There is an ongoing offer for all who would be willing to take this rest. No generation of people who are willing to exercise faith will be refused."

In the spirit of going on to perfection, we must be constantly doing those things that will provide us the spiritual rest. Throughout Hebrews there are ongoing appeals to the believer to do that which will insure one's continual rest. May we observe some of these. In Hebrews 10:22-25, we may note instructions, which will help us to continue in His rest. *"Let us draw near with a true heart in full assurance of faith, having our hearts sprinkled from an evil conscience, and our bodies washed with pure water. Let us hold fast the profession of our faith without wavering; (for he is faithful that promised;) And let us consider one another to provoke unto love and to good works: Not forsaking the assembling of ourselves together, as the manner of some is; but exhorting one another: and so much the more, as ye see the day approaching."*

The first appeal requires that we *"draw near."* One cannot rest lest he first is abiding with Christ. Abiding is an act of the believer's will for the purpose of drawing near with *"a true heart in full assurance of faith."* One cannot escape the importance of faith. Though these verses and chapters are removed in time from our present discussion, they connect back to the meaning of having the believers rest while also offering the support necessary to make it so.

We are also instructed to *"hold fast the profession of our faith without wavering."* One only needs to remember the way Israel kept reverting back from belief to unbelief. It seemed that every difficulty or obstacle that they encountered caused them to murmur and to complain. Each time they complained they were demonstrating that they were not experiencing nor enjoying the rest. They also were not exercising faith. Galatians 5:16-25 shows the contrast of those who are enjoying rest as opposed to those who are not. Israel was not at all being controlled by God, but by their own flesh. They preferred the garlic and the leeks to angel food. Notice these verses that show the graphic difference of those enjoying God's rest and those who were not. *"This I say then, Walk in the Spirit, and ye shall not fulfill the lust of the flesh. For the flesh lusteth against the Spirit, and the Spirit against the flesh: and these are contrary the one to the other: so that ye cannot do the things that ye would. But if ye be led of the Spirit, ye are not under the law. Now the works of the flesh are manifest, which are these; Adultery, fornication, uncleanness, lasciviousness, Idolatry, witchcraft, hatred, variance, emulations, wrath, strife, seditions, heresies, Envyings, murders, drunkenness, revellings, and such like: of the which I tell you before, as I have also told you in time past, that they which do such things shall not inherit the kingdom of God. But the fruit of the Spirit is love, joy, peace, longsuffering, gentleness, goodness, faith, Meekness, temperance: against such there is no law. And they that are Christ's have crucified the flesh with the affections and lusts. If we live in the Spirit, let us also walk in the Spirit"* (Galatians 5:16-25).

Practically, we must be led by the Spirit if we are to enjoy the blessings and the benefits of God's rest. We must not cast away our confidence that we have in Him (Hebrews 10:35), *"which hath great recompence of reward."* Throughout Hebrews there are challenges given to encourage us so that we might go on to receive the promise or the rest that God has for us (Hebrews 10:36). The same tragedy that befell the nation of Israel could happen in a salvation sense when there are: I. Those who are professors of religion but who have never known anything of true piety. II. Those that are expecting to be saved by their own works, and are looking forward to a world of rest on the ground of what their own hands can do. III. Those who defer attention to the subject from time to time until it becomes too late. They expect to reach Heaven, but they are not ready to give their hearts to God "now," and the subject is deferred from one period to another, until death arrests them unprepared. IV. Those who have been awakened to see their guilt and danger, and who have been almost but not quite ready to give up their hearts to God. Such were Agrippa, and Felix, the young ruler (Mark 10:21), and such are all those who are "almost" but not "quite" prepared to give up the world and to devote themselves to the Redeemer. To all these the promise of "rest" is made, if they will accept salvation as it is offered in the gospel; all of them cherish a hope that they will be saved; and all of them are destined alike to be disappointed. With what earnestness, therefore, should we strive that we may not fail of the grace of God (Barnes' notes on the Bible: Hebrews 4:1)!

B. The Triumph of Receiving the Rest. (4:7)

"Again, he limiteth a certain day, saying in David, To day, after so long a time; as it is said, To day if ye will hear his voice, harden not your hearts." In David's day, as quoted from Psalm 95, there was still an opportunity of rest. This verse emphasized that this *rest* was not limited to a prescribed time, but was available from King David approximately 500 years after it was first made available to the nation of Israel. It is still available, because the rest is based upon the concept of exercising faith, with its many spiritual benefits being ongoing. If the blessing was available in David's day, it meant that at the least there was a promise of the rest that is found only in Heaven. Yet there may have been pleasures and blessings beyond even that. David knew a relationship with God that could be described as rest. As quoted earlier in Psalm 37:7, *"Rest in the LORD, and wait patiently for him: fret not thyself because of him who prospereth in his way, because of the man who bringeth wicked devices to pass."*

The transitory benefits of God's blessing should give us reason to always triumph. To rest in God's plan and purpose means that one is always a victor. The song "Victory in Jesus" is an anthem to this truth. When one powerfully ministers the Word of God to the souls of men, he may rest confidently in knowing that what he has said will be blessed of God, just as will any Spirit-led ministry in which he involves himself. The rest of God must be understood to be more than just comfortably laying ones head on a pillar somewhere in a state of ease. It is the soul confidence and contentment that frees one from worry. It is the spiritual courage that allows one to stare opposition and conflict in the face without flinching.

The place of rest is located in the throne room. It is His room made available to us, Praise God! Verse 16 of this chapter teaches us this, *"Let us therefore come boldly unto the throne of grace, that we may obtain mercy, and find grace to help in time of need."* The place of rest is a place of grace, as well as a place of help in time of need.

It should be understood by now that Hebrews is a great book that emphasizes faith. All that we do and the rest that can be ours is dependent upon faith. Though we may have already considered this next thought somewhat, may we consider it in more detail as we conclude this study, *"There now remaineth a rest"* (Vv. 8-10).

III. THERE NOW REMAINETH A REST. (4:8-10)

A. It is True Logically. (4:8-9)

The text shows that Jesus (Joshua of the Old Testament) did not offer a complete and final rest, for had he done so there would not be the offer of another day. David recognized that there was to be another day, as did the writer of Hebrews. The writer of Hebrews is declaring that God is as great today as He ever was. The words *"another day"* are close kin to the old saying, "There's always tomorrow." The words *"another day"* are more promised than the old cliché "There's always tomorrow." For the believer who wishes to trust God, there still remains a rest.

Albert Barnes in his notes makes this observation: I. That there was a "rest" called "the rest of God" spoken of in the earliest period of the world, implying that God meant that it should be enjoyed; II. That the Israelites, to whom the promise was made, failed to obtain what was promised because of their unbelief; III. That God intended that "some" should enter into his rest, since it would not be provided in vain; IV. That long after the Israelites had fallen in the wilderness, we find the same reference to a rest which David in his time exhorts those whom he addressed to endeavor to obtain; V. That if all that had been meant by the word "rest," and by the promise, had been accomplished when Joshua conducted the Israelites to the land of Canaan, we should not have heard another day spoken of when it was possible to forfeit that rest by unbelief (Barnes' notes on the Bible: Hebrews). Simply put, there now remains a rest.

Verse nine thrills me in regards to Heaven. Heaven is a place of rest that remains to the people of God. It is a sure thing. Heaven is a place where the curse of laboring toil is removed. It will be a place of occupation, but not with fatigue and stress. Even as I am preparing this Hebrews study, it is with great joy that I do so. Yet there is a certain weariness that is attached to it. I have the thrill of pastoring a church, but there are also ongoing pressures and stress that marks the ministry. It is the same with Christian businessmen, and Christian bricklayers. The fatigue is there. Yet when we arrive in Heaven, the labor, as we know it here will be over. It will be that glorious ultimate place of rest that the Bible speaks of, that we shall enter.

B. It is True Practically. *(4:10)*

Verse nine says, *"There remaineth therefore a rest to the people of God."* The word *rest* is a different Greek word than we have previously considered when talking only of what is to be enjoyed here upon earth. The rest upon earth is, as we would use the word *repose*. The word used here is *sabbatismos*, which is of Hebrew origin and is a "sabatism", i.e. (figurative), the repose of Christianity (as a type of Heaven): -- rest. We must remember while contemplating this Sabbath rest that "the Scriptures constantly connect our faithfulness, obedience, and discipline on earth with our eternal condition and blessedness, with the reward which sovereign grace will assign to the heirs of life. They, who sow sparingly, reap sparingly; they, who sow abundantly, reap abundantly (Adolph Saphir; "Epistle to the Hebrews"; page 229).

How may we engage in the things of the Lord while going on unto perfection? In a practical sense; knowing the benefits of the faith life, knowing also the rest that comes with the faith life; we ought not to do anything that would even make us *"seem to come short"* (V. 1) of the rest that God has promised. Verse ten tells us, *"For he that is entered into his rest, he also hath ceased from his own works, as God did from his."* Believing this pictures Heaven for us who are believers, we should be challenged to do all that we can down here, realizing that our work here will soon be over.

For my reader, I must now confess. I do not write to be an author. I write with the intent of keeping myself under a discipline. I am investing at least twenty hours a week in this study. By doing so it keeps me in the Bible. In this way, I can always hope to have something fresh for the people whom I pastor. I am actively involved in my pastoral duties, but I am greatly impressed of the Lord, that for the most part I am the only one who will be standing in my pulpit to feed and meet the needs of my people on a regular basis. I am accountable to the Lord for this ministry; I wish to be faithful so that when I stand before Him I may fully enter into His rest and be found faithful to my calling down here.

If the Lord sees fit for these materials to be used in a fuller sense, then praise God for that. Another practical reason for my writing may be traced back to a quote that I heard many years ago. I cannot remember if I am repeating it correctly, nor to whom to attribute it. I believe it goes like this: "Reading maketh a learned man and writing maketh an exact man." As I preach God's Word, I wish to be exact and careful to deliver the truth. If writing helps me to achieve this, then I must praise God for that also.

Chapter Ten

CURE FOR UNBELIEF

Text: Hebrews 4:11-16

11 Let us labour therefore to enter into that rest, lest any man fall after the same example of unbelief.
12 For the word of God is quick, and powerful, and sharper than any twoedged sword, piercing even to the dividing asunder of soul and spirit, and of the joints and marrow, and is a discerner of the thoughts and intents of the heart.
13 Neither is there any creature that is not manifest in his sight: but all things are naked and opened unto the eyes of him with whom we have to do.
14 Seeing then that we have a great high priest, that is passed into the heavens, Jesus the Son of God, let us hold fast our profession.
15 For we have not an high priest which cannot be touched with the feeling of our infirmities; but was in all points tempted like as we are, yet without sin.
16 Let us therefore come boldly unto the throne of grace, that we may obtain mercy, and find grace to help in time of need.

There was only one thing that kept Israel out of the Promised Land. It was unbelief. Numbers 13 and 14 make it clear that unbelief was their problem. God told Moses that the land was theirs for the taking (Numbers 13:2). Yet, they would not take it. How much have we also forfeited simply because we would not take what God had for us?

The Bible could very easily be called the Promise Book, because it is full of promises. However, a promised blessing is of no value unless it is claimed. Israel had the land of promise lying before them. They may have been standing in the very portals, yet failed to step over and claim it by faith. Their unbelief kept them from going in, but also hindered their children from going in for up to 40 years. Those who were 19 years old when God told them that they would have to wait forty years before going in, would be almost 60 years of age when finally getting in. It is tragic when one imagines that his sin is only hurting himself. There are so many who are affected and hurting because of the sins of a few. The ten unbelieving spies brought the curse upon an entire nation.

For the purpose of being warned, it would do us well to analyze the sequence of events that led to and included Israel's sin of unbelief. The Lord gave instruction and a commission to Moses to send in spies. Deuteronomy 1:22 indicates that the people requested of the Lord that the spies be sent in, to which the Lord graciously agreed. There was a spy representing each of the 12 tribes. Joshua and Caleb were the only spies that exercised obedient faith. Moses gave the spies tactical instructions (Numbers 13:17-20) on how to spy out the land. Moses told them to exercise courage and to bring the fruit of the land back with them. It may be observed that there was no indication that the spies had faced any conflict with the inhabitants. When they returned, they began to describe the land as being a land that *"floweth with milk and honey."* They did not stop there though. They immediately began to focus on what they had perceived as problems. They began to magnify any potential problem. At the same time they excluded the fact that the Lord had commissioned them to take the land, and that He would be there for them making their claim successful.

In Numbers 13:33 we read, *"And there we saw the giants, the sons of Anak, which come of the giants: and we were in our own sight as grasshoppers, and so we were in their sight."* Being inspired by this verse, I prepared a message entitled "What happens when you start looking at the giants." In this message, I preached that looking at the giants can be devastating. You must remember that while you are looking at the giants you are not at the same time looking at the "giant killer." Keeping ones eyes fixed upon the Lord, keeps one from focusing upon the giants. We have many giants that come into our lives to bring fear and discouragement. The solution to such a reality is that we must keep our eyes fixed upon the Lord, our giant killer, and not look at the giants.

As we have already discovered from our study, much of the warning that is given in Hebrews refers directly to Israel's failure to enter into the promise land. The strong plea, which introduces the truth which we are now considering, tells us, *"Let us labour therefore to enter into that rest, lest any man fall after the same example of unbelief"* (V. 11). The word labour as used in our text means: to use speed, i.e. to make effort, to be prompt or earnest—to (give) diligence, be diligent (forward), endeavor, labor, study (Strong's). Gaining insight from the meaning of this definition, we may agree that as believers we must very diligently strive to enter that rest which is His rest. Spiritually, there is no true rest apart from that which may be found in Him. The same Greek word that is used here pertaining to the word labour appears in Ephesians 4:3: II Timothy 2:15; II Peter 1:10; 3:14.

The truth is plainly stated that every effort should be exercised to obtain the rest that is promised. There must be a personal act of discipline on the part of the believer to claim the rest that is found only in Christ Jesus. One does not strive to become saved; he strives because he is saved. His salvation experience alone with the Word of God should challenge him to go on unto perfection. Entering into God's rest should be a top priority for all those who are born again.

Yet all do not enter into nor desire to enter into God's rest. There is evidence that one can still be saved yet have no desire to enter into God's rest. This is certainly a mystery and probably describes the carnal believer of which Lot was a type. Remember, Lot began by looking towards Sodom before he actually lived in Sodom. His fatal leap began with a fatal look. Yet there are still safeguards against unbelief. We will observe two major cures for unbelief: I. God's Powerful Word is a Cure for Unbelief (Vv. 11-13); II. God's Priestly Work is a Cure for Unbelief (Vv. 14-16).

I. GOD'S POWERFUL WORD IS A CURE FOR UNBELIEF. (4:11-13)

A. Its Power to Reach. (4:11-12a)

Too much cannot be said about the value of the Word relative to faith. Christian faith does not just happen apart from the Word of God. It has inspirational qualities much greater than that which is found in the works of a human author. Sometimes we say that a particular writer was inspired as he wrote. Such is the case with William Shakespeare. When we speak this way, we are only describing that ability that can be attributed when describing human genius. It does not at all describe biblical inspiration. Biblical inspiration means that God has breathed the very words. The Bible is the only place where the very Words of God may be found. For the English-speaking people this is our treasured King James Bible.

The Word of God has changing qualities because it is alive. *"For the word of God is quick..."* The *quick* Word of God is lively. It is the lively living Word because God is alive. The word *quick* means: active, energizing and manifesting itself actively in the world and in men's hearts. The reaching hand of God's Word has the ability to reach way down in grace from that place of grace. How many derelicts have been picked up by God's Word? Not to mention the drunkards, the harlots, the liars and all others who are the victims of the sin curse. The Word of God could not be alive if it were not just that; the Word of God. It would be incapable of reaching into the very heart of man if it were not inspired (God breathed).

The term *inspiration* means, the divine influence which renders a speaker or writer of Scripture infallible in the communication of the Scriptures from God to man.

"The theological use of the term *inspiration* is a reference to that controlling influence which God exerted over the human authors by whom the Old and New Testaments were written. It has to do with the reception of the divine message and accuracy with which it is transcribed" (Chafer, Lewis Spery; "Systematic Theology, Dallas, TX: Dallas Seminary Press, 1947, Vol. 1, p. 61).

The term *inspiration* means "God-breathed." The Greek word for inspiration is *theopneustos*—"theo; God, pneus; breath, tos; the "tos" ending indicates the end result of what precedes it. The very living, breathing Spirit of God gave us His Words. Speech cannot be spoken apart from one's breath flowing past the vocal cords. My words are breathed from me. God's Words are His own words breathed out. This fact is documented in God's Word in II Timothy 3:16-17. *"All scripture is given by inspiration of God, and is profitable for doctrine, for reproof, for correction, for instruction in righteousness: That the man of God may be perfect, throughly furnished unto all good works."*

God initiated truth by speaking His Living Word to, and through men. These men were Holy men of God who *"spake as they were moved by the Holy Ghost"* (II Peter 1:21). *Moved* is a word, which means to "bear" or *"uphold."* It is used in Acts 27:17, *"Which when they had taken up, they used helps, undergirding the ship; and, fearing lest they should fall into the quicksands, strake sail, and so were driven."* In this verse the term *driven* is used of a ship driven by the wind. The tense of the term in Acts is passive showing that it was the wind that was driving the ship. The wind was sovereign; no one could tell the wind when and how to blow. Likewise, God alone blows His breath… Just as the ship was driven by the wind, the authors of the Scriptures were carried along and the Holy Ghost determined their course. Just as the wind will push along a ship with respect to its own style and design, so by the Holy Spirit were the authors chosen to use their own style and language. It is the breath of God that makes the words come alive. This is another argument against dynamic equivalency. No one has the right to tamper with the words of God by filtering them through his own polluted mind and restating what he supposes to be the equivalent expressions. Proponents of dynamic equivalency may argue with the way that I am expressing their definition, yet any changing of the Word makes it different and things that are different are certainly not the same.

Not only is the Word of God quick, it is powerful. The word *power* means, active, operative or effectual and powerful. The word *powerful* is a very expressive word. For if a man's word is to be respected and given consideration, it is on the basis of that man's own strength. If the man is weak in character and disposition; then such are his words. God's words are strong and powerful words; for so is God.

The translation issue must continue to be an issue. It should continue to be an issue because there are still people who are under the influence of Satan, who wish to water down the words of God, making them more generic to each of the different people groups. (I use the word *words* of God only to emphasize that the Word of God is comprised of words…do not bother or mess with His words!)

In recognizing that the Word of God is powerful, it should also be understood that its power lies also in its truthfulness. His Word is absolutely true and truth never changes. The immutability of God is passed on to His Word. God does not change, nor does His Word change. Barnes said in his notes on Hebrews, when describing the word *powerful*, "And powerful Mighty. Its power is seen in awakening the conscience; alarming the fears; laying bare the secret feelings of the heart, and causing the sinner to tremble with the apprehension of the coming judgment. All the great changes in the moral world for the better have been caused by the power of truth. They are such as the truth in its own nature is suited to effect, and if we may judge of its power by the greatness of the revolutions produced, no words can over-estimate the might of the truth which God has revealed" (Barnes).

If this summary statement by Barnes were not true regarding the awesome power of the Word, then we would not have a lasting foundation upon which to build our faith. Nor would there be a force, which drives our conscience to recognition of purity and truth. There is nothing, and there is no one that is beyond the reach of its energy. The energy of God's Word has a cutting power for it is described as being sharper than any twoedged sword. When the word is described as being "sharper than any twoedged sword" it is describing it maximum efficiency. By a sword's design, it can have one edge, but it can also have two edges. Having two edges speaks of its efficiency, only to be furthermore complimented by the fact that it is a *sharp* twoedged sword.

Lest we be lost to the true meaning of our verses under consideration, because of our great admiration and love for the Word, we must remember that *warring* words are used to describe the True Word of God. When thinking of the Word being likened unto a sword, what is the primary function of a sword? Ask a warrior, and with his two-edged, sharp sword he will tell you that he either defends himself or pursues the enemy. Could it be from our context that the seriousness of not entering by faith into God's rest is being shown by the metaphor of God's Word being a sword?

Psalm 7:11-12 shows what may be the proper interpretation of the sword being likened to God's Word. *"God judgeth the righteous, and God is angry with the wicked every day. If he turn not, he will whet his sword; he hath bent his bow, and made it ready."* In a very *manly* way (not in a weakly way) God deals with the sin of unbelief. Yet it also may be said that the sword can be used to describe the surgical means of exposing sin, so that the patient may appropriately deal with his sin.

B. Its Power to Reveal. (4:12b-13)

"For the word of God is quick, and powerful, and sharper than any twoedged sword, piercing even to the dividing asunder of soul and spirit, and of the joints and marrow, and is a discerner of the thoughts and intents of the heart" (Hebrews 4:12). The sword not only is sharp with its two edges but is also piercing sharp. It is, *"piercing even to the*

dividing asunder of soul and spirit, and of the joints and marrow, and is a discerner of the thoughts and intents of the heart." The Word is quick, powerful, and sharp having the ability to get into the innermost depths of one's being. It has the ability to filet and remove whatever it takes to bring about exposure. The Word being likened unto a sword affects the innermost parts of our being. The soul, the spirit, and the body are being referred to here. The word is exposing things that may be blamed on the body that could really be originating in the mind. We must remember, before we fail physically, we have already experienced failure in our mind. Unbelief is demonstrated by one's actions. The Word, as a surgical tool, is able to make the distinction. It can provide an accurate measure of what one's true motive is. The criterion of God's Word is an absolute standard not to be refuted when measuring motives.

When referring to the body, it is really more than that. It is a referral to the flesh instead. The word "flesh" as used here is used to denote corrupt human nature. The Word of God is quite able to reveal the motive and the intent of man. When man is operating in the energy of the flesh, in a carnal or fleshly manner, the Word will expose that kind of operation.

Everything we do has a motive attached to it. For something to be accomplished by faith it must be directed by the Word of God and led by the Spirit of God. Anything that is of the flesh will be exposed or revealed by the Word of God. The Word of God as previously noted is the true standard of comparison (criteria) that we are to operate by. It will reveal our true motive.

Verse 13 further shows how the all-knowing God will expose us completely and it is always in relationship to the Word of God. Every human is wholly known to God. Everything about him is known. This should serve as a warning reminding us that all our planning, thoughts, ambitions, concerns, feelings, passion, and moods, etc., are clearly known by the Lord. The phrase *"all things are naked and opened unto the eyes of him with whom we have to do."* The word *opened* is a word used in describing the slaughtering of an animal when removing the skin to expose what is on the inside. This was done when animals were sacrificed on the altar. The head was held back and the throat was slit, and the animal was skinned, thus exposing what was on the inside.

This is a very graphic word picture that shows how vulnerable the animal was to the blade. Likewise, God just as easily exposes us when He reveals who and what we are. There is nothing hidden from Him. May we be warned!

II. GOD'S PRIESTLY WORK. (4:14-16)

A. Look at Who He Is. (4:14a)

The writer of Hebrews references the subject which had been introduced in Hebrews 2:17 and Hebrews 3:1, and continues the study of the Priest to the end of Hebrews 10.

"Seeing then that we have a great high priest." Already we have learned much about the infinite greatness of Christ. We immediately learned that He was greater than the prophets of the Old Testament who had been given the privilege of speaking and of writing the oracles of God. By right and might of creation, He was greater than the angels, including Lucifer. He was greater than creation which *"shall wax old as doth a garment."* He was greater than even Moses. When just these comparisons are made, evidence is given that we have such a Great High Priest. Yet, He is also recognized to be greater than Joshua, which is a further declaration of His greatness.

In every realm of comparison, our High Priest, the Lord Jesus Christ is superior. His qualities and His qualifications are without comparison. Everything that has been presented in argument to show Christ's superiority now serves to characterize Him as the great High Priest. His greatness is without compromise, whether it be as Creator God, or as the Great High Priest.

It is extremely important that one knows the one that he is trusting. This speaks of that one knowing how to trust. If you do not know one's abilities or strengths, then how would you know when to place your trust and confidence in that one. Blanket trust can sometimes be a wonderful trust in that you trust without asking any questions. This sounds like the more spiritual way of trusting Christ, but I do not believe that it is. In this very study under our consideration, the nation of Israel was accused in this manner, *"They do always err in their heart; and they have not known my ways."* Notice carefully, *"they have not known my ways."* For trust to be verified in our practical

Christianity, it must be more than just trusting Him; we must know Him as well. We must know His ways. We learn of Him from the Scriptures. One's faith in our Great High Priest cannot be developed unless we learn of Him.

Matthew 11:28-30 speaks of the rest that is in Christ Jesus, and also tells us to learn of Him. Notice the wording of these verses. *"Come unto me, all ye that labour and are heavy laden, and I will give you rest. Take my yoke upon you, and learn of me; for I am meek and lowly in heart: and ye shall find rest unto your souls. For my yoke is easy, and my burden is light."* The word yoke here means, "the service of God as I teach it" which is a word that is used in association with the teacher, instead of a picture of the oxen being yoked together as commonly interpreted. Jesus is telling those who were labouring in the law, and were heavy laden that they could come to Him. When contrasting His teachings to the scribal teachings said, "my teaching" is a *light yoke* and "the current scribal teaching" is a *heavy yoke.* Jesus offers refreshment in His school and also promises to make the burden light, for He is a meek and humble Teacher.

Just because the burden of study is light does not mean that there is no labour at all. Charles H. Spurgeon gives wonderful insight concerning the truth of this passage. *"Take my yoke, and learn:* this is the second instruction; it brings with it a further rest which we *will examine.* The first rest he *gives* through his death; the second we find in copying his life, thereto. First, we *rest* by faith in Jesus, and next we *rest* through obedience to him. Rest from fear is followed by rest from the turbulence of inward passion, and the drudging of self. We are not only to bear a yoke, but his yoke; and we are not only to submit to it when it is laid upon us, but we are to *take it upon us.* We are to be workers, and *take his* yoke; and at the same time we are to be scholars, and *learn* from him as our Leader. We are to learn of Christ and also to learn Christ. He is both teacher and lesson. His gentleness of heart fits him to teach, to be the illustration of his own teaching, and to work in us his great design. If we can become as he is, we shall rest as he does. We shall not only rest from the guilt of sin—this he gives us; but we shall rest in the peace of holiness, which we find through obedience to him. It is the heart which makes or mars the rest of the man. Lord make us *lowly in heart,* and we shall be restful of heart. *Take my yoke.* The yoke in which we draw with Christ must needs be a happy one; and the burden which we carry *for* him is a blessed one. We rest in the fullest sense when we serve, if Jesus is the Master. We are unloaded by bearing his burden; we are rested by running on his errands" (Spurgeon: Commentary on Matthew).

So much of what Mr. Spurgeon said describes the believers rest and supports the thesis that our High Priest must be learned for us to trust or rest in Him. Spurgeon said that we are to "learn of Christ and also to learn Christ." He said that Christ is "both teacher and lesson." May we be good students.

B. Look at Where His Is. (4:14b)

"Seeing then that we have a great high priest, that is

passed into the heavens, Jesus the Son of God, let us hold fast our profession." Our Great High Priest is passed into the heavens. That is indeed a thrilling thought, just knowing that He is there. My, how wonderful; for that speaks of the promise that we also will one day be there. He is the Priest (bridge builder). He also is the Bridge Builder and the One who will carry us across. We will learn of the special work that He is doing in the most Holy of Holies on our behalf as we continue this study.

This study in showing Christ as being the better High Priest, shows that He is better in His place of offering. He made not His one, singular, sufficient offering in a temple made by human hands, but instead went into the very heavens created by Him, Himself. The Jews could only admit, if they would, that their priests were only of the lineage of Aaron, and were serving for a limited period of time. They could only annually put off the wrath of God. But Christ has once and for all passed into the heavens to finish the work of which the earthly priesthood was just a type.

Christianity is not inferior to the Jewish religion, but in every way superior. For the type and shadow in the old dispensation could only introduce the substance in the new dispensation. The writer of Hebrews will continue to develop and show the superiority of Christ Jesus who is our Great High Priest over the Jewish Aaronic system. This statement is not made in disrespect to that system, but only to contrast the better things of Hebrews.

On the Day of Atonement, the Jewish high priest went once a year into the most holy place in the temple for the purpose of putting off the wrath of God while in contrast our Great High Priest has gone into heaven to make intercession and to sprinkle the blood of the atonement on the mercy seat. He did this as Jesus the Son of God and not as a descendant of Aaron. This alone makes His priesthood a greater priesthood. When Christ did this great priestly work, He satisfied God's Holy requirements once and for all.

The challenge for our going on unto perfection is seen in the last part of this verse; *"let us hold fast our profession"* (V. 14b). Knowing the superiority of His priesthood, we are beckoned to hold onto, obtain, or retain… not let it go (our profession). This is not an effort for the purpose of keeping our salvation, but practically "working out" our salvation; not "working for" our salvation. In verse sixteen the admonition is, *"Let us therefore come boldly unto the throne of grace."* Our practice and faith should never be exercised with a spirit of timidity. May we have the spirit of Joshua and Caleb of old, and claim the believer's rest that is in Christ Jesus.

C. Look at What He Is. (4:15-16)

In explaining what He is, the writer began with a strong negative telling us assuredly what He was not. The way this negative is used has a very positive effect. It forms a sudden image of what our High Priest is not and then by doing so tells us what He really is. Notice the reading of the verse, *"For we have not an high priest which cannot be touched with the feeling of our infirmities; but was in all points tempted like as we are, yet without sin."*

We have a High Priest who knows who we are...every creature is manifest in His sight. By knowing us and having experienced walking as a man, He can sympathize with us. The Greeks saw God as a God of apathy. The writer of Hebrews is proving Him to be a God of sympathy. He is a God with feelings who is touched by the way we *feel*. What a Saviour! His coming to the earth served so many purposes. His incarnation involved so many theological and practical purposes. Yet most of what He did for us was in a condescending Spirit.

Though He was tempted in all points just as we are, He did not yield to the temptation. Though He did not sin, He still can and does sympathize with us. Because this is so, He challenges us to come boldly unto the throne of grace for help in time of need. His helping in the time of need could very well be interpreted as part of the rest spoken of earlier in our text. Christ, our Great High Priest, wants us to know not only that the rest is available, but that we should appropriate it with boldness.

This approach to the throne is not only superior to that which the Mosaic Law required, but is without the holy dread. The requirements for the Old Testament priest in his making the atonement were so demanding that there was always a dread that the priest faced while the Day of Atonement was approaching. The door of grace now swings open wide and is available to all who will believe. Once one steps through by faith, he may continue to enjoy the riches of God's grace without dread, but instead with delight.

Chapter Eleven

A FURTHER LOOK AT THE GREAT HIGH PRIEST

Text: Hebrews 5:1-5

1 For every high priest taken from among men is ordained for men in things pertaining to God, that he may offer both gifts and sacrifices for sins:
2 Who can have compassion on the ignorant, and on them that are out of the way; for that he himself also is compassed with infirmity.
3 And by reason hereof he ought, as for the people, so also for himself, to offer for sins.
4 And no man taketh this honour unto himself, but he that is called of God, as was Aaron.
5 So also Christ glorified not himself to be made an high priest; but he that said unto him, Thou art my Son, to day have I begotten thee.

We have a brief introduction of the high priest in Hebrews 2:17, and again in chapter four. The high priest will be the dominant theme of our study for the next several chapters. The high priest theme will continue beginning with the first verse of this chapter through chapter 10:39.

Judging from the amount of space given in Hebrews to this study, one may readily see the importance of understanding the priesthood as biblically presented. Rather than giving attention to the traditional, papal, or secular role of the priesthood, we will primarily consider how the high priest is described in the Word of God. We will consider how the Old Testament priest pictures Christ. We will do this by looking at the priest's garments and his consecration to the priesthood.

This study will continue in this manner through chapter ten. In order to build a foundation of understanding as it pertains to the priesthood, we will look at Aaron and his garments in detail as recorded in Exodus chapters 28 and 29. We will learn some very wonderful things about Christ, our Great High Priest.

As we consider the priestly garments, we will do so according to the materials that the garments were made of and the colors that were used. When studying the Word of God everything has significance. We also may recognize the value of typical significance as well. Closely noting the garments and the colors used will bring into focus the Person and the work of Jesus Christ. The fine white linen of which the garments were made, pictures the Lord's purity and His absence of sin (I Peter 2:22). The threads of the priestly garments were made with blue, purple, scarlet, and gold thread (Exodus 28:5). The color blue is a color that is used in association with heaven. When one looks up to the blue sky he is reminded of heaven, just as the threads were a reminder of Christ's heavenly origin and now His present position seated on the right hand of the Father (I Corinthians 15:47). His royalty is pictured by the purple thread. When one thinks of Christ in His royalty, he must be reminded that He is King of Kings and Lord of Lords.

The scarlet threads speak of Christ as being our sin bearer (Isaiah 1:18). *"Come now, and let us reason together, saith the Lord: though your sins be as scarlet, they shall be as white as snow; though they be red like crimson, they shall be as wool."* The gold thread speaks of Christ's deity; Jesus is God (I Timothy 3:16).

The robe of the high priest was blue as a reminder that the robe, though being worn only by a man who was of the earth, was doing a work that was commissioned from Heaven. Also, those who saw him who was dressed in blue should recognize that he was representing the man of the earth to the God of Heaven. Thus, the Latin word *pontifex* which is the word for priest, means bridge builder. Christ alone is the true Pontifex. Only in type could a man of the order of Aaron represent man to God. Yet our Great High Priest, Christ Jesus, fulfilled the type in every way.

Looking closer at the robe, one might notice that upon the hem of the robe were sewn blue, purple, and scarlet pomegranates. Pomegranates are a very unusual fruit; their seed that is encased in a sweet nectar pulp reminds us of the fruitfulness of Christ. Even as a child, when I first opened up a pomegranate, I was amazed at the shiny red seeds that glittered in the sun. Those seeds could very well picture the multitudes that are in Christ Jesus.

Between the pomegranates were seven gold bells. These bells would ring as the priest conducted his services. The bells were heard by the people as the high priest was doing his work in the holy place. Our High Priest has gone to Heaven to serve on our behalf; once and for all the bells represent the testimony of the Holy Spirit in agreement with the Word of God as it relates to us the work of Christ Jesus.

A girdle was used to secure the robe (Exodus 28:6-14). The girdle was commonly used to gird the loins of the wearer to make him more effective in his personal service or in his warfare. By strengthening the midsection, one was able to carry a heavier load or fight with greater stability. This pictures Christ the warrior, and Christ the servant. In regards to the priest it was a visual reminder that priestly service is very demanding and requiring. The labor may have been more intense than we would think it to be. For sure, the priestly work on the Day of Atonement was for the purpose of putting off the wrath of God. The annual accumulation of all the sins was symbolically taken by the priest into the Holy of Holies. This pictured the burden of our sins resting upon Jesus as He entered that holy place of sacrifice and slaughter at Mount Calvary. What a weight it was, not to be compared to the Day of Atonement. Yet the Day of Atonement, in miniscule proportions as compared to what Christ did, was typified as a day of burdens as the girdle symbolized.

The ephod (Exodus 28:6-14) was put in place over the head and shoulders of the high priest. Again the colorful symbolism is seen as the ephod was made of fine linen with gold, blue, purple, and scarlet colors woven in it (Exodus 28:6, 39:2-5). Christ's deity was represented by the gold, with again the blue representing heaven; the purple, His royalty; the scarlet, His sacrificial atonement;

the white linen; His pure, sinless nature (Hebrews 7:26).

The onyx stone also had a definite purpose in the priestly attire. They were to be found on the shoulders of the ephod. They were set in gold having the names of the tribes of Israel engraved therein (Exodus 28:9-12; 39:6-7). These stones represent believers who are kept secure and held up under the strong shoulders of Christ Jesus. Christ alone should be our strength. Everything we accomplish should be done by His power and might.

Closely connected to the symbolism of the onyx stone is the picture of the twelve precious stones in four rows of three each, with each having one of the twelve tribes engraved. The orderly arrangement showed that each tribe had its place upon the heart of the high priest, just as each believer has a special place in Christ's heart (Ephesians 3:17-19).

Resting upon the head of the high priest was a priestly crown, or mitre, made of fine white linen (Exodus 28:36-39). The crown is worn primarily by a king, thus the teaching here is that Christ Jesus who is our Great High Priest is also our King.

It may also be noted that upon the front of the mitre was a golden plate which had been engraved with the words "Holiness to the Lord." This speaks of the total dedication that Christ had for doing His Father's will. Exodus 28:38 says that the golden plate was always upon Aaron's forehead to insure that the people might be accepted before God.

The high priests were not only dressed according to

God's sovereign purpose, they were to be consecrated in every way. They were first washed with water (Exodus 29:4). With water being a type of the Word of God, it illustrates God's requirements of God's Word for practical dedication and consecration. As believers we are to be consecrated in our service to Him. To further picture the work of consecration the priest was clothed and anointed with oil (Exodus 29:5-7). (Notes gleaned from: "Way of Life Encyclopedia of the Bible and Christianity" by David W. Cloud).

Realizing how important this section on the high priest is should explain the purpose for departing from our usual format to consider briefly the attire and the consecration of the high priest. May we now continue our more structured format as we indeed take a further look at the Great High Priest. As mentioned, this begins the largest section involving the dominant theme of the priesthood (Hebrews 5:1-10:39). In this study we will consider three things. I. The Ordination of the High Priest (V. 1); II. The Administration of the High Priest (Vv. 2, 3); III. The Glorification of the High Priest (Vv. 4, 5).

I. THE ORDINATION OF THE HIGH PRIEST. (5:1)

A. **The High Priest is Selected From Among Men.**

(5:1a)

This first verse shows the foundational requirements for the priesthood. The first great principle is that the priest must be taken from among men to serve men. This is a very important issue regarding the priesthood and must be understood in order to appreciate the greater work of Christ, our High Priest. In the Old Testament, much explanation and attention is given regarding the attire, the consecration, and the function of the priesthood. Though the priest is taken from among men, it has been said that there were 146 external requirements that the priest had to meet and maintain to be duly qualified. These requirements show that the call to service is a serious call in that it typifies Christ who is absolutely without blemish. God did not find it wise to select the priest from among the angels. Angels have not the capacity to sense or feel human weaknesses. Moses was not chosen to be the first priest, perhaps because he did not live entirely among the people that he was to represent. Aaron did, however. Aaron worked as a laborer while the Israelites made bricks. During much of this time Moses was living within the palace walls. For this reason, it seems that Aaron was taken more definitely from among their ranks to carefully sense their needs.

The first mention of the high priest in the scriptures show his being positioned "among his brethren" (Leviticus 21:10). "All the males of the family of Aaron were equal, and brethren, as to the priesthood; but there was one who was the head and prince of the rest, whose office was not distinct from theirs, but in the discharge of it, and preparation for it there were many things peculiarly appropriated unto him. And these things are distinctly appointed and enunciated in several places. The whole office was firstly vested in him, the remainder of the priests being as it were his present assistants, and a nursery for a future succession. The whole nature of the type was preserved in him alone. But as in one case our apostle tells us of these high priests themselves, that by the law they 'were many.' That is, succession one after another, 'because they were not suffered to continue by reason of death' (Hebrews 7:23)." ("The Works of John Owen: An Exposition of the Epistle to the Hebrews).

The phrase "taken among men" must emphasize as the old writers, such as John Owens understood, that it was only in the realm of the human family that the high priest could be found. There would have been a pronounced terror and awe had the selection originated and continued in someone other than man. Angels would not have, as mentioned, been sympathetic as a fellow human being would. Their earthly existence would be foreign to that of man, remembering that the angels were specially created and never could die.

B. The High Priest is Serving Among Men. (5:1b)

"Is ordained for men..." The high priest was distinctly set apart or consecrated for the special and solemn benefit of the people. The solemnity of this occasion is shown in Exodus chapter 29.

Keeping in mind that God had to establish a means of

approach for the benefit of sinful man, God chose as a representative a priest. On a more permanent and a more spiritual plane, Christ became that totally accepted bridge builder (pontifex) that could both condescend to man and be exalted back to God. Christ Jesus was suitable before God to make the one singular offering for this purpose.

John Calvin says that, "it was necessary for Christ to be a real man." He went on to say, "Hence, that the Son of God has a nature in common with us, does not diminish his deity, but commends it more to us; for he is fitted to reconcile us to God, because he is a man." He was *"taken from among men... for men."*

We must be dependent upon our High Priest realizing that in and of ourselves we have absolutely nothing to offer. The earthly high priest had so many human limitations that plagued his office. There must have been an awful holy dread that overshadowed the high priest while the Day of Atonement was approaching.

The high priest had the responsibility of offering both "gifts and sacrifices for sins:" In this verse we notice the third requirement of "every high priest." First, he was *"taken from among men"*; second, *"is ordained of men in things pertaining to God"*; third, *"that he may offer both gifts and sacrifices for sins:"*

This third truth indicates that there must be a prescribed payment offered to put off the wrath of God for a little while. This was all that could be expected from an earthly priest. Yet, the priesthood of Christ will be shown to be entirely adequate to reconcile us to God forever. The gifts that were offered may have been given out of the gratitude of the grateful priest and the people showing that God once more was willing to put off His anger. A parallel to the offering of sacrifices and gifts today would be salvation and service. Salvation requires that one accept by faith the offering of Christ Jesus, who was our Sacrifice. Service should be offered in a *delightful way* rather than in a *dutiful way* just as the gifts were offered by the high priest.

One thing that we who are members of His Church should be mindful of is that this letter was written to those who were converted from Judaism. It is not certain that they had a favorable memory of and recollection of the Jewish priesthood because of the terrible abuses by such priests as Caiaphas. Caiaphas was a very wicked and uncaring priest who was consumed by greed. When Jesus cleansed the temple it was due to the wicked taking of money from the poor, when they were charged exorbitant prices for the sacrificed animals.

The wording of the Hebrew letter does not maliciously attack the Jewish system, but does make a comparison showing how much better Christ the High Priest is in both order and service. The comparison is to show Christ's superiority over the human order while showing at the same time that the human order was only temporary.

II. THE ADMINISTRATION OF THE PRIEST.

(5:2-3)

A. The Compassion That the Priest Must Have. (5:2)

"Who can have compassion on the ignorant, and on them that are out of the way; for that he himself also is compassed with infirmity." As the high priest would prepare himself for his solemn duty, he must be aware as he dressed himself with his priestly attire and went through the consecration ceremony, that he had a grave duty to perform. He was not to be the people's judge. He was not to be a harsh ruler, for he struggled with the same sins for which he was making atonement. He was to deal gently as he exercised his office. Even this is in contrast to the better *way* Christ deals with sin.

It is true that Christ deals graciously with the sinners, but He also deals in a very firm manner as it pertains to sin: *"It is a fearful thing to fall into the hands of the living God"* (Hebrews 10:31). Mere mortal men have no right to judge this way; only Christ can.

The word *compassion* is a key word in this verse. It carries the meaning of gentleness. This gentleness is to be exercised towards those who are *"ignorant, and on them that are out of the way"* (V. 2). R.C.H. Lenski says this about the "gentle" priest; "Flagrant sinners, open violators were cut off from Israel without atonement and were cursed of God. Only those who erred in ignorance and thus had sins resting on them were freed on the Day of Atonement, for despite all the daily sacrifices such sins still remained, and the high priest acted for the people as a whole, for any and for all such sins. Although he had to deal with sin, the high priest was not to be harsh and severe and act the part of a stern judge. He was 'to be moderate.' This term is carefully chosen. He was not to ignore the sins (for he was to make atonement for them as being sins), nor was he to condemn these sins to their proper punishment (for it was his part to make atonement for them)." ("Interpretation of Hebrews" James; Lenski; p. 156).

Showing that the priesthood included men who were not only subject to sin but also to failure, we have a historical record. Such was alluded to when Caiaphas the high priest was mentioned. The last part of verse two shows that the high priest, *"also is compassed with infirmity."* Just as the priest was to minister with gentleness, so is the pastor. This does not mean nor does it imply any compromise by the pastor. It is dreadful however, when pastors lose the gentleness and tear into their flock with absolutely no mercy nor compassion. There are those who think that if the pastor does not mimic or pattern himself after the street people, then he is nothing more than a "wimp." Only time and eternity will reveal how detrimental such a spirit is to the cause of Christ. It is only by God's grace that I am able to stand at all before my people—and with my people! Such should be the spirit of all of God's men.

B. The Character That the Priest Must Have. (5:3)

"And by reason hereof he ought, as for the people, so also for himself, to offer for sins." The priest "ought" to offer for himself as for the people realizing that he also is

subject to sinning; He is subject to temptation; he must die, and appear before God. With this being true, it must be understood that he being an imperfect priest must offer expiation for sins. When he preaches to others, he must be mindful that he is a sinner and include himself in his preaching.

John Owens calls attention to three types of offerings that the high priest had to offer for himself. "But besides this there were three sorts of offerings that were peculiar unto him, wherein he offered for himself distinctly or separately:

> The solemn offering that ensued immediately on his inauguration: Leviticus 9:2, *"And he said unto Aaron, Take thee a young calf for a sin-offering, and a ram for a burnt-offering, without blemish, and offer them before the LORD."* This was for himself, as it is expressed, verse eight. *"Aaron therefore went unto the altar, and slew the calf of the sin offering, which was for himself."* After this he offered distinctly for the people *"a kid of the goats for a sin-offering"* verses 3,15. And this was for an expiation of former sins, expressing the sanctification and holiness that ought to be in them that draw nigh unto God.

> There was an occasional offering or sacrifice which he was to offer distinctly for himself, upon the breach of any of God's commandments by ignorance, or any actual sin: Leviticus 4:3, *"If the priest that is anointed do sin according to the sin of the people;"* (that is, in like manner as any of the people do sin), *"then let him bring for his sin, which he hath sinned, a young bullock*

without blemish unto the LORD for a sin-offering." After which there is a sacrifice appointed of the like nature, and in like manner to be observed, (1.) For the sin of the whole people, verse 13; and then (2.) For the sin of any individual person, verse 27. And hereby the constant application that we are, on all actual sins, to make unto the blood of Christ for pardon and purification was prefigured.

There was enjoined him another solemn offering, or the annual feast, or day of expiation, which he was to begin the solemn service of that great day withal: Leviticus 16:3, *"Thus shall Aaron come into the holy place: with a young bullock for a sin-offering, and a ram for a burnt-offering."* After this, he offers also on the same day, for the sins of the people, verse 15; a bullock for himself, and a goat for the people. And this solemn sacrifice respecting all sins and sorts of them, known and unknown, great and small, in general and particular represents our solemn application unto Christ for pardon and sanctification: which as to the sense of them may be frequently renewed" (The Works of John Owens; p. 581).

No parallel exists in this section pertaining to Christ having to offer a sacrifice for His own sins. Obviously, this third verse pertains to the earthly priesthood. There are those who portray Christ as a sinner. Hollywood produced a blasphemous movie that portrayed Christ as a sinner. The movie is wicked in that it portrayed Christ as being a sinner. Christ is *"holy, harmless, undefiled, separate from sinners"* (Hebrews 7:26-27).

Not only does Hollywood portray Christ as a sinner, ancient theologians did also and more recent theologians do so as well. When Christ was *"made sin for us"* and he was made a *"sacrifice for sin,"* it did not mean that He was made sinful as us.

III. THE GLORIFICATION OF THE PRIEST. (5:4-5)

A. The Appointment Was of God the Father. (5:4)

"And no man taketh this honour unto himself, but he that is called of God, as was Aaron." The high priest had to be lawfully called, meaning that one could not initiate himself into the priesthood. The Roman priesthood that is in effect today is not a God-appointed priesthood; it is a religious invention with no scriptural significance. Our text is referring to the God-ordained system that required a God appointed priest as was Aaron. The Word of God qualifies his appointment and those who succeeded him. There are scriptural examples of those who intruded into the priestly office and met the sure judgment of God as did King Uzziah (II Chronicles 26:16-23). Another example was when "strange fire" was offered, again attended by God's judgment.

We are told that, *"no man taketh this honor unto*

himself." The honor spoken of here could be either the *office* itself or the *dignity* of the office. Even though the Priesthood of Christ is superior to the priesthood of Aaron, that does not mean that the priesthood of Aaron was without honor. It retained great honor as long as the office was not being abused.

The abuse and the dishonor came when the qualifications of the office were de-valued. Again, making a parallel to the office of the pastor, that office has much dignity when it is properly maintained and is being exercised according to God's Word. Any deviation from the Word of God brings dishonor. Men today are still guilty of intruding into the office that has not been consecrated unto them, or either guilty of offering strange fire. Just as the priest's office could be violated by an intruder, so might the office of the pastor. No one has a right to intrude into the office of the pastor. In a sense the pastor is a bridge builder, with the bridge being the Word of God. But the pastor absolutely is not a bridge builder in the same sense as Aaron the high priest.

B. The Appointment Also Came to God the Son. (5:5)

"So also Christ glorified not himself to be made an high priest; but he that said unto him, Thou art my Son, to day have I begotten thee." This verse is amazing in that it shows that Christ did not violate His own constitution by intruding into the priest's office. He could not enter into the

priestly office by succession because he was not of the tribe of Levi and of the family of Aaron. Christ Jesus was very protective of the priestly office recognizing its constitutional existence. It was constituted by God, and there were not to be any appointments made that were not prescribed or directed by God. Christ borrows from a Messianic Psalm, and gives His right to His priesthood; He was appointed by the Father, *"Thou art my son, to day have I begotten thee."*

Without violating God's predetermined purpose, Christ did not and could not have taken upon himself the priesthood. The priesthood was a sacred trust that had to be given according to God's original and intended purpose. Spiritual authority and spiritual order must be kept in check by even Christ. The Jew would not accept anyone, Christ included, taking the office to Himself. Yet, realizing that the priesthood was originally designed and ordered by God, He had the right to give the office to Christ. By doing so, He sanctified the office to Christ alone. This permitted His priesthood to be superior to and different than Aaron's. To make the break was necessary to sanctify or set it apart as a uniquely different office. With all that has been said being true, the word *honour* as used in the fourth verse previously considered, takes on special significance.

He alone is honored with His particular and His unique office. His priesthood is His alone, meaning that it will not change by reason of death nor by reason of defilement. We have a Priest who is alive for evermore to intercede on our behalf and help in the time of need.

Chapter Twelve

THE ORDER OF MELCHISEDEC

Text: Hebrews 5:6-10

6 As he saith also in another place, Thou art a priest for ever after the order of Melchisedec.
7 Who in the days of his flesh, when he had offered up prayers and supplications with strong crying and tears unto him that was able to save him from death, and was heard in that he feared;
8 Though he were a Son, yet learned he obedience by the things which he suffered;
9 And being made perfect, he became the author of eternal salvation unto all them that obey him;
10 Called of God an high priest after the order of Melchisedec.

For the next several chapters the study of the priesthood will become more intense and more clearly defined in respect to our Great High Priest, the Lord Jesus Christ. God chose to give us a detailed study of the priestly order, in respect to Aaron and Melchisedec, with both being types of Christ, our High Priest. A study of either of these priestly personalities, to the exclusion of the other, will not give us a clear working knowledge of the way

Christ Jesus set up His priesthood. It is required that we study both just as they were given to us.

Our study will show that Christ is preferred to Aaron as God the Father appointed Him a priest of a higher order than that of Aaron. In our previous study, we gave emphasis to Aaron. Now, we must look more carefully at Melchisedec. When we look at Melchisedec, we will actually learn more about Christ Jesus who is a priest after the order of Melchisedec (V. 10).

Concerning Christ, may we consider these three things: I. The Duration of His Priesthood (V.6); II. The Development of His Priesthood (Vv. 7-8); III. The Distinction of His Priesthood (Vv. 9-10).

I. THE DURATION OF HIS PRIESTHOOD. (5:6)

A. The Time Given. (5:6a)

"Thou art a priest for ever after the order of Melchisedec." This verse is a quote from Psalm 110:4. This Messianic psalm, penned by David, makes a clear distinction as to how long the priest will hold his office. Though Aaron is not mentioned in the psalm, it is already understood that Aaron's priesthood was a priesthood that changed either by the death, by the disqualification of, or by the aging of the priest. Thus, there were many priests serving in succession after Aaron.

We have learned that Christ serves after the pattern

of Aaron, but now we learn that Christ serves after the order of Melchizedec. Verse six begins this way, *"As he saith also in another place."* There is no clearer prophecy concerning Christ's eternal priesthood than that found in this already mentioned psalm (Psalm 110). How thrilling that David was given a prophetic glimpse of what the priesthood of Christ was going to be like in regards to time. His office will never be destroyed, nor will it cease to exist. The book of Hebrews, by divine inspiration, has things to say about Melchisedec that can be found nowhere else. Yet there are those who call themselves historians that try to explain this additional information by saying it is a quote from other writings, or from tradition. I could quote some of these, but simply saying the writer of Hebrews was inspired to write the additional information, should suffice for those who are truly Bible believers (Hebrews 7:1-28).

Abraham first confronts Melchisedec in Genesis 14:18, *"And Melchisedek king of Salem brought forth bread and wine: and he was the priest of the most high God."* This was after Abram rescued his nephew Lot. The priest who was also king of Salem (Jerusalem), blessed Abram, recognizing Abram to be *"of the most high God."* Abram received and acknowledged Melchisedec and showed it by giving him *"tithes of all"* (Genesis 14:20). Very little is said in Genesis upon the first appearance of Melchisedec. This will contribute to a better understanding of this Old Testament priest being presented as a type of Christ, with Christ being appointed a priest after the order of Melchisedec with no successors. A mystery surrounds this priestly–king named Melchisedec.

Melchisedec will be shown to be superior to Aaron, but Christ will be shown to be superior even to Melchisedec in such language as this: *"Now of the things which we have spoken this is the sum: We have such an high priest, who is set on the right hand of the throne of the Majesty in the heavens;"* (Hebrews 8:1).

The writer of Hebrews will continue through chapter seven in showing the superiority of Melchisedec to Aaron, and then beginning in chapter eight the focus will be on Christ our High Priest.

Looking again at this sixth verse, please notice the clause, *"Thou art a priest for ever."* The great strength of Christ's priesthood is that it is an everlasting priesthood. I do not believe anyone really knows the magnitude of this truth. There is so much about *eternity* that is only hinted at in the Scriptures. There seems to be support that the priesthood of Christ will be an everlasting, ever expanding priesthood. As a Kingly Priest, knowing that His kingdom is without end, there is no way to comprehend the extent of His government, nor the requirement of His ongoing priesthood.

B. A Type Given. (5:6b)

Students of the Scriptures often and for many centuries have recognized Bible types. There is no more sterling type pertaining to the priesthood of Christ than that of Melchisedec. Before we consider the typology of

Melchisedec may we briefly examine Bible types in general.

First, the type does not receive greater magnitude than what it pictures (its anti-type). There are some features that are distinctly given in the type that clearly points one in his thinking from the lesser to the greater, with the lesser being the type and the greater being the substance. An example of this would be of David being a type of Christ, and the giant being a type of Satan. David's conflict with Goliath is similar, but less in magnitude than that of Christ being in conflict with Satan.

Another truth regarding the type, the type may picture more than one quality. It is commonly understood that Canaan Land or Beulah Land is a type of the Spirit-filled life. This would be the greater teaching, yet Canaan to a lesser degree pictures Heaven. This is not true in a perfect sense. No types measure up absolutely to the substance. Joseph is a type of Christ, yet lacks something that keeps him from being a perfect type; he is human and not deity. The type is not an exact clone of that which it represents, but is only a picture of the actual.

Canaan is a type of Heaven because it pictures the believer's rest as referred to in Hebrews chapter three. In a greater way, however, Canaan pictures the Spirit-filled life with all of its struggles. Upon entering Canaan there were still battles to be won and wars to be fought, just as there is when we walk in the Spirit.

A third consideration involving types is that the type may have many components to make up the whole. This may be true because Christ in His splendor is many faceted, like a diamond refracting light with all of its brilliance. Noah's ark is a type of Christ. When considering the ark and its design, remember it had only one door which granted Noah and his family access into God's safety. There were no back doors in which to climb. Christ Jesus is the only Door that opens to salvation. The ark had three levels that pictured the Trinity. It was covered with pitch which is a type of Christ's blood. It was made of wood which is a type of Christ's humanity. This one vessel of safety had many types that formed a composite of the whole; again, that whole is Christ.

A fourth consideration is that types are uniquely placed in the canon of Scriptures to help develop doctrinal truth. God's Word is absolutely complete, with nothing lacking. As the Scriptures were inspired, the types found in the Scriptures were placed in a proper sequence. The types given may contribute to a doctrinal climax, involving what we refer to as the "progressive mention principle." An example which would support this statement is a study involving the *Lamb of God*. Each time the lamb appears in the Scriptures as a type of Christ there is a progressive revealing of truth. Beginning with Abel's lamb, one may be taught that Christ died for one person. The Passover lamb shows that Christ died for one family and the lamb in Isaiah chapter 53 shows that Christ died for one nation. In John chapter one, the Lamb is shown to be dying for the world. In each of these examples briefly considered, each lamb is a type of the Sacrificial Lamb (Saviour), but with a slight difference. These differences progressively help develop the truth pertaining to Christ who is the Lamb being pictured.

For our final consideration, types may be referred back to for a correct interpretation. Proper interpretation is a safeguard against heresy. God has given us many such safeguards in the Scriptures to help us to properly interpret sound doctrine. We must be careful to never let the type have greater significance than that which it represents. Yet, it is proper and helpful in one's study to venture back to the type that the truth represents. Considering the type, ask any question that will help make truth more clearly understood. For example, when considering the Spirit-filled life and its type, which is Canaan Land, one may ask the question, "What example of conflict as found in Canaan Land will better help me to deal with my own conflict?"

Having considered the way that types may be used, may we now observe from typology how Melchisedec is a picture of Christ. First, Melchisedec was not numbered with the Levitical priests, and his office would be described differently than theirs. Because so little is said of him, students may only speculate beyond what the Scriptures tell us. The historian Flavius Josephus said simply that he was "a pious Canaanitish prince; a person eminently endowed by God, and who acted as the priest of the people. That he combined in himself the offices of priest and king, furnished to the apostle a beautiful illustration of the offices sustained by the Redeemer, and was in this respect, perhaps, the only one whose history is recorded in the Old Testament who would furnish such an illustration. That his genealogy was not recorded, while that of every other priest mentioned was so carefully traced and preserved, furnished another striking illusion. In this respect, like the Son of God, he stood alone" (Barnes).

Melchisedec is distinguished as a type of Christ in the respect that he did not have a mentioned, recorded Hebrew genealogy. He, like Christ, stood alone. Christ's name is not recorded in the priestly lineage. Though Christ's genealogy was recorded, He had no genealogical record "as a priest." Again, as we explained, Melchisedec is not a perfect or exact replica in type of Christ, but he is still a very clear type of Christ.

II. THE DEVELOPMENT OF HIS PRIESTHOOD. (5:7-8)

A. His Priesthood is Developed Through Personal Prayer. (5:7)

"Who in the days of his flesh, when he had offered up prayers and supplications with strong crying and tears unto him that was able to save him from death, and was heard in that he feared;" Prayer has significance. Prayer was important to our Great High Priest. Our scripture indicates the passion that our Priest had as he prayed. Prayer is an activity that measures one's sincerity, and by this I recognize how sincere He is. His praying showed the gravity of the office. His praying shows just how human

He is without Him being any less than God. If prayer has such a meaningful place in the life of Christ, should we not pause and consider it more carefully at this time?

Also realizing how broad the scope of prayer is, we will restrict our comments to how prayer is used in our text. Beginning this way, *"Who in the days of his flesh..."* The first thing that we might learn from this statement is that Christ Jesus prayed while in the flesh. We all must relate to this. Our prayer is being made while we are in the flesh, while we yet have our earthy existence. Whether we pray beyond our earthy pilgrimage, I am not sure, but I am sure that while we have our being in this world, we must pray.

The weakness of our flesh requires that we pray. Prayer admits and acknowledges this weakness and beckons the Lord for strength to endure. Suffering must be crowned with prayer, and in this way the Lord learned obedience by the things which He suffered (V. 8). He says that while in the flesh He suffered, and while in the flesh He prayed. Prayer contributed to His development. Prayer asks for strength, recognizing at the same time one's weakness; in this way even Christ prayed.

The second ingredient from our text that should mark one's prayer is sincerity or a fervent cry. Prayer must be real. For prayer to be real it must be based upon the belief that there is One who can answer. There are the examples from the Scriptures that witness to the sincerity of our Saviour while He was praying. He prayed and His sweat was as great drops of blood falling to the ground which indicated how earnest His prayer was. When He prayed like this, there was an angel from Heaven that strengthened Him. Notice these verses that testified to His fervent prayer. *"And he came out, and went, as he was wont, to the mount of Olives; and his disciples also followed him. And when he was at the place, he said unto them, Pray that ye enter not into temptation. And he was withdrawn from them about a stone's cast, and kneeled down, and prayed, Saying, Father, if thou be willing, remove this cup from me: nevertheless not my will, but thine, be done. And there appeared an angel unto him from heaven, strengthening him. And being in an agony he prayed more earnestly: and his sweat was as it were great drops of blood falling down to the ground"* (Luke 22:39-44).

The sincerity and the intensity of Christ Jesus' praying was shown in our text by His strong crying and tears being made unto His Father. This ingredient of prayer shows the Person to whom prayer is made. As our High Priest, the Lord Jesus Christ may intercede on our behalf and pray to the Father, even as He prayed to the Father upon this earth. We too must have God the Father as the one to whom we pray. We pray to Him through His Son Jesus Christ. We can pray, as Jesus did, to the Father because He is able.

B. The Priesthood is Developed Through Peril. (5:8)

"Though he were a Son, yet learned he obedience by the things which he suffered;" The phrase, *"Though he were a Son,"* shows that even though Jesus was the Son of

God, and very God, He chose to become man that He might be touched by the feeling of our infirmities. In this, He both can be identified with man and suffer as a man. This makes Him a High Priest capable of being touched by the feelings of our infirmities (Hebrews 4:14-16).

Christ suffered and His ministry was developed as He did suffer; we too may mature through our own perils. Testing and trials come in our own lives for the purpose of maturing us and making us more like Christ. David was so developed; He matured through brokenness as Psalm 119:65-72 teaches us. *"Thou has dealt well with thy servant, O LORD, according unto thy word. Teach me good judgment and knowledge: for I have believed thy commandments. Before I was afflicted I went astray: but now have I kept thy word. Thou art good, and doest good; teach me thy statutes. The proud have forged a lie against me: but I will keep thy precepts with my whole heart. Their heart is as fat as grease; but I delight in thy law. It is good for me that I have been afflicted; that I might learn thy statutes. The law of thy mouth is better unto me than thousands of gold and silver."*

This passage of scripture shows exactly the means whereby David had been spiritually strengthened by his own affliction. He recommended, *"It is good for me that I have been afflicted: that I might learn thy statutes"* (V. 71). We also could say that many of our greatest lessons are learned in the school of adversity. The trials that we face in this life are under the stroke of God's providence. God can develop us through the storms that we face, thereby causing us to be more sensitive to others who suffer a similar fate. God may permit us to be broken as a means of discipline. The brokenness may also come about as a form of chastisement to correct us.

Christ did not sin, but He still suffered in the flesh as well as on the cross experiencing much of the grief that we experience as sinners. Considering the totality of His suffering, He suffered as no man ever suffered. He learned obedience by those things that He suffered (V. 8). This was part of His kenosis, in that He limited Himself to experience, as man does, the stages of development that comes only from suffering. In His case His response to suffering was always a correct response. His deity was never compromised.

III. THE DISTINCTION OF HIS PRIESTHOOD.
(5:9-10)

A. There is a Distinction in the Way He Saves. (5:9)

"And being made perfect, he became the author of eternal salvation unto all them that obey him;" "Being made perfect," signifies that Christ was consummated, and fully consecrated by the Father to serve as a priest over mankind with the requirement of having been taken from men to serve among men. His being made perfect was not made true in a human sense, for He who is God is already perfect. The language of our text indicates that He met all of the demands and the requirements of the Father to

present Himself as the Author of "eternal salvation". Being in this sovereign state according to God's purpose, He is absolutely qualified to serve as the High Priest. He cannot be disqualified by lack of identification. Philippians chapter two certainly expresses this truth. If it were not for the plain teachings relating to Christ's humility and His humanity as taught in Philippians chapter two, we would find it more difficult to understand the truth of what we are studying here.

Looking at Philippians 2:7, there is an interesting word, the word *made*. This word also appears in Hebrews 5:9. The word as used in these places means to "be ordained to be." It was God's purpose for His Son *to be ordained to be* exactly what was required for Him to fulfill His purpose as Kinsman Redeemer and High Priest. With these earthly requirements being met, He (Christ) was highly exalted and given a name which was above every name (Philippians 2:9).

When our text says that He was made perfect, it cannot be supposed that He was in any way imperfect; but practically and experimentally He was consecrated for this particular ministry of High Priest. Following God's plan, Christ Jesus was consecrated also to become the Author of "eternal salvation" (V. 9).

No other priest had the rights to this claim. No other religious system has a qualified Saviour as Christ. He is qualified uniquely by right of inheritance. As we learned in Hebrews 1:2, Christ was appointed heir of all things. He obtained by inheritance a more excellent name than the angels. Christ was given the appointed right to serve and to serve with all authority. As Priestly-King, Christ was given an eternal throne (Hebrews 1:8). Jesus was made a little lower than the angels so that He might suffer death and then He later was crowned with glory and honor (Hebrews 2:9). All of this parallels the truth taught and explained in Philippians chapter two. In all things, Christ was faithful to Him that appointed Him (Hebrews 3:2).

As one might notice I am showing the progression of how the Scriptures reveal Christ Jesus being "made" the Author of eternal salvation. He is qualified by right of His personal suffering and His sacrificial death. He suffered, and He sacrificed. His suffering was demonstrated by what happened to His body. His sacrificing was demonstrated by what happened to His blood. His body was bruised; His blood was shed. Only His body and His blood could satisfy the demands of the Father. He had to be given a body for the purpose of His humility. Without a body He could neither be the One who sacrificed, nor the Sacrifice. Only as the resurrected Saviour could He take His own blood into the very presence of God. Can we but comprehend such a magnanimous truth? Christ is both the Sacrifice and the Giver of that sacrifice. He as the Great High Priest delivers His own blood to the Father. This is a further reason Christ Jesus had to arise from the dead. Had He not risen, the blood could not have been delivered, for no earthly priest, after the pattern of Aaron, could have achieved this. Therefore, His Priesthood is above all others.

He is qualified to become the High Priest of eternal salvation to those *"that obey him."* This does not imply a works salvation as some would certainly teach. It describes instead the *proving attitude* and the *particular action* of one who is eternally saved. That means that true believers are marked by obedience, because chiefly they became obedient to the Gospel of Christ.

Upon recognizing that Christ was obedient unto death to the will of His Father, should inspire us to do likewise as we imitate Him. It should be our sacred purpose and sacred goal to imitate Christ. How much practical Christianity could be achieved if we would do that!

B. There is a Distinction in the Way He Serves. (5:10)

"Called of God an high priest after the order of Melchisedec." The call and the simply prescribed way in which Christ was called is given in this tenth verse. He was called of God. Psalm 110 had predicted this event and now in verse ten we read that He is actually called of God. This call demonstrates above all else that God the Father was pleased with His Son. If Christ Jesus in any respect had been blemished, then the Father would not have called Him. The call showed that the Father was "well pleased," as the Gospels teach us. The 146 external requirements that had to be met to qualify the Aaronic priesthood foreshadowed God's perfect Son. We must remember that the type can only hold a lesser position than that which it represents. In the priestly sense, all priests have come short of the glory of God just as the rest of the human family.

Not only did God's call show that the Father was well pleased, but the call also proved that the legal requirements of having Christ serve had been met. God had His own law and requirements and as students we must agree that God did not break His own law in letting Christ serve. For Christ declared His own purpose and intent in regards to the law where He said, *"Think not that I am come to destroy the law, or the prophets: I am not come to destroy, but to fulfil"* (Matthew 5:17).

His call of God was after the order of Melchisedec. We may remind ourselves that He could not serve as a Levitical priest because He was of the tribe of Judah (Hebrews 7:14). Moses did not even suggest that a priest would come forth from the tribe of Judah. The similarities of Melchisedec and Christ are these: They both were men (Hebrews 7:14; I Timothy 2:5); They both served as priestly-kings (Genesis 14:18; Zechariah 6:12, 13); they both were appointed by God directly (Hebrews 7:21); they also carried the same title of "King of righteousness" and the King of peace" (Hebrews 7:2, Isaiah 11:5-9).

Though there are similarities, there are vast differences in Christ and Melchisedec, as well. Immediately as chapter eight begins, a quick recognizable difference is given. It appears in this fashion, *"We have such an high priest, who is set on the right hand of the throne of the Majesty in the heavens."* This could not ever be said about Melchisedec. Even though Melchisedec was not exalted to the place of Christ, he upon both his person and office received great honor because he was a representative type of the Person and the Priesthood of the Lord Jesus Christ.

There seems to be a gentle argument and development of that argument as it pertains to Christ being a Priest superior to both Aaron and Melchisedec, and now it is being said that Christ was definitely called of God, and also served after the order of Melchisedec. This approach initially was for the benefit of the Jewish mind. Even if one would read some of the writings by the Jews, they will find that Melchisedec is referred to as a prince of God rather than a priest of God. This is an indication of how the truth was defined by the Jew. The writer of Hebrews is careful of the way the Jew thinks as he embraces his tradition. There was the concern as it was so in the letter to the Galatians that there would be those who were converted from Judaism, that they might be tempted to revert back. Now, with a practical and current addressing of truth as found in Hebrews, we must be mindful that Christ is superior and qualified in His priestly service. May we serve Him well, as He has us.

Chapter Thirteen

WHEN TRUTH IS NEGLECTED

Text: Hebrews 5:10-14

10 Called of God an high priest after the order of Melchisedec.
11 Of whom we have many things to say, and hard to be uttered, seeing ye are dull of hearing.
12 For when for the time ye ought to be teachers, ye have need that one teach you again which be the first principles of the oracles of God; and are become such as have need of milk, and not of strong meat.
13 For every one that useth milk is unskilful in the word of righteousness: for he is a babe.
14 But strong meat belongeth to them that are of full age, even those who by reason of use have their senses exercised to discern both good and evil.

For one to have the availability of truth and then neglect it is not much different than not having truth at all. The second chapter of Hebrews has already warned us of the dangers of *hearing* truth but not *heeding* it. Sometimes we neglect to hear truth because we are not ready to hear. Ecclesiastes 5:1 tells us that when we go to the house of God we should be "ready to hear." Many times we are incapable of hearing the truth because we are not ready to hear.

There are ways that we should prepare ourselves to hear. Mark 4:24 tells us to, *"Take heed what ye hear."* Remember also, *"So then faith cometh by hearing, and hearing by the word of God"* (Romans 10:17). It is clearly apparent that the Word of God has much to say about hearing. When preparing ourselves we realize the importance of hearing to the development of our faith.

Hearing takes place in one's soul. We describe the soul in this manner. It is composed of three parts; there is the will of man, the intellect of man, and the emotional part of man. We will look at these three parts in respect to *hearing preparation.*

We shall first consider the value of the intellect in one's hearing. From our warning in Mark 4:24, when a person has the intellect to hear, it simply means that he has the capacity to hear and to learn. One needs to be careful and discerning as he listens. There are so many things that can impede one's ability to properly hear. After all, we do live in a very noisy world. We live in a world that suffers from noise pollution. So much that is being said in this world is not worthy of being heard. Therefore, one must be careful to either turn the volume down or turn off all that would be offensive to one's spiritual maturity. This may prove very difficult, but it certainly is necessary.

In taking heed to what one hears, there must also be a criterion for hearing. It should begin by one first being tuned into what God is saying. The importance of this cannot be over-estimated. When one intently considers what God is saying, then He has a perfect reference point to measure what He is otherwise hearing. For this reason, we must continue to insist that we do not at all tamper with the Word of God (The King James Bible).

Luke 8:18 tells us to, *"Take heed therefore how ye hear."* This tells us that there is an emotional part involving our hearing. You may refuse to hear because you do not like what you are hearing. There may be emotional reasons for this. I have talked to people who have been hurt by someone, and their emotional pain is so intense that they refuse to listen. A person like this must prepare himself to listen by getting over whatever is hurting him and then start listening.

Believers may have suffered some form of emotional crisis that hinders their ability or either their desire to listen. A person may find himself emotionally cluttered to the extent that it is impossible to hear clearly until some of the clutter is removed.

When preparing oneself for worship, there may need to be a quieting down first before that one can hear. As a pastor, I recognize how difficult it is to step out of the noisy world into a quite sanctuary of truth. In contrast to what is being heard out in the world, the church certainly ought to be a haven of rest. We have found that in preparing oneself to hear, both the intellect and the will is involved in our hearing.

The will can be a strong positive or negative force in our hearing. Some do not hear because they do not want to hear. As simple as this statement may be, it certainly is true. The will, the intellect, and the emotional part of man are fused together with each affecting the other. For one to exercise his will, he must have his intellect and his emotions at work. This being so, one then wills to think or to act in a prescribed way.

One also wills to hear what he wants to hear. In regards to the believer, while preparing one's heart to hear, it would be appropriate to pray that we may have the will to hear what God has to say lest we neglect the truth by being dull of hearing. In this study, we will look at three things regarding our hearing. May we notice: I. A Dullness of Hearing (V. 11); II. A Declining in Hearing (V. 12); III. A Discernment by Hearing (Vv. 13-14).

I. A DULLNESS OF HEARING. (5:11)

A. The Dullness That Characterized the People. (5:11)

The word "dull" *nothros* as used only here and in 6:12 in Hebrews means; *slow, sluggish, and indolent.* The word "hearing" is a plural word. The meaning is that after hearing the blessed truth over and over again, they had become listless and slow. One may sense the frustration of the writer upon recognizing their condition. The writer of Hebrews had wonderful truth pertaining to the priest-king,

Melchisedec, yet they could not receive it. The problem was not with the truth being too complex, but with the people being too unwilling to receive what the writer needed to say because of their indolence.

The Jews may have been dull of hearing because they were becoming guilty of taking their eyes off of Jesus as indicated especially in Hebrews 11. Though hearing and seeing are not the same, when one takes his eyes off of Jesus it will affect all of the senses including the hearing.

Since "dullness of hearing" describes the historical readers of the Hebrew letter, it would also behoove us to look at different aspects of being dull in our hearing. The first thought that we might consider is, the amount of additional effort that is required to communicate when a person has dullness of hearing. *"Of whom we have many things to say"* (V. 11), clues us in to the extra energy or effort that is required to communicate the truth when one has his attention divided; he does not clearly receive what he is hearing. We often use the phrase in normal communication, "stay focused." When one is not focused he does not hear. When Hebrews reminds us to keep our eyes upon Jesus, it is for the purpose of keeping us focused. I have a hearing problem and I have difficulty understanding words. It helps when I look into the face of the one who is speaking. Our spiritual hearing would improve tremendously if we would keep our eyes upon Jesus.

My mother used to say to me when I was being either stubborn or indolent, "Max, I talk to you until I am blue in the face and you do not listen." The writer of Hebrews would have known the way that my mother felt I am sure.

Another consideration involving dullness of hearing is that the one speaking has a much greater concern and a much greater awareness of what is being communicated than those listening. Quite often when one is crusading for something dear to one's heart and he senses that no one feels the intensity that he feels as he communicates, he may say that his listeners are dull of hearing. I just recently found myself sharing my burden with a group, and did so with passion and feeling only to recognize that my listeners were not hearing. I then, as our text suggests, had to do much talking to get the group interested in what I had to say. Likewise, the minister has the enormous task of raising the dead and of awakening the sleepy in thirty minutes or so.

A third consideration involving "dullness of hearing" is that, when one does not hear well his faith does not increase. Satan certainly has his sleeping pills to make you sleepy around God's Word. He also knows that *"faith cometh by hearing."* This section of our study is a warning section reminding us to very carefully hear and process the truth, allowing God to incorporate it into our faith. To not let this happen will cost us dearly. We will now consider, "The dullness that cost the people."

B. The Dullness That Cost the People. (5:11b)

The *dullness* of the people who were being addressed

meant that their "souls were not keeping pace with the doctrines and exhortations that were delivered unto them" (Clarke). They were dwarfs instead of giants. So much had been said, with so little being comprehended that they were said to be "slow." This was not an indictment against them intellectually, but instead an indictment against their cooled down spiritual state.

These Palestinian Christians were not simply babies, but old babies who had been introduced to Christ for 10 to 30 years, and were not maturing, but worst than that they were retrogressing. There is certainly a high cost involved when one remains a spiritual infant. We will consider several ways in which it will cost one who is spiritually dull.

First, a person who does not mature cannot do anything that requires maturity. A child cannot pilot a jet aircraft, nor can a spiritual infant exercise and perform spiritual tasks. Paul, when he wrote to the church at Thessalonica, had the strong desire that those to whom he was writing might be perfected in the faith. Notice this verse, *"Night and day praying exceedingly that we might see your face, and might perfect that which is lacking in your faith?"* (I Thessalonians 3:10). Paul was challenging this church in much the same way as the Hebrew Christians were being challenged when he said, *"Therefore let us not sleep, as do others; but let us watch and be sober"* (I Thessalonians 5:6).

Those who pastor our churches, and lead our congregations should be especially mindful of not being dull of hearing. The example of leadership is needed both to inspire and to challenge. Unless our spiritual teachers are being taught and going on to perfection, how can we expect our followers to do any better. A dynamic, functional faith must be present for one to perform great things for God.

Another consideration is that one who is dull of hearing lacks not only the maturity, but also the endurance to run the race. Race running should mark the spiritual man. There are many races to be run.

We should press on for Christ, without casting away our confidence. Confidence builds confidence. When we have our confidence in Christ, we have a "forerunner" or a "captain" who is able to challenge us as our leader. Those who are dull of hearing have gotten out of the race. Their spiritual legs grow weary and they no longer have the endurance to run. When they lack endurance, it is easy for their desire to fail. Another cost that is imposed upon the dull of hearing is that they must give account for that which they did not receive by their refusing to hear. We certainly ought to be mindful that there is the Judgment Seat of Christ waiting for all believers who must give an account of their obedience to the Word of God. When truth is given, and it involves instruction, and those instructions are not followed, then that constitutes disobedience.

I recall telling my father a number of times that I did not hear him when he had told me to do something. That certainly was no excuse for him. Neither will it be at the Judgment Seat of Christ, for we must all give an account of the things done (or not done) in the body. There will be many lost rewards for those who are dull of hearing.

II. A DECLINE IN HEARING THE TRUTH. (5:12-13)

A. Their Condition Described. (5:12a)

"For when for the time ye ought to be teachers, ye have need that one teach you again which be the first principles of the oracles of God; and are become such as have need of milk, and not of strong meat." The apostolic rebuke is strongly given in this verse. The writer sternly rebukes them for wasting valuable time. How precious is our lifetime upon this earth; it is not to be wasted. Yet that is exactly what is happening here. The students had learned and then by neglect they had let the truths that they had been taught "slip" out of their minds, as chapter two had warned. This warning, as given in chapter 2:1, certainly applies to this situation. Carefully attend to what is being said; *"Therefore we ought to give the more earnest heed to the things which we have heard, lest at any time we should let them slip"* (Hebrews 2:1).

Very gradually, all that they had learned was being lost. Initially, the Hebrew converts had learned rapidly, because of their familiarity with the Old Testament. That which they had previously learned in the Old Testament served as a foundation for their now being taught New Testament truth. Yet, with the passing of time that which had become familiar to them was being neglected, and then forgotten. This is part of the reason they were being told they had to learn again the first principles of the oracles of God. This would be like being told one must learn his "ABCs" all over again.

When we look at these Hebrew students, we may observe a few things about them and apply it as needed for ourselves. First we see the principle, "use it or lose it." When we fail to exercise our bodies, atrophy sets in and our muscle tone is lost as well as muscle strength. Likewise, when one fails to exercise his mind the same will happen to the mind. No greater is this truth recognized as it is when one begins to *"neglect so great salvation."* The principle is the same. As mentioned earlier, one does not only fail to grow, one will actually retrogress or go back, losing what had previously been taught and learned.

They were also losing what they had by being careless. In other words, they had gotten to the place that they could not care less. The discipline of study was no longer theirs; they did not give the things of God a strong priority. They apparently were not at all walking by faith, for in chapter 11 an entire chapter is given to inspire and rebuke them. For those who were pricked in their conscience, they were being challenged in chapter 10 not to cast away their confidence and then in chapter 11 were being instructed and were being told what faith was. Then in chapter 12 they were being told to turn their eyes back on Jesus.

The third thing that needs to be said about these early Hebrew students is that they did not acknowledge the true worth of that which they had learned. They were losing by neglect, *"the oracles of God."* In a practical application of this today, Satan blinds the minds of believers and they do not recognize the value of their church, nor its teachings. Again, this may come about when the pastor loses his zeal and begins to personally retrogress before his people. He could very well be holding the position, while his position no longer holds him. Each pastor must strive to burn with desire and passion for the knowledge and the application of truth.

In verse 12 the word *time* is used in this manner, *"For when for the time ye ought to be teachers."* This should stir us today as we handle the oracles of God, knowing that we have the privilege to do so for only a small period of time. We constantly ought to be moved to further advance the cause of Christ, by each tick of the clock. The passing of time should stir us to remove ourselves from a life of slothfulness. Each tick of the clock should be a sharp goad to rouse us from our sleep. It is time that we have, but it is time that we also lose. We are losing the time and then fail as good stewards to redeem the time that we have remaining while here upon this earth.

B. Their Crisis Defined. (5:12b-13)

"For when for the time ye ought to be teachers, ye have need that one teach you again which be the first principles of the oracles of God; and are become such as have need of milk, and not of strong meat." Again, may we notice the last part of this verse that tells us that these Hebrew students, *"are become such as have need of milk, and not of strong meat."* The Apostle Paul used the same metaphor

in I Corinthians 3:1-2 to rebuke the carnal Corinthians. Our text is not a rebuke to normal Christian growth, but instead it is a rebuke when one returns to a child-like grasp of the Word of God, being unable to spiritually stand or walk. The milk pictures the elementary doctrines, which are needful for beginning growth, but not for sustained growth.

Notice the contrast of "milk" to "strong meat." The listings of these ingredients that pertain to growth are given to form a mental picture that we may comment on. Milk, as used by a baby for its nourishment is very necessary. Before the child has developed to a certain point, the child would find it an impossibility to eat and digest "strong meat." One does not take the baby directly from the birthing room to the local steakhouse to eat prime rib. Likewise, a child of God when birthed must begin with a diet that is suitable to his beginning spiritual state. When there is spiritual maturity taking place, one then has the privilege and the responsibility to take on the heavier matters of the faith. Natural spiritual growth is a process just as is physical growth.

Once the process has begun and the believer has matured, he need not start over with the elementary rudiments of the faith, no more than an adult should go back to a baby bottle and back to eating baby food.

Next, notice the suggestion that appetite plays an important part in one's growth. Just how important is a proper appetite for spiritual growth. It is a sign of sickness when a person loses his appetite. The same may be said of the believer. When one has no hunger for the things of God, you may say that the person is spiritually ill. Appetite is a wonderful thing.

I recall early in my ministry visiting an old man named Mr. Pruitt who had lost his appetite. I felt that if I could just get him to eat that he would get better. I remember getting him a milkshake thinking that no one could turn that down, only to have him refuse it after only a swallow or two. Many are like that when it comes to the things of God. They have no appetite for the nourishment that comes from the Word of God.

They neglect their Bible study and become unfaithful to the House of God. They are "dull of hearing" and have no hunger for the Word being preached. We should remind ourselves that the beatitudes say, *"Blessed are they which do hunger and thirst after righteousness: for they shall be filled"* (Matthew 5:6).

In I Peter 2:2-3, appetite is used to express how one should desire Christ Jesus. It uses the appetite of a newborn baby to picture what should be our appetite for the Word with normal growth being implied. *"As newborn babes, desire the sincere milk of the word, that ye may grow thereby: If so be ye have tasted that the Lord is gracious."*

One is in a very serious state spiritually when there is no appetite or either there is only an appetite for milk. The value of a healthy appetite for one's spiritual growth cannot be over stated. For if a person finds himself in such a state that leaves him "dull of hearing," that person is in need of critical care. In our hospitals we have Intensive Care Wards, and also Critical Care Wards for the infirmed. Many believers are close to a terminal state because they have allowed themselves to become weakened by their inactivity as it pertains to spiritual things. They are curled up in their inactivity as little babies sleeping the day away. I have also seen people reach a terminal state because of some dreaded disease, only to complete their life upon this earth sleeping with no strength to do anything else. Their desires and ambitions fail them as they find themselves with no more dreams or goals in life. We must guard against this happening to us spiritually.

The thirteenth verse says, *"For everyone that useth milk is unskilful in the word of righteousness: for he is a babe."* This conveys to us another aspect of the crisis of being "dull of hearing." One who uses milk has no skill in handling Bible doctrine. Doctrine involves teaching. Those who use milk require teaching and have no ability to expound precious truth. Truth expounders must be eating of the strong meat to feed others. Those who desire that their ears be tickled, having "itching ears" (II Timothy 4:3), have no desire for strong doctrinal teaching. Much of the truth found in the writings of Paul and the Pastoral Epistles warn of the dangers of not exercising spiritual maturity. Paul's dilemma, at times, seems to be the frustration of not being able to expound doctrine because his hearers were incapable of receiving the meat of God's Word.

The phrase *"word of righteousness"* as used in verse 13 is a way of referencing doctrine. Therefore, one might say in particular that an unskilled person is unable to teach basic doctrines pertaining to salvation. Salvation is the starting point for all theology. With this being so, those who are dull of hearing have absolutely no ability to relate truth, for their own slothfulness has eroded their ability to do anything spiritually.

III. A DISCERNMENT BY HEARING THE TRUTH. (5:14)

A. Those Who Do Not Hear Lack Discernment. (5:14)

"But strong meat belongeth to them that are of full age, even those who by reason of use have their senses exercised to discern both good and evil." Spiritual discernment demands the exercising of biblical truth. *"Strong meat belongeth to them that are of full age."* This expression refers to those who have grown up and are applying the Word in their personal lives to discern that which is either good or evil.

We know that the unregenerate person has no ability to discern the things of the Spirit of God (I Corinthians 2:14), but the spiritually-immature Christian has the same problem. The Spirit of God is within man to recall to his senses the things of God according to the Word, but the dull of hearing do not have this ability.

The dull of hearing do not exercise their senses. They have not the capacity. Yet many such people are dangerously put into places of responsibility and they depend upon their intellectual acumen or their gifted personality to operate the things of God. They shortcut

God's requirements and substitute their own devices, while depending upon their own strengths rather than God's power. A wise person, in biblical terms, is one who has his senses exercised by God's Word to discern both good and evil. The non-discerner is at a lost as to God's requirements concerning his dress, testimony, use of time, use of talents, etc. He has instead been programmed by the world, and forfeited having the mind of Christ.

B. **Those Who Do Hear Exercise Discernment.**

(5:14 cont.)

Those who have grown to the level of maturity that is being described here did not achieve it overnight. I recall on more than one occasion Evangelist C.L. Roach telling me, "some things you only get by getting older." How true that statement is. Christians with the long experience of growing in grace reach the place of being able to understand the more elevated doctrines of Christianity; they have a settled sense and purpose about them that carries them through their trials and difficulties while staying clearly focused, and while trusting God all the way. They are operating on a spiritual plane that gives them confidence while carrying out the will and the purposes of God.

James 1:5 says, *"If any of you lack wisdom, let him ask of God, that giveth to all men liberally and upbraideth not; and it shall be given him."* The Lord desires for you to want what

He has to give. Just as salvation is made available, so is spiritual wisdom and spiritual discernment. May we be challenged by this study to "go on unto perfection" and not to be "dull of hearing."

Chapter Fourteen

LET US GO ON

Text: Hebrews 6:1-6

1 Therefore leaving the principles of the doctrine of Christ, let us go on unto perfection; not laying again the foundation of repentance from dead works, and of faith toward God,
2 Of the doctrine of baptisms, and of laying on of hands, and of resurrection of the dead, and of eternal judgment.
3 And this will we do, if God permit.
4 For it is impossible for those who were once enlightened, and have tasted of the heavenly gift, and were made partakers of the Holy Ghost,
5 And have tasted the good word of God, and the powers of the world to come,
6 If they shall fall away, to renew them again unto repentance; seeing they crucify to themselves the Son of God afresh, and put him to an open shame.

Growth is normally a very subtle event. It is difficult to notice growth taking place even by constant observation. Normally to reference something that is growing involves making a time comparison. A good example of this would be by taking a picture of a child just before he has a growth spurt. Then several months later, take another picture and then make a comparison. On a personal basis, when one is measuring his spiritual growth, he should do it by looking into the mirror of God's Word; God's Word has a perfect reference point.

Our study under consideration will consider the doctrine of growing. In this study we will see how one should experience a complete growth. The word *perfection* as it appears in our text comes from the root Greek word *telios*. This word means: complete (in various applications of labor, growth, mental and moral character, etc.); neuter (as noun, with completeness, of full age, man, perfect). The similar word was used when Christ cried, "It is finished."

With our challenge to go on to maturity (perfection), we will look at three things: I. The Exhortation To Be Mature (Vv. 1-3); II. The Explanation For the Mature (Vv. 4-6a); III. The Revelation About the Mature (V. 6b).

I. THE EXHORTATION TO BE MATURE. (6:1-3)

A. The Standard For the Challenge Given. (6:1-2)

"Therefore leaving the principles of the doctrine of Christ, let us go on unto perfection; not laying again the foundation of repentance from dead works, and of faith toward God, Of the doctrine of baptisms, and of laying on of hands, and of resurrection of the dead, and of eternal

judgment." Many students stumble when they come to this great sixth chapter. Proper hermeneutical skills should help one to avoid this being such a frightful chapter. Some have been taught that the chapter teaches that one can lose his salvation. Nothing could be further from the truth. When studying this chapter, one needs to study it as he would the rest of the book. As he studies He should keep the converted Jew in mind, who is being tempted to revert back to Judaism. Then from a more practical and more contemporary position, one needs to keep in mind the "dull of hearing" of any age which have been converted to Christ, but have neglected the growth that God intended for them.

The dominant concern that the writer is expressing in this study is that the people to whom he is writing are not advancing according to God's plan and purpose. He is challenging them, not to get saved again, but to function as a saved person should. When this thought is kept intact, there will be less difficulty in arriving at a proper interpretation.

The Bible identifies three groups of people in I Corinthians chapters two and three. The first is the natural man which *"receiveth not the things of the Spirit of God."* This first group identified as the "natural man" has no capacity to receive the spiritual things of God. He is sensual and operates according to his own senses. He would make up the chaff or the goats within the Kingdom of God. He may be able to mimic, as did the Pharisee, certain religious characteristics. Christ, however, saw them only as "whited sepulchres." He called them hypocrites. The natural man also may make no attempt at all to be *religious*. He may be motivated only by his sinful lusts and passions. He may be of high moral persuasion, and be intellectually refined, yet operating only by his natural senses. In no way is the natural man being referred to in our Hebrews study. The writer is not challenging an unbeliever (natural man) to go on to perfection. Nor does the spiritual man revert back to a natural unregenerate state.

The second group we may refer to is the *spiritual*. The *"spiritual judgeth all things"* (I Corinthians 2:15). The spiritual person has become such, only by regeneration. When one is born again, he becomes a spiritual being having a spiritual existence. When he is in a spiritual state of maturity, he is thriving on the things of God. He has the ability to get in focus spiritually and to stay in focus. He is, as Hebrews 5:14 tells us, of *"full age"* and *"have their senses exercised to discern both good and evil."*

One may be only converted, but not maturing. This person would be called a carnal man or a carnal person. I Corinthians 3:1 says, *"And I, brethren, could not speak unto you as unto spiritual, but as unto carnal, even as unto babes in Christ."* The next verse continues, *"I have fed you with milk, and not with meat: for hitherto ye were not able to bear it, neither yet now are ye able."*

The Greek word for carnal is *sarkinos* which means "fleshly" or "of the flesh", This word carries the idea of weakness, and willfulness. These babies, are as Hebrews tell us, babies who cannot comprehend, nor apprehend the deeper truths of God. For a baby to achieve maturity, the baby must be put on a proper diet suited to the baby's growth. Also, the child must be taught those things that will properly formulate the baby's thinking and activity. Then, there needs to be healthy exercise to develop the muscles. All of this is true in regards to spiritual growth. If any of these ingredients are lacking, proper growth will not be achieved. An unattended and undisciplined child will express that state in its personal weakness and its personal willfulness.

To illustrate this, our granddaughter Camrey recently stayed with us for nearly two weeks. During this time we emphasized the importance of good and correct manners. She is three years old and is very impressionable. She went to see her maternal grandparents after being with us. I called her grandparents to ask how she was doing since she had returned home. Her grandmother said, "We want Camrey to stay with you more often." She has come back a different child, saying such things as, "Thank you" to me and "Yes ma'am" to her great-grandmother, etc.

Yet, this same child if left to herself will become *weak* and *willful*. In the book of Proverbs this truth is stated, *"The rod and reproof give wisdom: but a child left to himself bringeth his mother to shame"* (Proverbs 29:15). In the eighteenth verse of this same chapter we read, *"Where there is no vision, the people perish: but he that keepeth the law, happy is he."* The word *vision* means, "God ordained plan, or strategy." The word of God is that strategy of which we speak. For proper growth to take place there *must* be a plan of action. What better way than God's Word; it is the only way!

This chapter, as previously mentioned, begins with a challenge, not to someone who is in an unregenerated, natural state, for this would be impossible. Yet, the challenge is to the weak and willful who are in a *baby state*. The standard for what must be achieved is conveyed by the word "perfection." As we have already considered, this word involves having a goal that leads to completion or maturity. A grape that only remains as a bud, has not achieved its purpose until it goes beyond the bud, and the blossom to the actual fruit. The vine's purpose in the vineyard is to yield its fruit. Likewise, Christ wants us to go beyond just the blossom to the actual fruit bearing.

The word "therefore" as it appears in verse one is one of the many transitional words used in Hebrews. Only the first chapter and the last chapter do not use such transitional words when the chapter is being introduced. It is almost like the entire book of Hebrews is one ongoing sentence. The word "therefore" is a signal to "leave" and to "let." The meaning being, *leave* where you began and *let* a new ambition characterize your existence. Then there are several things mentioned that should be left behind. They can be divided into seven groups which are: *1. "Learning the principles of the doctrine of Christ," 2. "Repentance from dead works," 3. "Faith towards God," 4. "Doctrine of baptisms," 5. "Laying on of hands," 6. "Resurrection of the dead," 7. "Eternal judgment."*

All of the above are very important, but they each have their particular place. They have a restricted place and purpose. When building a house, each component is very important. One does not perpetually build or lay the foundation. Once the important process of putting in the foundation has been completed, the builder goes on to the next stage. Think how absurd it would be to never get beyond the foundation. The building will never be perfected or completed. A completion requires successive steps with a goal in mind. The same may be said in regards to spiritual maturity.

May we briefly comment on these seven stages mentioned that should be left behind while going on to perfection. The first mentioned, *"learning the principles of the doctrine of Christ."* This refers to those things which are first required in a beginning relationship with Christ. If Christ is accepted as He should be, as the true and the only Saviour, then He should be known in a primary sense beginning at salvation. Once one is saved, the primary teachings pertaining to Christ are to be expounded upon and developed to a more mature apprehension of who Christ really is. A.W. Tozier desired and taught that men might *learn* to really know Him. Should we not strive to know Him more nearly, know Him more clearly, and know Him more dearly?

Before the Jew would make a radical departure from Judaism, he had to have an elementary or foundational knowledge of Christ and the way Christianity is different from his own system. Once this difference is learned, then there are new lessons to be learned. Paul recognized that the Jew in his faith, had *"a zeal of God, but not according to knowledge* (Romans 10:1-4). The Jewish system defined its righteousness according to laws and ceremonies. They were ignorant of the fact that *"Christ is the end of the law for righteousness to every one that believeth."* They knew that Moses had described the *"righteousness which is of the law, That the man which doeth those things shall live by them"* (Romans 10:4,5). The plea is now given by the writer to go beyond the elementary teachings concerning Christ.

The second item mentioned not to be repeated, *"not laying again the foundation of repentance from dead works."* The key word in this thought is the word *foundation*. Two thoughts may be given about this word. First, the foundation is known to support the building that rests upon it, and the foundation comes first. In respect to Judaism, as pertaining to the laws given by Moses, they were very much necessary. Yet, once given, they did not need to be given again, no more than should the foundation be laid more than once.

Just as Paul knew that the early Christian Jews were being tempted to return back to "dead works," as given in the book of Galatians, so sensed the writer of Hebrews. The dead works were those works that could only be accomplished in the flesh. The writer was challenging his readers to continue in a lively manner by being energized by the Holy Spirit. Sadly, so much of our present church activities are being performed in a cold, lifeless manner, while at the same time not even suspecting that there is no life there.

The third item is *"faith toward God."* Again, thinking with a Jewish mindset, it was the Jew who exercised his faith towards God, even having *"a zeal of God, but not according to knowledge."* Yet, now a distinction is being made. Our worship is to be addressed not to God in a generic sense, but to Christ in a particular sense. All of our worship should center on Christ. The language of our text is pointing to exactly what Hebrews 12:2 teaches, when it says, *"Looking unto Jesus the author and finisher of our faith"* (Hebrews 12:2a). It is as though the writer keeps telling his reader, "change your focus...keep your eyes on the new economy." Keep your eyes on Him!

The fourth expression, "of the doctrine of baptisms," pertains to teachings having to do with ceremonial washings that were elaborately taught. In Hebrews 9:10 it is *"meats and drinks, and divers washings, and carnal (fleshly) ordinances"* concerning which it is said, they were *"imposed... until the time of reformation."* These passages refer back to the Levitical system as outlined in Exodus 30:18-19; Leviticus 16:4; Numbers 19:19. All of these plural baptisms (washings) were necessarily taught to teach and foreshadow the perfect cleansing that would be in Christ Jesus. The argument is that no one needed to go back to the shadow when we have the substance. Again, the challenge speaks of leaving the old economy of law and entering the new economy of grace.

The fifth expression, *"and of laying on of hands,"* again keeping the Jewish mindset intact certainly yields a correct understanding of what is being said. A.W. Pink has clear insight to the meaning in his studies; "The older commentators quite missed the reference here. Supposing the previous clause was concerned with the Christian baptisms recorded in the Acts, they appealed to such passages as Acts 8:17; 19:6, etc. But those passages have no bearing at all on the verse before us. They were exceptional cases where the supernatural "gifts" of the Spirit were imparted by communication from the apostles. The absence of this "laying on of hands" in Acts 2:41; 8:38; 16:33, shows plainly that, normally, the Holy Spirit was given by God altogether apart from the instrumentally of His servants. The "laying on of hands" is not, and never was, a distinctive Christian ordinance. In such passages as Acts 6:6; 9:17; 13:3, the act was simply a mark of identification, as is sufficiently clear from the last reference.

"And of laying on of hands." The key which unlocks the real meaning of this expression is to be found in the Old Testament, to which each and all of the seven things here mentioned by the apostle, refer or look back. Necessarily so, for the apostle is here making mention of those things which characterized Judaism, which the Hebrews upon their profession of their personal faith in Christ, had "left."

The "laying on of hands" to which the apostle refers is described in Leviticus 16:21, *"And Aaron shall lay both his hands upon the head of the live goat, and confess over him all the iniquities of the children of Israel, and all their transgressions in all their sins, putting them upon the head of the goat, and shall send him away by the hand of a fit man into the wilderness."* This was an essential part of the ritual on the annual Day of Atonement. Of this the Hebrews would naturally think when the apostle here makes mention of the *doctrine* (teaching)...of laying on of hands" (Pink).

The sixth expression, *"and of resurrection of the dead"* is a return to emphasizing a combined resurrection of the *just and unjust.* When we perfect or complete this teaching, we learn to know that there will be the Judgment Seat of Christ and the Great White Throne Judgment. The Great White Throne Judgment will be for the wicked dead (Revelation

20:11-15) and the Judgment Seat of Christ for the believers (II Corinthians 5:10-11). Perhaps what the writer is emphasizing is that these Jewish Christians were embracing their previous teachings while lacking the revelation that had come through Christ Jesus. This began with His resurrection and was hinted at with the raising of Lazarus. Notice what Martha said, *"Martha saith unto Him, I know that he shall rise again in the resurrection at the last day"* (John 11:24). This "going back" illustrates again how truth is able to "slip" away.

The seventh expression, *"and of eternal judgment,"* has been mostly dealt with when considering the sixth expression. To achieve perfection means the setting aside of at least these seven mentioned principles. The first statement made, involving "learning the principles of the doctrine of Christ" embodies the other six. The setting aside of these is not in any way a suggestion that these things did not serve a valid purpose, but that the purpose had already been served in a previous economy. The superior way offered by Christ permits one to enjoy a greater degree of development that never could be obtained in the old economy. Our next consideration will show where the strength comes from to meet the challenge of going on to perfection.

B. The Strength of the Challenge Given. (6:3)

The writer is challenging the indolent, the dull of hearing with respect to their sin problem. The Christian has no permitted right to do wrong. It is God's purpose and desire for the Christian that he goes on to maturity. This verse shows however that one may not always exercise that right. One may reach a point in time, when it will be too late to recover from his slothfulness and that person will not have the opportunity to yield the fruit that is expected of him. Yet, that does not mean that it was not God's will for him to mature; it simply means that he forfeited the will of God.

The third verse says it like this, *"And this will we do, if God permit."* The writer of Hebrews is saying "go on," realizing all the while that it may not be in God's sovereign will and purpose to permit it. The shameful state that these souls had fallen was an ongoing reproach to the cause and to the name of Christ. The writer is expressing how critical their present state had become.

The will of God has a mysterious element about it. The Word of God clearly gives us the body of truth from which the will of God is determined. Yet, the manner in which the will of God is realized is according to His sovereign purposes. In His providence and by His sovereign design is His will manifested. The statement, *"And this will we do, if God permit"* is a most sobering statement. It shows the respect the writer had for the God whom He was writing about. This brief verse shows in just a few words that they were in such a dangerous state. This expression should remind us of the first warning section in Hebrews that asks, *"How shall we escape, if we neglect so great salvation…?"* (Hebrews 2:3).

II. THE EXPLANATION FOR THE MATURE.

(6:4-6a)

A. An Impossible Scenario. (6:4-5)

"For it is impossible for those who were once enlightened, and have tasted of the heavenly gift, and were made partakers of the Holy Ghost, and had tasted the good word of God, and the powers of the world to come." When reading these verses, it is almost like reading a courtroom briefing that describes a trial lawyer as he lays out his evidences to support his case. The evidence is in. A strong opening statement is made to prove that the said evidence is available. Listen as the writer speaks, *"For it is impossible..."* He prefaces his argument with such strong language. The statement made under divine inspiration leaves no room for debate.

May we take each argument and analyze it in such a way to gain a proper interpretation of this great chapter. The first phrase involves those *"who were once enlightened."* Jesus Himself described those who walk in the light in this manner. *"And this is the condemnation, that light is come into the world, and men loved darkness rather than light, because their deeds were evil. For every one that doeth evil hateth the light, neither cometh to the light, lest his deeds should be reproved. But he that doeth truth cometh to the light, that his deeds may be made manifest, that they are wrought in God"* (John 3:19-21). He that *"doeth truth cometh to the light."* One cannot be enlightened unless that one comes to the Light (John 1:4-12). Christ Jesus is the only one that can open up one's heart of unbelief and let the light in. To be enlightened means to be born again. When one comes to Jesus as Saviour, he leaves his state of darkness. With light being contrasted to darkness, one is able to picture how radical the new birth is. The new birth is the only means whereby one is able to detect God's truth. Paul, writing to the church at Corinth called this enlightenment, discernment. The words that Paul gave us in I Corinthians 2:10-16 is worthy of being placed here in our study. *"But God hath revealed them unto us by his Spirit: for the Spirit searcheth all things, yea, the deep things of God. For what man knoweth the things of a man, save the spirit of man which is in him? even so the things of God knoweth no man, but the Spirit of God. Now we have received, not the spirit of the world, but the spirit which is of God; that we might know the things that are freely given to us of God. Which things also we speak, not in the words which man's wisdom teacheth, but which the Holy Ghost teacheth; comparing spiritual things with spiritual. But the natural man receiveth not the things of the Spirit of God: for they are foolishness unto him: neither can he know them, because they are spiritually discerned. But he that is spiritual judgeth all things, yet he himself is judged of no man. For who hath known the mind of the Lord, that he may instruct him? But we have the mind of Christ."*

The key to being enlightened or having discernment is to have the mind of Christ. This occurs at salvation. When one is saved, he has the capacity to learn the ways of God. The Word of God becomes his text for learning. An unregenerate person has not this capacity for enlightenment. The writer of Hebrews is saying that one can be "dull of hearing," but after he has been enlightened does not entirely lose that capacity. This capacity comes at the time of the new birth, and one cannot become unborn.

Though Romans eight does not directly relate to this text, there is a principle that is relative to this study in regards to our being His children. Romans 8:14-16 tells us, *"For as many as are led by the Spirit of God, they are the sons of God. For ye have not received the spirit of bondage again to fear; but ye have received the Spirit of adoption, whereby we cry, Abba, Father. The Spirit itself beareth witness with our spirit, that we are the children of God:"*

In the fifteenth verse we note that the believer receives the Spirit of adoption. Adoption is the act of God that places the believer in His family as an adult son (Romans 8:23; 9:4; Galatians 4:5; Ephesians 1:5). At the same time, the new birth takes place. His *position*, at the time of adoption, is that of full privilege; when the new birth takes place there must be the *practice* which involves growing in grace. The writer of Hebrews recognized this principle when he saw that growth was no longer taking place and referred to the spiritually-immature Christians as "babes" (Hebrews 5:12-13).

This first statement conveys simply that those who have been enlightened cannot become unenlightened. The second statement that we will consider speaks of those who "have tasted of the heavenly gift"—the same rule applies. But just what does it mean to taste of the heavenly gift?

Tasting of the heavenly gift is a most descriptive way of describing the enjoyment that comes when one is birthed into God's family. If anyone should have had a "good taste" in their mouth, it should have been the converted Jews. All that could have been experienced under the heavy demanding requirements of the law had been lifted. Now the new economy of Grace had been ushered in and certainly must have "tasted good." Again, this is an expression that relates to the eating of strong meat versus only the drinking of milk. Even though their appetite had diminished and they are now being referred to as babies, they did at one time experience, by having tasted of the heavenly gift, the good things of the Lord. Our text shows how easy it is to experience the better things of Christ and then take these better things for granted.

Even so, once a person has experienced the better things of Christ, that experience cannot be destroyed. To taste of the heavenly gift is to accept a gift that cannot be taken away. The writer is showing by these illustrations that one does not lose his salvation, but loses the full expression of it. This brings us to the third ingredient in the argument. The expression, "were made partakers of the Holy Ghost" certainly characterizes the believer. Only the believer can be indwelt by the Holy Ghost. The Spirit is given at conversion. The sanctification of the Spirit takes place with first the call of the Gospel and the believing of the truth as taught in II Thessalonians 2:13-14. *"But we are bound to give thanks alway to God for you, brethren beloved of the Lord, because God hath from the beginning chosen you to salvation through sanctification of the Spirit and belief of the truth: Whereunto he called you by our gospel, to the obtaining of the glory of our Lord Jesus Christ."*

The argument pertaining to the Holy Ghost should be considered in respect to the fact that the Holy Ghost is absolutely necessary for one's salvation. The work of the Holy Ghost is necessary for the new birth; so also to be understood is that when one is born he does not become unborn.

As the argument continues, one's attitude towards the Word of God should be of great joy and delight. A love for the Word of God should characterize the newborn in the faith. Sin can diminish one's joy and spiritual effectiveness, but positionally once one has tasted the good Word of God the spiritual palate has been touched forever. One's love or respect for God's Word is directly connected to whether that one has been converted; this theme will appear throughout the study of Hebrews.

The final argument involves experiencing "the powers of the world to come." All power and authority originates from the throne room. The child of God directly benefits from this relationship he has to the Person on the throne. The believer does not have to wait until he gets to Heaven to enjoy the blessings from Heaven. Ephesians 2:5-7 shows how we have been saved and God *"hath raised us up together, and made us sit together in heavenly places in Christ Jesus."* Also, God will *"shew the exceeding riches of his grace in his kindness toward us through Christ Jesus."* The only ones that may "taste the powers of the world to come" are believers. Again, these arguments are describing true believers who have neglected so great a salvation. This brings us to our next consideration.

B. An Inconceivable State. (6:6a)

"If they shall fall away, to renew them again unto repentance." So begins this verse, and so begins a debate that has been ongoing for hundreds of years. Does a person lose his salvation by apostatizing? Apostasy takes place in its beginning form when one drifts first from the Word of God. In its earliest stages it may be those who are 'dull of hearing" that have a lesser respect for the true Word of God and begin to depart from the Bible to the perverted translations. Once the move has been made in that way, the flood gates are opened. Then when a generation finds itself without the true Word of God, it can do nothing but apostatize. Apostasy is deterred by having the true Bible. This continues to be a reason that I embrace only the King James Bible for the English speaking people.

Some interpret the falling away as being a renouncing of Christianity, resulting in their perishing eternally. Yet, a clear, contextual study will reveal that the "if" makes the reading hypothetical for the sake of developing an interpretation that shows how absurd it would be if such happened. If it could happen (it cannot) then Christ would have to begin the redemption process all over again. This will never happen as we will examine.

III. THE REVELATION ABOUT THE MATURE.

(6:6b)

A. The Saviour on the Cross. (6:6b)

"...seeing they crucify to themselves the Son of God afresh..." The very spirit of what is being said shows the impossibility of having the Son of God crucified afresh. Yet this is what would need to transpire for a person to lose his salvation and hope to recover. Some would argue that there would be no opportunity to recover once the apostasy has taken place. My belief is that apostasy is a drifting that begins when one has a lesser appreciation of the Scriptures than he should, and with the passage of time there is a total rejection of truth. I do not believe that the Scripture at all supports apostasy as being an event that happens to a saved person. The Scriptures state that the Lord is able to keep His sheep. He only had to go to the cross one time and will never return. Praise God!

B. The Shame of the Cross. (6:6c)

"...and put him to an open shame." Never again will Christ occupy a place of open shame. The humility that was a part of His kenosis is never to be repeated. If it was repeated it would destroy the integrity of God's Word and require that all the types be done away with as well. The writer of Hebrews is legally showing that the word "if" can only introduce a hypothetical part of the argument to show how impossible it would be for a saved person to become lost

again. *If* men could fall away in regards to salvation, the argument states that the Son of God would have to be crucified again and be put to "an open shame." This will never again happen.

Chapter Fifteen

THE RAIN, THE SEED, AND THE ANCHOR

Text: Hebrews 6:7-20

7 For the earth which drinketh in the rain that cometh oft upon it, and bringeth forth herbs meet for them by whom it is dressed, receiveth blessing from God:
8 But that which beareth thorns and briers is rejected, and is nigh unto cursing; whose end is to be burned.
9 But, beloved, we are persuaded better things of you, and things that accompany salvation, though we thus speak.
10 For God is not unrighteous to forget your work and labour of love, which ye have shewed toward his name, in that ye have ministered to the saints, and do minister.
11 And we desire that every one of you do shew the same diligence to the full assurance of hope unto the end:
12 That ye be not slothful, but followers of them who through faith and patience inherit the promises.
13 For when God made promise to Abraham, because he could swear by no greater, he sware by himself,
14 Saying, Surely blessing I will bless thee, and multiplying I will multiply thee.
15 And so, after he had patiently endured, he obtained the promise.
16 For men verily swear by the greater: and an oath for confirmation is to them an end of all strife.

17 Wherein God, willing more abundantly to shew unto the heirs of promise the immutability of his counsel, confirmed it by an oath:
18 That by two immutable things, in which it was impossible for God to lie, we might have a strong consolation, who have fled for refuge to lay hold upon the hope set before us:
19 Which hope we have as an anchor of the soul, both sure and stedfast, and which entereth into that within the veil;
20 Whither the forerunner is for us entered, even Jesus, made an high priest for ever after the order of Melchisedec.

A common illustration from nature will occupy our thoughts as we enter into our present study. There is nothing more common or vital to nature than rain. *"For the earth which drinketh in the rain..."* (V. 7a); at this point we will begin our study.

1. *Rain* is necessary. No one should argue this. It may at the same time be understood that too much rain makes swamps, and too little rain makes deserts. Yet, rain is necessary. All life is dependent upon water. Even if there is some organism that is to be found that is not directly dependent upon water for its existence, it is at least indirectly dependent. Even our own bodies are mostly water. It only takes several hours without water for one to begin to experience the ill effects of deprivation. Water is a type of the Word of God. Just as water is necessary to our physical survival, so is the Word of God necessary for our spiritual survival.

To be removed from the Word of God will immediately cause one to be in a dry and thirsty land. One should thirst and long for the falling rain of God's Word, even as a farmer would want the showers to bless his land; for rain is necessary.

2. *Rain* **has its own sovereignty.** Just as one does not tell the wind when to blow, one cannot tell the rain when to fall. I understand that silver nitrate has been used to "seed" rain clouds with hopes that the clouds will drop their moisture. Yet, there still must be conditions suitable for this to ever happen. This reminds me of how we sometimes attempt to help God. The rain falls at the pleasure of God. Psalm 65:9-10 reads, *"Thou visitest the earth, and waterest it: thou greatly enrichest it with the river of God, which is full of water: thou preparest them corn, when thou hast so provided for it. Thou waterest the ridges thereof abundantly: thou settlest the furrows thereof: thou makest it soft with showers: thou blessest the springing thereof."*

The Lord gives us rain. We pray for rain; He gives us rain even if we do not pray for it. God has set in effect the ecosystem, the weather system, and has given us certain laws that allow us some degree of predictability for our existence. We cannot dial in or program rain at our own will. The rain is sovereign. We may, however, pray for rain. God may intervene in the scheme of things to meet the desires of our hearts. Old time prayer meetings are still appropriate. God is still willing to answer our prayers if we are willing to repent. II Chronicles 7:13-14 tells us that God can shut the heavens up *"that there be no rain"* or will *"hear from heaven." "If I shut up heaven that there be no rain, or if I command the locusts to devour the land, or if I send pestilence among my people; If my people, which are called by my name, shall humble themselves, and pray, and seek my face, and turn from their wicked ways; then will I hear from heaven, and will forgive their sin, and will heal their land."* Just as rain has sovereignty about it, so does the Gospel. The rain falls in different degrees; so does the Gospel.

3. *Rain* may fall more at some times than others. Rain may mist, sprinkle, shower or even flood. There could be practical significance to this. Think about what it is like when a drought comes, with no rain for an extended period of time, and then it only sprinkles. Every drop is a blessing from Heaven with hope of much more. Perhaps the Lord does this at times to make us more appreciative of all that we either have or have been blessed with previously. There is purpose in every drop of rain, as there is in every other ongoing event of our lives.

It may also be said that the Lord seems to bless His people in regards to the Gospel. In association with the Gospel, there seems to be times that the Gospel falls as showers of rain, and then at other times there seems to be only a sprinkle. There seems to be an element of mystery surrounding the event of rain, even as it is concerning the Gospel.

4. *Rain* produces different results. This is the way our text introduces the event of rain. On good seed the good rain falls and produces good fruit. The same good rain falling on thorns and briars produces the same thorns and briars. That brings us to the understanding that the problem was not with the rain; it was with the seed. We shall further examine this concept as we continue our study. We will notice the following three things that have to do with "Continuing": I. A Continuing People (Vv. 7-11); II. A Continuing Promise (Vv. 12-18); III. A Continuing Priesthood (Vv. 19-20).

I. A CONTINUING PEOPLE. (6:7-11)

A. Notice How They are Different. (6:7-8)

"For the earth which drinketh in the rain that cometh oft upon it, and bringeth forth herbs meet for them by whom it is dressed, receiveth blessing from God: But that which beareth thorns and briers is rejected, and is nigh unto cursing; whose end is to be burned." The spiritual difference found in people is indicated by the illustration of the different kinds of seed. The seed is the principle of all living things. The word *seed*, because of its life association, is used to describe that most necessary part of the new birth. The Scriptures tell us, *"Being born again, not of corruptible seed, but of incorruptible, by the word of God, which liveth and abideth for ever"* (I Peter 1:23). In our

text, the seed is implied. The rain that falls upon the earth on the first mentioned group (of seeds) *"bringeth forth herbs meet for them by whom it is dressed, receiveth blessing from God:"* In the second group (of seeds), as shown in verse eight, it says *"But that which beareth thorns and briers is rejected, and is nigh unto cursing; whose end is to be burned."* These are the two distinct groups of seeds alluded to with their respective issue (fruit). May we pause at this point and examine as we did "rain," and look at the spiritual significance of *seed* as it is mentioned in the Bible and as the seed appears in nature.

1. *Seed* has distinct life characteristics of its own.

When we consider human life we find that life has its own genetic code. The human cell has chromosomes that determine the heredity traits that are passed on to its offspring. The seed has deposited within its own kernel all the mimicked qualities of the seed that preceded it. The kernel of corn will only yield corn. For this reason the farmer is able to forecast qualitatively what will come up once the seed is planted. Quantitatively the farmer has no guarantee of how much will come up, but he certainly knows *what* will come up. This expressed law gives us an understanding of the nature of good seed and the nature of bad seed as relative to our text. Good fruit will not come up from bad seed.

Spiritually, the seed of Christ must indwell the believer for spiritual fruit to be yielded. I Peter 1:23, tells us that we are born again by the *"incorruptible seed."* The seed mentioned here is Christ Jesus. Galatians 3:16 tells us that Christ is the seed, *"Now to Abraham and his seed were the promises made. He saith not, And to seeds, as of many; but as of one, And to thy seed, which is Christ."* The theology of this truth needs to be clearly understood. We must understand that embedded within every believer is the spiritual seed of Christ; apart from His seed being within the believer there can be no spiritual life at all.

2. *Seed* must be acted upon by an outward force for there to be life continuing.

The seeds after they have been produced remain in a state of dormancy. They can remain dormant for varying periods of time and still remain viable. In general, the period of viability ranges from a few weeks to fifty years. I recall reading where some seeds had remained in one of the Egyptian pyramids for around 4,000 years. After their discovery they were planted and germinated. Scientists found that dormant lotus seeds could germinate after thousands of years if conditions were favorable for growth.

Generally, seed germination needs certain requirements to be met. These requirements include abundant water, an adequate supply of oxygen, and proper temperatures. The water causes many chemical changes to take place inside the seed. Likewise, the Word of God causes spiritual things to happen on good ground to good seed. Though a step by step comparison cannot be made with the natural seed to the spiritual seed, there are enough similarities to use the rain and the seed to illustrate what is going on spiritually.

3. *Seed* refers to family descendants in the Scriptures.

A clear example of this is referred to in John 7:42, when it says, *"That Christ cometh of the seed of David."* The Bible also refers to *"seed of evildoers"* (Isaiah 1:4; 14:20), and *"a godly seed"* (Malachi 2:15). The seed may have different meanings in the Scriptures; in Luke 8:11 the seed is the *"word of God."*

In our text, the rain falls on two classes of people, the saved and the lost. In a Jewish sense it falls on those who accept the economy of Christ, and those who reject the new economy of Christ. The argument of the writer of Hebrews is that the old economy is dead; it has been replaced with that which is better. When one has the attitude of either staying in the old economy, or either reverting back to it, such is to be *"rejected," "cursed"* and *"whose end is to be burned"* (V. 8). This speaks of the severity of not continuing in Christ.

In a general sense, when thinking of the attitude that people have to the Word, there are many opportunities being given to hear the preached Word, yet so many are rejecting it as they hear it. But to those who do receive it, as showers of blessings, they will indeed be blessed as the fruit comes forth.

B. Notice How They are Diligent. (6:9-11)

"But, beloved, we are persuaded better things of you, and things that accompany salvation, though we thus speak. For God is not unrighteous to forget your work and labour of love, which ye have shewed toward his name, in that ye have ministered to the saints, and do minister. And we desire that every one of you do shew the same diligence to the full assurance of hope unto the end:"

After dealing firmly, the writer now seems to be dealing more tenderly to encourage those who have a mind to continue. The tenderness of the writer's speech shows this, *"But, beloved..."* The challenge is for these Jewish Christians to accept the better things and to be identified by having operational in their lives those things which accompany salvation. It is my belief that not only is this chapter a very pivotal chapter, but this verse and also verse one are very pivotal. Everything regarding their continuing hinges upon *going on unto perfection having those things that will accompany their salvation.*

An interesting study would be for the serious student to take every *command* or *instruction* that appears from this ninth verse on and consider those as being the things which accompanies one's salvation. An example of this would be found in our present chapter in verse 11, *"And we desire that every one of you do shew the same diligence to the full assurance of hope unto the end."* The key phrase, *"do shew the same diligence"* is a request that would provide for one's continuing. II Peter 1:5 uses this expression, *"And beside this, giving all diligence, add to your faith virtue; and to virtue knowledge;"* Diligence marks the believer, or at least should.

Another example of the way the writer challenges us is found in Hebrews 10:22, *"Let us draw near with a true heart in full assurance of faith, having our hearts sprinkled from an evil conscience, and our bodies washed with pure water."* The clause, *"Let us hold fast the profession of our faith without wavering"* is another similar challenge that should accompany one's salvation as he is going on to perfection. Many such challenges will be found by the careful student in his *continuing*.

The writer is, as mentioned, speaking more tenderly to those who are weak. He wants them to be diligent in showing the *"full assurance of hope unto the end"* (V. 11), *"without wavering"* (10:23). He knows that he is writing to those who are genuine but feeble in spirit and in their faith. There has come then into his heart as he writes, what someone referred to as "a rush of affection." Just as he strongly warned his readers of the dire and tragic consequences of unbelief, he now wants to encourage and comfort them to continue, and to be benefactors of God's blessings.

He tells them that God will not forget their work and labor of love (V. 10). This is a challenge that tells them that there are great rewards for doing right and continuing in the faith. When we, in our contemporary society become discouraged, we must remind ourselves, as the writer reminded these feeble Christian Jews, that we must not be unbelieving, but trusting. The rewards are there for those who "go on unto perfection." The writer commends these feeble Jews for their ministering *"to the saints."* The word rendered "ministered" is the verb *diakoneo,* from which we get our word "deacon." This word translates the idea of waiting upon others, attending to them in their needs, rendering assistance, helping in any way to serve another's interests, supplying their needs, and relieving their distress.

This group appears to be sincerely serving others, yet at the same time in violation of believing as they should. Wisely, the writer commended them for what they were doing, but challenged them to *"shew the same diligence to the full assurance of hope unto the end:"* We have looked at a Continuing People; now may we consider a Continuous Promise.

II. A CONTINUING PROMISE. (6:12-17)

"That ye be not slothful, but followers of them who through faith and patience inherit the promises. For when God made promise to Abraham, because he could swear by no greater, he sware by himself. Saying, Surely blessing I will bless thee, and multiplying I will multiply thee. And so, after he had patiently endured, he obtained the promise. For men verily swear by the greater: an oath for confirmation is to them an end of all strife. Wherein God, willing more abundantly to shew unto the heirs of promise the immutability of his counsel, confirmed it by an oath:"

There are promises belonging to the redeemed. The Bible has been called *God's Promise Book*—continuing in the faith demonstrates the reality of our profession. There are multitudes of people who profess Christ yet continue in a course of self-will and self-pleasing. *"There is a generation that are pure in their own eyes, and yet is not washed from their filthiness"* (Proverbs 30:12). It is the redeemed only that receives the grand promise of salvation.

The lofty, biblical concept of Christianity has been so compromised by those who entertain the idea that they are bound for Heaven while living as a *child of Hell*. Christ Jesus came to this earth to save His people *"from their sins"* (Matthew 1:21), not in their sins. A clear distinction must be made in our theology, that the person who is truly birthed into the family of God is radically marked by change. For one to be a benefactor of the promises of God, he must be one of God's own elect. We will now consider who the real benefactors of God's promises are.

A. The Benefactors of God's Promises.

1. They are those people who endeavor in the things of God.

Would it not be contrary to God's Holiness for God to reward those who never really endeavor in the things of God? Should they live a life that is contrary to the Scriptures, and pattern their living after the world, and expect God's reward? The Scriptures do not teach this. We are told that *"the world passeth away, and the lust thereof: but he that doeth the will of God abideth for ever"* (I John 2:17). When one lives being satisfied by the lust of the world, he is showing that he is not born of God (I John 3:9).

The Bible is very clear in identifying those who are the children of God. I John 3:10 says, *"In this the children of God are manifest, and the children of the devil: whosoever doeth not righteousness is not of God, neither he that loveth not his brother."* Throughout the Scriptures the teaching is very plain, that the children of God carry the distinguishing marks of Christ. To believe and practice otherwise is contrary to the Scriptures.

2. They are those which doeth righteousness.

"Little children, let no man deceive you: he that doeth righteousness is righteous, even as he is righteous" (1 John 3:7). As this Scripture tells us, there is the distinct possibility of being deceived. One of Satan's primary tactics is deception. He wants people to think that they can practice their unrighteousness and still be counted worthy to have the righteousness of God. *"He that committeth sin is of the devil…"* (I John 3:8a). The word commit does not refer to a single act, but to a continual practice. It is careless and dangerous to excuse one's sinning by saying, "Everyone sins." Though that statement is true, one's attitude should not be an attempt to excuse sin, but instead an attitude to not sin. Every sinful act upon the part of the

believer should be followed by extreme remorse, and then a repentant spirit that is shown in one's practice. People are deceived in thinking that they are not all that bad, yet fail to compare themselves to God's righteousness and also do not pattern themselves according to the Word of God. The person who comes to the place of having a godly sorrow in his repentance follows a pattern as shown in II Corinthians 7:10-11. *"For godly sorrow worketh repentance to salvation not to be repented of: but the sorrow of the world worketh death. For behold this selfsame thing, that ye sorrowed after a godly sort, what carefulness it wrought in you, yea, what clearing of yourselves, yea, what indignation, yea, what fear, yea, what vehement desire, yea, what zeal, yea, what revenge! In all things ye have approved yourselves to be clear in this matter."*

When one sorrows after a godly sort resulting in one's repentance, there is a remarkable and notable change as indicated from this passage of scripture.

3. They, like Abraham, are those who believe God.

Abraham expressed his belief by what he did. Had he not obeyed God there would have been no evidence to support his belief. When Abraham believed God it was accounted to him for righteousness. Yet, he signified that belief by the things which he did. He said, *"order my steps in thy word, and let not any iniquity have dominion over me"* (Psalm 119: 133).

It may be said that David sinned in a most wicked way, and he did; yet Psalm 51 is in the Bible telling us that he yearned for a restoration. Abraham stumbled, and had his lapse of faith, but was an overcomer. True believers will not habitually practice sin, but will turn in repentance from their sinning, back to the Lord. If Abraham only had faith without works, his faith would have been dead. *"For as the body without the spirit is dead, so faith without works is dead also"* (James 2:26).

We are challenged to be as Abraham; we are to be *"followers of them who through faith and patience inherit the promises"* (V. 12). The writer is relating back to the Old Testament believers who trusted in the predicted events pertaining to Christ, and to Abraham in particular who God *"swear by himself."* God made a covenant or a promise to Abraham. It is commonly referred to as the Abrahamic Covenant. Just as Abraham had a promise, the language of the writer indicates that the Palestinian Jewish believers also had a promise, and by application all believers have a promise. God made the promise, and God keeps his promises. The oath that God took had Him saying in affect that if He did not keep His oath, then let Him no longer be God (Vv. 16-17).

B. The Consolation From the Promise. (6:18)

"That by two immutable things, in which it was impossible for God to lie, we might have a strong consolation, who have fled for refuge to lay hold upon the hope set before us:" The strong consolation comes from the fact that it is *"impossible for God to lie"* (V. 18). Men may lie, papers

may lie; but God cannot lie. The very foundation upon which our hope rests is the integrity of God. The fact being, not only is Abraham an heir of His promise, but the promise is unto all of God's elect. Romans 4:16 tells us this plainly. Verse 16 is worthy to be studied as a proof text for the above statement. Verse sixteen says, *"Therefore it is of faith, that it might be by grace; to the end the promise might be sure to all the seed; not to that only which is of the law, but to that also which is of the faith of Abraham; who is the father of us all,"*

To flee for refuge (V. 18) is the true attitude of the believer. The believer recognizes Christ Jesus to be that One who may be approached by faith for the purpose of soul safety. Notice now as we consider *Christ our refuge*.

1. He is a very present help in the time of need.

Never does one need to wait in line for His help. Hebrews 4:16 told us to come in this manner, *"Let us therefore come boldly unto the throne of grace, that we may obtain mercy, and find grace to help in time of need." "In the time of need,"* means anytime!

Great and wonderful consolation comes in just knowing that Christ can be our Refuge. In my personal experiences, the pressures and difficulties of life certainly warrants having a place of escape. My escape is the Lord. Psalm 46:1-3 supports this statement. *"God is our refuge and strength, a very present help in trouble. Therefore will not we fear, though the earth be removed, and though the mountains be carried into the midst of the sea; Though the waters thereof roar and be troubled, though the mountains shake with the swelling thereof. Selah."*

2. He is a strong refuge during the time of need.

Psalm 27:1 has often comforted me, *"The LORD is my light and my salvation; whom shall I fear? the LORD is the strength of my life; of whom shall I be afraid?"* Nearly 30 years ago, I preached my first sermon in my first church from this text. It was such a comfort then, and it still is a comfort to my soul knowing that I have a strong refuge in which to flee.

3. He is a very legal refuge.

This may seem strange, saying that He is a *legal* refuge, but that is an important issue to be considered. Criminals have been known to flee for a refuge that was not legal. Christ Jesus is that refuge that is completely legal according to the demands of the law and according to the holy requirements of the Father. Our text tells us not only is He legal, but He cannot lie, and He also is immutable in His counsel. He also is available as a continuing Priesthood.

III. A CONTINUING PRIESHOOD/AN ANCHOR OF THE SOUL. (6:19-20)

"Which hope we have as an anchor of the soul, both sure and stedfast, and which entereth into that within the veil; Whither the forerunner is for us entered, even Jesus, made an high priest for ever after the order of Melchisedec."
"This world is as a sea; the church in it, and so every believer, is as a ship; the port that is bound unto is heaven; Christ is the pilot, and hope is the anchor: an anchor is cast on a bottom, out of sight; and when the ship is in a calm, or in danger of a rock, or near the shore; but is of no service without a cable: and when cast aright, keeps the ship steady: so hope is cast on Christ; whence he is often called hope itself, because he is the ground and foundation of it, and who is at present unseen to bodily eyes; and the anchor of hope without the cable of faith is of little service; but being cast aright on Christ, keeps the soul steady and immovable: in some things there is a difference between hope as an anchor; an anchor is not of so much use in tempests as in a calm, but hope is; the cable may be cut or broke, and so the anchor to be useless, but so it cannot be with faith and hope; when the ship is at anchor, it does not move forward, but it is not so with the soul, when hope is in exercise; the anchor of hope is not cast on anything below, but above; and here it is called the anchor of the soul, to distinguish it from any other, and to show the peculiar benefit of it to the soul. Pythagoras makes use of the same metaphor; Riches (he says) are a weak anchor, glory: is yet weaker; the body likewise; principalities, honors, all these are weak and without strength; what then are strong anchors? Prudence, magnanimity, fortitude, these no tempest shakes" (John Gill). The above was

written several hundred years ago by John Gill who preceded Charles Spurgeon as the pastor of the Strict Baptist Church from 1720 to 1771. The church eventually would evolve into the Metropolitan Tabernacle. Charles Spurgeon pastored there for over 35 years. John Gill well describes the anchor of hope as being none other than the Lord Jesus Christ. The expression *"anchor of the soul"* is worthy of our consideration.

A. It is an Anchor For the Living.

The ship on the sea is not embedded in concrete; it has life in the sense that it is not still, it is moving. The movement must be controlled. When that ship is cut loose and is left unattended, there is no control. The ship when it is anchored is held in safety so as to maintain that control. We also are alive. The word *soul* speaks of this. Man's soul is comprised of intellect, emotions, and will.

Our intellect needs its anchor. What better way for one to be stable in his mind than for Christ to be in one's mind. Philippians 2:5 says, *"Let this mind be in you, which was also in Christ Jesus:"* God created man with intellect; by this, man has the capacity to acquire knowledge. The Spirit of Christ Jesus should, by His Word, hold our acquiring of knowledge in check. We will call this anchor, the *anchor of discernment*. There are things that we should not put into our minds, and there also should be a transformation by the renewing of our minds (Romans 12:2). The anchor of discernment should come by learning His Word. When one lets the Word of God correct and also direct, then he will find himself certainly to be anchored. James 1:8 tells us that, *"A double minded man is unstable in all his ways."* It could be said as well, that an unanchored man *"is unstable in all his ways."* The chain that connects us to the anchor is the Truth. It is Christ the Word that holds us at bay. We can be stedfast, unmovable in the things of God, while at the same time still exhibiting life. Spiritual life has movement and also stability when connected to Christ the Anchor.

B. It is an Anchor That is Hidden But Serves a Visible Purpose.

I Peter 2:4 gives us this principle, *"But let it be the hidden man of the heart, in that which is not corruptible, even the ornament of a meek and quiet spirit, which is in the sight of God of great price."* Just as the anchor is attached quietly and secretly to the ship, so also does the inward man Christ Jesus lie quietly tucked away in man's spirit. The holding strength of the anchor serves a very humble, yet very important part in assuring the ship's stability. The ship upon the surface remains calm because there is something hidden underneath that holds. My, how wonderful it is to view that person who is firmly attached by faith to the anchor that holds. The winds of adversity may blow against the believer thus described, yet the believer does not move. He cannot move as long as the anchor holds. Guess how long that is.

There is no way to calculate the holding power of God's presence. Just as our intellect needs an anchor, so do our emotions. Emotionally, it is of great benefit to know that there is a hidden anchor available when stress or uncertainties cause us to be challenged in the area of our feelings. We do have feelings and our feelings can be hurt. This happens when we do not by faith acknowledge the anchor that is able to hold our feeling in check. Our will or drive requires the benefit of the anchor. The will is very strong and needs to be under the control of God's Spirit. The anchor can keep the will in check as well as the intellect and the emotions.

C. The Anchor's Name is Hope.

Knowing that the anchor's name is *hope*, one is able to rest even when there seems to be no hope. Hope gives you confidence, and a sense of good expectancy. The stronger one's faith, the greater is one's hope. Hope and faith are fused together. When one has hope, it is because he has faith. The principle for obtaining and enlarging upon one's hope is by having faith in the Word of God.

Where would we be if it were not for the anchor of hope? The ship may be found tossed about upon the open sea, but it is held even as it is tossed. God may let us feel the effects of the blowing wind, while sensing the holding presence of the anchor of hope. As long as the anchor holds there is no need for alarm.

D. This Anchor is Different in the Place That It is Anchored.

Praise God, this anchor of Hope is not cast into the murk and the mire of the earth within its deep, dark, slimy waters. It is anchored in God's immutability, anchored in God's unchanging Word; it is anchored in Heaven! Instead of there being a downward tug, there is an upward pull. Though the anchor is hidden, it is still there. The believer's hope rests not upon being firmly attached to the world but eternally attached to Heaven. Our anchor rests in the throne room of God's presence. Our Anchor is seated at the Father's right hand. Remember, no pull or force will remove the Anchor from His rightful place.

E. An Anchor That is Sure. (6:19b)

This term speaks of the anchor's quality. To say that it is a sure anchor is to say that it is an anchor of quality. We will consider some truths relating to this anchor being sure. For an anchor to be sure it must be strong. We have heard the term "stronghold." In a different capacity, the anchor must be a strong hold. For a ship's anchor to serve its purpose and for it to do its job, it must be of strong composition. Any trash in the composite material would greatly weaken its use and strength.

Christ Jesus, our Anchor, is of perfect composition. He is

the Strong One. The Psalmist recognized His singular strength in Psalm 89:8, *"O LORD God of Hosts, who is a strong LORD like unto thee? or to thy faithfulness round about thee?"* The way something is composed determines its strength. As a student of metallurgy, I learned the value of correct composition. The chemistry of the metal affected its malleability, its ductility, its strength, its hardness, and its weight. When these qualities were known and applied, then there was the likelihood of predictability. The metal had its recognizable characteristics revealed by either testing or by usage. The Lord has shown Himself to be strong with a perfect composition. He is the only "fine flour" of Leviticus. He is without blemish. He is the all-together lovely One.

F. For an Anchor to be Sure It Must be Dependable.

Dependability is a quality that is admired in both people and in things. Likewise, the sailor must be able to depend upon his anchor to hold. In two cases he will use the anchor. In one case he uses the anchor to help him ride out a storm. This is especially the case if there are cliffs, or coral reefs to be avoided. The anchor helps keep the ship from meeting disaster. Another time that the anchor is let down is when the ship comes into safe harbor. The harbor would not seem to be a place of danger, but it is potentially. A lesson that could be learned from this is that we need Christ the Anchor even when it seems that we do not. Christ not only can be, but must be depended upon.

G. An Anchor That is Stedfast. (6:19c-20).

When we are told to be stedfast, as in I Corinthians 15:58, it is upon the basis that we may be attached to the One who is stedfast. If the anchor was of perfect composition but had no firm attachment then the hold would be weak.

1. An anchor must be fixed to something as strong as itself to hold.

The ship's anchor will either need to be buried or attached to a rock in order for it to hold. When meditating on the truth that the anchor must be fixed or attached to something as strong as itself, I came to the realization that Christ is both the Anchor and the Rock. "On Christ the Solid Rock I stand all other Ground is Sinking Sand." Knowing that Christ is the Anchor that is sure and the Rock that makes the anchor stedfast, one can have great hope.

H. The Anchor is Available Forever.

Certainly, as we conclude this study in chapter six it is wonderful knowing that we will be safe forever. The Anchor tells the believer his soul is safe forever. Knowing this, there is peace in the midst of the storm—our Anchor holds! The Forerunner has gone before, assuring the believer that he will soon follow.

When God swore to Abraham, making His covenant with him, (Genesis 15) it was as though God was telling Abraham, "If I do not keep my word then I am not God." Even as strong as the oath was given to Abraham, God was *"willing more abundantly to shew unto the heirs of promise the immutability of his counsel."*

Chapter Sixteen

LET MELCHISEDEC SHOW YOU JESUS

Text: Hebrews 7:1-28

1 For this Melchisedec, king of Salem, priest of the most high God, who met Abraham returning from the slaughter of the kings, and blessed him;
2 To whom also Abraham gave a tenth part of all; first being by interpretation King of righteousness, and after that also King of Salem, which is, King of peace;
3 Without father, without mother, without descent, having neither beginning of days, nor end of life; but made like unto the Son of God; abideth a priest continually.
4 Now consider how great this man was, unto whom even the patriarch Abraham gave the tenth of the spoils.
5 And verily they that are of the sons of Levi, who receive the office of the priesthood, have a commandment to take tithes of the people according to the law, that is, of their brethren, though they come out of the loins of Abraham:
6 But he whose descent is not counted from them received tithes of Abraham, and blessed him that had the promises.
7 And without all contradiction the less is blessed of the better.
8 And here men that die receive tithes; but there he receiveth them, of whom it is witnessed that he liveth.
9 And as I may so say, Levi also, who receiveth tithes,

payed tithes in Abraham.
10 For he was yet in the loins of his father, when Melchisedec met him.
11 If therefore perfection were by the Levitical priesthood, (for under it the people received the law,) what further need was there that another priest should rise after the order of Melchisedec, and not be called after the order of Aaron?
12 For the priesthood being changed, there is made of necessity a change also of the law.
13 For he of whom these things are spoken pertaineth to another tribe, of which no man gave attendance at the altar.
14 For it is evident that our Lord sprang out of Juda; of which tribe Moses spake nothing concerning priesthood.
15 And it is yet far more evident: for that after the similitude of Melchisedec there ariseth another priest,
16 Who is made, not after the law of a carnal commandment, but after the power of an endless life.
17 For he testifieth, Thou art a priest for ever after the order of Melchisedec.

18 For there is verily a disannulling of the commandment going before for the weakness and unprofitableness thereof.
19 For the law made nothing perfect, but the bringing in of a better hope did; by the which we draw nigh unto God.
20 And inasmuch as not without an oath he was made priest:
21 (For those priests were made without an oath; but this with an oath by him that said unto him, The Lord sware and will not repent, Thou art a priest for ever after the

order of Melchisedec:)
22 By so much was Jesus made a surety of a better testament.
23 And they truly were many priests, because they were not suffered to continue by reason of death:
24 But this man, because he continueth ever, hath an unchangeable priesthood.
25 Wherefore he is able also to save them to the uttermost that come unto God by him, seeing he ever liveth to make intercession for them.
26 For such an high priest became us, who is holy, harmless, undefiled, separate from sinners, and made higher than the heavens;
27 Who needeth not daily, as those high priests, to offer up sacrifice, first for his own sins, and then for the people's: for this he did once, when he offered up himself.
28 For the law maketh men high priests which have infirmity; but the word of the oath, which was since the law, maketh the Son, who is consecrated for evermore.

The writer of Hebrews has concluded his warning which was followed by an exhortation challenging one to consider more in depth how Christ is superior in the order of His priesthood. Clearly understanding Christ's superiority, means having a better understanding of those to whom He is superior. We will now enter back into an in-depth study of Melchisedec for the purpose of understanding more clearly Christ and His superior priesthood. There are three thoughts that we will look at: I. The Priesthood of Melchisedec Considered (Vv. 1-4); II. The Priesthood of Melchisedec Compared (Vv. 5-10); and III. The Priesthood of Melchisedec Changed (Vv. 11-28).

I. THE PRIESTHOOD OF MELCHISEDEC CONSIDERED. (7:1-4)

"For this Melchisedec, king of Salem, priest of the most high God, who met Abraham returning from the slaughter of the kings, and blessed him; To whom also Abraham gave a tenth part of all; first being by interpretation King of righteousness, and after that also King of Salem, which is, King of peace; Without father, without mother, without descent, having neither beginning of days, nor end of life; but made like unto the Son of God; abideth a priest continually. Now consider how great this man was, unto whom even the patriarch Abraham gave the tenth of the spoils."

A. Melchisedec Considered Uniquely (7:1-3a).

Refreshing our memories, Christ Jesus was introduced in Hebrews 2:17 as "a merciful and faithful high priest in things pertaining to God." Then in Hebrews 3:1 the plea is given to those who are partakers of the heavenly calling to "consider the Apostle and High Priest of our profession." The challenge further communicates that "we have a great high priest, that is passed into the heavens, Jesus the Son of

God." We also were told that we have a High Priest who can be touched with the feelings of our infirmities. Then a comparison was made to the Aaronic priesthood, to whom Christ was found to be superior. Finally, we discovered that the Lord Jesus was, "Called of God an high priest after the order of Melchizedec" (Hebrews 5:10). Now, may we look at some unique things about Melchisedec.

1. Notice when Melchisedec appears in the Biblical record.

The account of Melchisedec is very brief. There are only three places in the Holy Scriptures that Melchisedec is to be observed. The first account is Genesis 14:18-20. His name then occurs in Psalms 110:4, and also in this Hebrew Epistle.

Genesis 14 shows how four allied kings had strategically positioned themselves around the area of Sodom. Their aggression had caused them to raid, to plunder, and to carry off a large number of captives among whom was Abraham's nephew Lot. When word got back to Abraham, who was in Mamre near Hebron, he rallied more than 300 of his trained men to fight and to rescue Lot. He fought courageously and recovered the stolen goods; he also delivered the prisoners. His journey involved him going from Hebron, through Judaea, Samaria, Galilee, and over the Syrian border to Damascus.

Upon his return, *"Melchizedek king of Salem brought forth bread and wine: and he was the priest of the most high God. And he blessed him, and said, Blessed be Abram of the most high God, possessor of heaven and earth:"* (Genesis 14:18-19).

As Melchisedec approached Abraham, Melchisedec was *exercising* his priesthood. When Abraham gave him tithes, he was *recognizing* Melchisedec's priesthood, "And he gave him tithes of all" (Genesis 14:20b). The giving of the tithes was also a means whereby Abraham was able to publicly express his gratitude to Melchisedec for providing him with sanctuary considering the hermeneutical principle called, "the law of first mention." May we note that this is the first mention in the Scriptures of the tithe being given, and may we further comment on this.

a. The tithe was freely given.

There is no hint that the tithe was required of Abraham, although the giving of the tithe may have already been culturally practiced. The fact that the tithe was freely given strongly expresses that Abraham was deeply grateful to the Lord for his being blessed, to both conquer the foe and to rescue Lot. Even though the tithe is scripturally required, there should be an ongoing grateful heart each time the tithe is given. If Abraham was delivered from an earthly enemy, and he showed his gratitude, should we not continually express our gratitude for being eternally delivered from our enemy, the devil?

b. The tithe was given to Melchisedec who is a

representative type of Christ.

Abraham knew that the Lord had helped him, and he also knew that Melchisedec was a representative of the Lord. His gift of the tithe expressed this belief. When people have a heart to give unto the Lord, they are simply expressing their belief in the Lord. As we give through the ministries of our local churches, we should be mindful that our giving is preeminently to the Lord. The Law of Moses later teaches this truth in Leviticus 27:30-33. *"And all the tithe of the land, whether of the seed of the land, or of the fruit of the tree, is the LORD's: it is holy unto the LORD. And if a man will at all redeem ought of his tithes, he shall add thereto the fifth part thereof. And concerning the tithe of the herd, or of the flock, even of whatsoever passeth under the rod, the tenth shall be holy unto the LORD. He shall not search whether it be good or bad, neither shall he change it: and if he change it at all, then both it and the change thereof shall be holy; it shall not be redeemed."* The tithe here is said to be the Lord's; it is also holy unto the Lord (Leviticus 27:30). Abraham's same spirit of giving should be transmitted from people to people.

c. The giving of the tithe came after Abraham was

blessed.

The blessings and the refreshments were given by Melchisedec in a manner which portrays a most correct order. Melchisedec gave bread and wine with bread being mentioned first. The bread symbolizes Christ Jesus as being the "Bread of Life." The wine symbolizes the Spirit-filled life which produces joy in service.

Now, get the picture. Abraham comes to Melchisedec as a type of the weary pilgrim soldier, who conquers Satan by the power and the presence of the Lord. His salvation is of the Lord. He can rejoice in His salvation even as Paul told the church at Philippi to "rejoice in the Lord" (Philippians 3:1).

In the fifteenth chapter of Genesis, the Lord told Abraham in a vision, *"Fear not, Abram: I am thy shield, and thy exceeding great reward"* (Genesis 15:1). If Abraham was either putting too much confidence in himself (which I think not) or showing fear now that the battle was over (which is often common), the Lord reminded him that He was both his Reward and his Protection. This certainly was a reminder especially if Abraham was being tempted to forget that the Lord was all that he needed. He had demonstrated that he believed this when he gave the tithes to Melchisedec.

2. Notice the honor given to Melchisedec.

He is introduced as both "King of Salem" and "priest of the most high God," but in verse two it says, by interpretation, that he is King of righteousness, and King of Peace. The divine order is once again demonstrated. There can be no peace before there is first righteousness. One must be right with God, before he may enjoy the peace of God. Melchisedec as the priest king is illustrating such as the king of righteousness, and as the king of peace.

Melchisedec's honor is unique in that his priesthood preceded that of the Aaronic priesthood. Also, the priesthood of Aaron was a restricted and a shared priesthood. The pattern of Aaron's priesthood was established, which provided for a priestly successor. This was not the case with Melchisedec. Melchisedec served independently of all the other priests. Some embrace the teaching that Melchisedec was a Christophany. This may be rejected scripturally on the basis that he would have needed to have been incarnated to qualify as having been taken from among men (Hebrews 5:1). There would have had to be two virgin births for this to have happened, and one could only imagine the many problems that this would have created. Another way that Melchisedec could have served would have meant the elimination of the scriptural requirement pertaining to the priest being taken from among men. All of the above arguments give evidence to how difficult it would have been for Melchisedec to have been the Lord Jesus Christ. The absence of a genealogical record further shows that his priesthood did not have the same genealogical requirements as the Aaronic priesthood, and that both priesthoods served a different purpose in the portraying of Christ and in the serving of God. Both the qualities of the Aaronic Priesthood and the Melchisedec Priesthood were fulfilled in Christ through His own Priesthood.

B. Melchisedec Considered Typically (7:3b-4).

"Without father, without mother, without descent, having neither beginning of days, nor end of life; but made like unto the Son of God; abideth a priest continually. Now consider how great this man was, unto whom even the patriarch Abraham gave the tenth of the spoils." The phrase "without father" carries several meanings. It means literally one who has no father; one also who has lost his father; one who is an orphan. It also refers to one born after the death of his father. Another meaning is when the father is unknown. The meaning of our text is neither of these, but the text only seems to be stated as such because of the uniqueness of his priesthood. A distinctive feature of the Aaronic priesthood is a carefully recognized genealogical record, without which a man could not serve unless it could be proven that he was a proper descendant of Aaron. In the case of Melchisedec, the meaning is clearly shown that he is not of the pattern of Aaron. This shows Melchisedec as standing alone with no ties to either a priest before and to a priest after. This way Christ is not connected in any direction, thus He stands entirely alone. The scripture states Christ as being after the order of Melchisedec, without being actually connected to Melchisedec.

The old puritan writer John Gill had this to say about the phrase, "without father, without mother, without descent," etc.; "which is to be understood not of his person, but of his priesthood; that his father was not a priest, nor did his mother descend from any in that office; nor had he either a predecessor or a successor in it, as appears from any authentic accounts: or this is to be interpreted, not of his natural, but scriptural being; for no doubt, as he was a mere man, he had a father and a mother, and a natural lineage and descent; but of these no mention is made in Scripture, and therefore said to be without them; and so the Syrian version renders it; whose father and mother are not written in the genealogies; or there is no genealogical account of them" (Gill).

Hebrews 7:3b continues, "without descent, having neither beginning of days, nor end of life." By this statement there was no account which showed when Melchisedec was born, or when he died. In this way Melchisedec is a type of Christ who has no beginning of days; Christ is the Alpha and the Omega and everything in between. In a pure sense Christ is everything that Melchisedec could only picture while being only a type of Christ.

"Abideth a priest continually"; not in his person, but performed in his ante-type Christ Jesus, there will never be a change in the priesthood of Christ, nor will it ever be transferred to another. The full extent of this statement is a mystery; its fullness cannot be fathomed, only imagined. The blood of Christ Jesus is placed in the most holy presence of God the Father, and in the presence of the Lamb. Christ Jesus will, as High Priest, have an eternal responsibility back to His own blood. The full significance of the blood can also only be imagined. Yet, there is evidence that the blood will have a purpose that goes beyond the purpose of souls being saved in this dispensation of grace. The blood will certainly have the value of being an eternal testimony to the full payment that was made for our redemption.

In verse five, the writer of Hebrews is asking his reader to consider just how great Melchisedec is. If one could have a proper appreciation of the greatness of Melchisedec, he then could more respectfully consider the greatness of Melchisedec's ante-type, Jesus Christ. As an argument to induce one to properly consider the greatness of Melchisedec, the Scriptures tell us that "Abraham gave the tenth of the spoils" (V. 4). This demonstrates that Abraham acknowledged Melchisedec to be a greater than he, "priest-king". Abraham respected his greatness, yet the writer of Hebrews is going to prove that Christ is superior to even Melchisedec, as great as he was.

II. THE PRIESTHOOD OF MELCHISEDEC COMPARED. (7:5-10)

"And verily they that are of the sons of Levi, who receive the office of the priesthood, have a commandment to take tithes of the people according to the law, that is, of their brethren, though they come out of the loins of Abraham: But he whose descent is not counted from them received tithes of Abraham, and blessed him that had the promises. And without all contradiction the less is blessed of the better. And here men that die receive tithes; but there he receiveth them, of whom it is witnessed that he liveth. And as I may so say, Levi also, who receiveth tithes, payed tithes in Abraham. For he was yet in the loins of his father, when Melchisedec met him."

A. The Priesthood Compared to Those Who Make Up the Present (7:5-8).

John Owens described Abraham as "the stock and root of the whole people, their common father, in whom they were first separated from the other nations to be a people of themselves." Abraham as the leader by example, certainly set a good one. He recognized the rightful place of Melchisedec in the economy of God. Abraham by his practices was also setting a strong example that would be passed on as a blessing to his posterity. There is no better way to bless those who follow you than by giving them a clear path in which to walk. Abraham certainly did this by acknowledging Melchisedec's purpose within the economy of God's purpose, in that he was both recognized and reverenced by Abraham. The Levites, who were benefactors of the law, could expect by commandment to receive the tithes as verse five shows. *"And verily they that are of the sons of Levi, who receive the office of the priesthood, have a commandment to take tithes of the people according to the law, that is, of their brethren, though they come out of the loins of Abraham:"* Yet Abraham gave to Melchisedec without the coercion and the requirements of the law. Abraham gave freely, and appreciatively. He offered thanksgiving, as already shown, for having the protection and the presence of the Lord, while rescuing Lot. By doing this, Abraham not only showed a clear example for his immediate posterity, but also for those who are his spiritual descendants as well. The far reaching effects of Abraham's example are still being felt. Abraham recognized Melchisedec as being a person of superiority or of preference to himself. As Abraham recognized the superiority of Melchisedec to himself, we must recognize the superiority of Christ over Melchisedec. As great as Melchisedec was, he was only a type of Christ. Christ, the anti-type of Melchisedec is far superior. This is certainly in agreement with the major theme of Hebrews which presents Christ as having the better priesthood.

In Abraham's present tense he was making a gift personally to Melchisedec. He also was giving in a future tense to Levi. The same Levi also *"who receiveth tithes, paid tithes in Abraham. For he was yet in the loins of his father, when Melchisedec met him"* (Hebrews 7:9b-10).

B. The Priesthood Compared to Those Who Make Up the Future (7:9-10).

The expression, *"For he was yet in the loins of his father"* (V. 10), and the expression, *"paid tithes in Abraham,"* in the previous verse, speaks of that which was yet future in regards to father Abraham. This verse proves that our life has an ongoing effect to the yet unborn. This is an awesome truth. We must be mindful of this as we live out our lives. We should always be conscious of the reality of impacting future generations either in a positive or in a negative way.

By this above expression, and also in support of the priesthood of Melchisedec being preferred above the Levitical system, it is said that not only did Abraham offer tithes to Melchisedec, but so did his posterity. This is not to say that each descendant or even any descendant of Abraham was accountable to the individual acts of Abraham. The truth being conveyed is that the lineage of Abraham, which supports the Levitical system through Levi, does not tie back to Melchisedec. Melchisedec stands alone. Even more so, and in a superior position to even Melchisedec, Christ our High Priest stands alone.

III. THE PRIESTHOOD CHANGED. (7:11-17)

"If therefore perfection were by the Levitical priesthood, (for under it the people received the law,) what further need was there that another priest should rise after the order of Melchisedec, and not be called after the order of Aaron? For the priesthood being changed, there is made of necessity a change also of the law. For he of whom these things are spoken pertaineth to another tribe, of which no man gave attendance at the altar. For it is evident that our Lord sprang out of Juda; of which tribe Moses spake nothing concerning priesthood. And it is yet far more evident: for that after the similitude of Melchisedec there ariseth another priest, Who is made, not after the law of a carnal commandment, but after the power of an endless life. For he testifieth, Thou art a priest for ever after the order of Melchisedec."

A. The Change That Involved Necessity (7:11-14).

Verse eleven begins proving the need for change by demonstrating that the Levitical system was flawed. With pure logic, the question is asked, *"If therefore perfection were by the Levitical priesthood, (for under it the people received the law), what further need was there that another priest should rise after the order of Melchisedec, and not be called after the order of Aaron?"* As great as the earlier systems may have been, they were followed by a much better priesthood, and a much better economy. The better priesthood was born out of necessity. The Law of Moses served a necessary purpose in setting boundaries. For man to be aware of having transgressed the law, he had to know where the boundaries were. There had to be a clear line of demarcation to define this. God gave the law. Yet man was also shown that he was incapable of keeping the law. The law could not give the people perfection. Verse eleven proves this. *"If therefore perfection were by the Levitical priesthood, (for under it the people received the law,) what further need was there that another priest should rise after the order of Melchisedec, and not be called after the order of Aaron?"* The clause *"what further need was there that another priest should rise after the order of Melchisedec, and not be called after the order of Aaron?"* uses the rhetorical method of argumentation to support the need for a superior and a perfect priesthood. With the priesthood being changed, by necessity the Law of Moses was to change. Verse 12 says, *"For the priesthood being changed, there is made of necessity a change also of the law."*

John 1:17 says, *"For the law was given by Moses, but grace and truth came by Jesus Christ."* This verse has always intrigued me. I believe that John is making both a contrast and a subtle comparison of the new economy to the old. He tells us that *"the law was given by Moses,"* and in contrast to that he tells us that *"grace...came by Jesus Christ."* There a different word is used, which takes away the harshness of the word *law*. The word *truth* is not removed in meaning from the word *law*, but makes a better statement concerning the law. The *"change of the law"* did not at all mean the putting away of the law, for the law is good. The Psalmist said, in reference to the Word of God, that the law is perfect, sure, right, pure, true, and righteous. *"The law of the LORD is perfect, converting the soul: the testimony of the LORD is sure, making wise the simple. The statutes of the LORD are right, rejoicing the heart: the commandment of the LORD is pure, enlightening the eyes. The fear of the LORD is clean, enduring for ever: the judgments of the LORD are true and righteous altogether. More to be desired are they than gold, yea, than much fine gold: sweeter also than honey and the honeycomb. Moreover by them is thy servant warned: and in keeping of them there is great reward"* (Psalm 19:7-11).

In Matthew's Gospel, we learn that the Lord did not come to destroy the law, or the prophets, but to fulfill. Jesus is speaking here, *"Think not that I am come to destroy the law, or the prophets: I am not come to destroy, but to fulfil. For verily I say unto you, Till heaven and earth pass, one jot or one tittle shall in no wise pass from the law, till all be fulfilled. Whosoever therefore shall break one of these least commandments, and shall teach men so, he shall be called the least in the kingdom of heaven: but whosoever shall do and teach them, the same shall be called great in the kingdom of heaven. For I say unto you, That except your righteousness shall exceed the righteousness of the scribes and Pharisees, ye shall in no case enter into the kingdom of heaven"* (Matthew 5:17-20). He is describing His mission as the Great High Priest. The change made in the law was relative to the change in the Priesthood. The Aaronic Priesthood had many legal requirements that pertained to only that order and discipline. Our High Priest did not need to exercise that which was required of a sinful, earthly priest; His priesthood is perfect even as He is perfect.

Our High Priest is not subject to the law and indeed cannot be. He is superior to the law. The Old Testament priest had 146 external legal requirements that he had to meet to be qualified to serve. These rigid requirements show typically that the Lord Jesus always meets the requirements of the Father. Remember, His Father was *"well pleased"* with His Son.

There was a necessary change in the law because Jesus began to serve continuously, and forever. There was no further need for a law to be required for one who was incapable of breaking the law. The *"law of a carnal commandment"* has no effect upon Him (V. 16).

B. The Change That Involved Eternality (7:15-17).

A major change has taken place when the Lord *"sprang out of Juda"* instead of the tribe of Levi. His priesthood was both different and better. His priesthood was based on *"the power of an endless life"* (V. 16). Ultimately every believer will enjoy an endless life. Yet, Christ our High Priest is the originator of that possibility for He is eternal. For the believer to enjoy eternity, it has to be given to him by Christ Jesus. He, only, has the power to give eternal life.

The Priesthood of Christ being both different and eternal is such because He is availing Himself to serve a people who will live forever. There is still much about the Priesthood of Christ that we do not know, but it will be revealed in the *"ages to come"* (Ephesians 2:7). He will have His trophies of grace on display for all eternity, during which time He will be revealing to them His power and His grace.

Mankind, even from days of old, has searched for youth and eternality. Early in our nation's history the early explorer thought he had found the fountain of youth. Yet, Ponce de Leon only lived as a common man with no added years to his credit. Scientists today are studying the effects of aging and how to combat it, but to no avail. There are those hopefuls, who employ cryogenics for the purpose of freezing their bodies thinking that technology will one day bring them back.

For those who really desire to live forever, there is a way. That Way is Jesus. Jesus is our High Priest who ever liveth to make intercession.

C. The Change That Involved Immutability. (7:18-28)

Immutability is an expression that can only belong to God in the eternal sense. Verse 24 tells us that Christ has "an unchangeable priesthood", with that priesthood being described as being "holy, harmless, undefiled, separate from sinners, and made higher than the heavens;" (V. 26). Within the scope of his immutability it is comforting to know that He is "holy." Can you but imagine how awful it would be if He was unchangeable and unholy. His attribute of holiness is what makes him different from the common man and every other priest that served in the priesthood. If He were only holy on a part time basis, that would be totally inadequate. The holy demands of the Father would accept nothing less than a holy priesthood that is incapable of any change. The law made nothing perfect (v.19), but Christ makes everything perfect as He orders it. He also is "harmless." Harm is a byproduct of sin. He does not bring harm to the priesthood. There may have been those who had embraced a priesthood that referred back to Aaron who thought that the priesthood of Christ was to bring harm both spiritually and structurally. That simply is not so. His priesthood only complemented and made better what no other man could do.

His priesthood is undefiled. Thank God that this is not only so, but it is so without change. The defiling characteristics of sin and sinning has no effect upon this Priest or Priesthood forever. These are all strong arguments that prove why this Priesthood is so much better. In addition to these characteristics that describe the priesthood of Christ, He is also separate from sinners and higher than the heavens. This expresses that His priesthood is not contaminated by the earthy sin curse. This is just another way that clearly demonstrates that His priesthood is better and it also is immutable, meaning that it will continue to remain that way.

Chapter Seventeen

GOOD MATH

Text: Hebrews 8: 1-13

1 Now of the things which we have spoken this is the sum: We have such an high priest, who is set on the right hand of the throne of the Majesty in the heavens;
2 A minister of the sanctuary, and of the true tabernacle, which the Lord pitched, and not man.
3 For every high priest is ordained to offer gifts and sacrifices: wherefore it is of necessity that this man have somewhat also to offer.
4 For if he were on earth, he should not be a priest, seeing that there are priests that offer gifts according to the law:
5 Who serve unto the example and shadow of heavenly things, as Moses was admonished of God when he was about to make the tabernacle: for, See, saith he, that thou make all things according to the pattern shewed to thee in the mount.
6 But now hath he obtained a more excellent ministry, by how much also he is the mediator of a better covenant, which was established upon better promises.
7 For if that first covenant had been faultless, then should no place have been sought for the second.
8 For finding fault with them, he saith, Behold, the days come, saith the Lord, when I will make a new covenant with the house of Israel and with the house of Judah:

9 Not according to the covenant that I made with their fathers in the day when I took them by the hand to lead them out of the land of Egypt; because they continued not in my covenant, and I regarded them not, saith the Lord.
10 For this is the covenant that I will make with the house of Israel after those days, saith the Lord; I will put my laws into their mind, and write them in their hearts: and I will be to them a God, and they shall be to me a people:
11 And they shall not teach every man his neighbour, and every man his brother, saying, Know the Lord: for all shall know me, from the least to the greatest.
12 For I will be merciful to their unrighteousness, and their sins and their iniquities will I remember no more.
13 In that he saith, A new covenant, he hath made the first old. Now that which decayeth and waxeth old is ready to vanish away.

The writer of Hebrews is bringing the study of the better priesthood, as it pertains to Melchisedec, into sharp focus. The lumens of truth are shinning brightly as the discourse continues. Everything better has been said about this unchanging priesthood. He now delivers the summation or the chief point to his readers by saying, *"Now of the things which we have spoken this is the sum."* This is good math… Everything about Christ certainly adds up. There is not one truth missing from the formula. The priesthood prior to His was flawed because it was built entirely on a human system, even though God designed it. Remember, God designed it but man functioned in it. There was always something lacking, but not so with His priesthood.

The writer exclaims, *"We have such an high priest."* What a wonderful way to make a distinction of His priesthood. His priesthood is being further characterized in summary form in these first six verses. In the ninth chapter there will be a further discourse on how His priesthood excels the earthly priesthood, but now may we look at the way the writer shows this priesthood to be different, as verse 26 in chapter 7 indicates to us, *"For such an high priest became us, who is holy, harmless, undefiled, separate from sinners, and made higher than the heavens;"*

I. THE CHARACTER OF THIS HIGH PRIEST SUMMARIZED. (8:1-6)

Character marks us all. We characterize those whom we either belong to or by whom we are influenced. This Priest is the "express image of his person". For the reason just mentioned, we know this Priest to be "holy, harmless, undefiled, separate from sinners and made higher than the heavens" (7:26). He is, as we learned earlier in this study, delivering the essence of the Father straight to the human family. His priestly work is characterized in this divine manner. We will further discover that this Priest is characterized or revealed further by: I. His Position, II. His Purpose, III. His Peculiarity, and IV. His Preeminence.

A. The Position of this High Priest. (8:1)

"who is set on the right hand of the throne of the Majesty in the heavens;"

The fact that this Priest is seated declares that His priestly work has been finished. The image of the priest has never been that of one who is seated. The priest was always pictured in such a way as to show him busily engaged with his responsibilities. This Priest is different. He has concluded the sacrificial work that was required of Him and His being seated indicates this. Another important truth to be noted is that His place of being seated is not on the earth. This also makes His work much different than the Aaronic priesthood.

The seated Priest is a testimony to the finished work of Christ Jesus that should inspire confidence in each of us that there is nothing more that needs to be done. The holy requirements that involved both heaven and earth have all been met and the Father is completely satisfied. The Heavenly Father demonstrated His satisfaction of His Son Jesus at His baptism. It was there that the Father said, *"Thou art my beloved Son; in thee I am well pleased."* (Luke 3:22).

How sad it is that the Heavenly Father is well pleased with His Son, the Lord Jesus Christ, while there are so many wicked upon this earth that curse His name rather than revere it. The names of Christ are precious and communicate something about His character, even as His three-fold compound name says something about His priestly work. The name *Lord* speaks of His ownership and majesty. The name *Jesus* speaks of Him as being the Saviour and His name *Christ* speaks of Him as being the Anointed One who keeps. This is His priestly name and speaks of the ability that He has to do His job and finish it in such a way that it never will need to be repeated again. Praise God for His keeping power!

B. The Purpose of this High Priest. (8:2)

This second verse is part of the summary statement that tells of the purpose of the High Priest. He is *"A minister of the sanctuary, and of the true tabernacle, which the Lord pitched, and not man."* This one statement puts His priesthood in a class all of its own. There has never been, to His exception, one priestly offering made in a tabernacle that the Lord pitched, and not man, until the one described here. The Lord gave very careful instructions for the way that the earthly tabernacle was pitched by man, but this true tabernacle was pitched in Heaven by the Lord. Revelation chapter 11 gives indication of a future tabernacle that will be built during the tribulation in which the Jews will worship during the first part of the tribulation. Due to their rejecting Christ as the Messiah, the Jews will continue to worship as they did during the Old Testament. The Jews will be worshipping in such a manner because they have never accepted Christ as the Messiah. They are presently blinded to the real truth. This blindness of theirs will continue right up to the time that they truly recognize Christ as the Messiah. Worshipping in the temple will not grant them salvation. Salvation is in Christ alone. Paul told us in Romans 10:1-3, that Israel had a zeal of God, but not according to knowledge.

The temple that will be built by the Jews during the tribulation will not be of the same value as that which was *pitched by the Lord.* I will quote from my Revelation commentary regarding the measuring of the temple. "This chapter begins with the temple being mentioned, immediately being followed by the mentioning of the two witnesses. There seems to be significance to this being so. I would suggest that this is because God is going to show that the temple worship has been replaced by the actual worshipping of the Lamb. It will take some dramatic events for these lost Jews to get to the place that they will be willing to cast aside their religious system. The witnesses that come on the scene will contribute to them eventually rejecting the temple worship in preference to worshipping Christ the Messiah.

In verse one it says, 'And there was given me a reed like unto a rod: and the angel stood, saying, Rise, and measure the temple of God, and the altar, and them that worship therein.' It is like the measuring is taking place to see if both the temple and they that worship there measure up to God's standards. We know that His standards are absolutely perfect and *the reed like unto a rod* could picture the true standard, which is the Word of God. The word *reed* is the original word which the Septuagint uses for the Hebrew word kaneh, from which comes our word "canon." That is the reason that the Old and New Testaments are called the canon (or rule) of Scriptures.

The Lord will carefully define what His law is in respect to man's inability to keep it. The rules will be the same, *"For all have sinned and come short..."* The Jews will discover and be shown that they also do not measure up. In every dispensation, this has been the case. Some theologians believe that the worship setting for the Jewish temple will be "pure grace." It will be safe to say that there is much that we do not understand about the temple worship during the tribulation, except to say that as in every dispensation, they too, will come up short." (Revelation: Seeing Christ More Clearly," Alderman 204, 205)

In verse two, we are told that Christ is, *"A minister of*

the sanctuary, and of the true tabernacle, which the Lord pitched, and not man." The important concern that we must recognize and have here is that the priesthood of Christ is not an earth-originating or an earth-based priesthood, but a heavenly one. The distinction is given in order to clarify His purpose of ministry. His ministry will not be in the realm of the earth curse, but in the presence of the Heavenly Father. It was a most holy offering that Christ made when He offered up His own shed blood and He offered it in the most Holy place. I believe that the Lord Jesus Christ offered His blood in the presence of God, the saints, and the angels of Heaven.

Every earthly offering had its attachments to this earth with all of the defilement that is found both on the offering and the place of the offering. When Christ died and rose from the dead, He took His perfect blood into the presence of the Heavenly Father and made His blood offering as a suitable sacrifice. The Scriptures greatly declare this: Hebrews 9:12 tells us, *"Neither by the blood of goats and calves, but by his own blood he entered in once into the holy place, having obtained eternal redemption for us."* We are told also in Colossians 1:14, *"In whom we have redemption through his blood, even the forgiveness of sins."*

The purpose of our High Priest is to make an offering that only He could offer. He offered His own blood. He only had to make one offering because His was a Suitable Sacrifice. He perfectly suited the requirements of the Heavenly Father. The Jewish offerings and ours all come up short according to the book of Romans.

C. The Peculiarity of this High Priest. (8:4)

In every way, it would have either been contrary to the requirements of the priesthood or cumbersome for Jesus to have served as a priest. The law specified that the priest serve out of the lineage of Aaron and not Judah. Jesus, our High Priest, was able to do once in purpose what the previous priests could only do in type, and they also had to do it over and over again. The legal requirements of the law would have prevented Jesus from having served upon the earth, but by Him offering an offering that satisfied eternally the requirements of the Heavenly Father, there was no further need for any sacrifices to be made.

Not in a bad way, but in a better way the offerings that Jesus made were once and for all offered and then stopped, because there was no further need for them. We do not benefit from having an earthly priesthood because of what our better Priest did. There are entire religious systems that are operating on the bases of having a pontiff or priest for their worship efforts, but God has given us the opportunity through His Son, the Lord Jesus Christ, to come boldly to the throne of Grace in the time of need.

Due to the fact that Christ's Priesthood is different from all that preceded Him, His indeed is a peculiar priesthood.

D. The Preeminence of this Christ. (8:5-6).

The key words in verses five and six are "shadow" and "example," which at best can only describe the superior work of Christ who is our High Priest. This is all that they were capable of accomplishing. In their long earthly priestly lineage, this is the most that they could ever hope to accomplish. Every type and every shadow in the Scriptures could only portray in a very limited and weak manner the work of the Greater Priest. These shadows serve as a contrast to the better priesthood.

Knowing that Christ is the Preeminent One, we should be practically challenged in the same manner as when Paul told the church at Colosse, to set their affections on things above. *"If ye then be risen with Christ, seek those things which are above, where Christ sitteth on the right hand of God. Set your affection on things above, not on things on the earth."* (Colossians 3:1-2).

II. THE COVENANT OF THIS HIGH PRIEST STATED. (8:6-13)

This next section considers the covenant and its necessary importance to the economy of God. The word *covenant* means *a cutting*. This refers back to the way a covenant was established. Notice the way that the covenant was originally carried out in this given illustration; "a covenant is of force (or firm) over the dead," as meaning that the covenant is established on the ground of sacrifice, that sacrifice representing the death of the maker of the covenant. The allusion may be further explained by a reference to Genesis 15:9-10,17, which has generally been considered as illustrating the ancient Semitic method of making a covenant: the sacrificial animals being divided, and the parties passing between the pieces, implying that they deserved death if they broke the engagement. The technical Hebrew phrase for making a covenant is "to cut a covenant."

This should show us how serious the covenant is to God. We should also know that this covenant is a better covenant.

A. It is a Covenant that is Better. (8:6-9)

Just as the priesthood is better, so is the covenant which is called *a better covenant.* It is better for a number of reasons. The primary reason would be that it has a better Mediator. Christ is the Mediator of this better covenant. Moses was the mediator of the Old Covenant. The Old Covenant was tied directly back into the law, whereas this new covenant is tied into the economy of grace. Moses was very qualified, as man is concerned, to mediate the Old Covenant; yet he did not measure up to the quality of the Son of God. No one does. All that Moses could do in the spirit of the Old Covenant was only a shadow of what Christ made available to us in the New Covenant. The way that the Old Covenant was structured, it could only convey in type the substance and the potential of the New Covenant. There was fear and trepidation associated with the Old Covenant, whereas there is peace and liberty associated with the New Covenant. Christ having obtained "a more excellent ministry" had it established on better promises. Christ places His signature on this covenant, by going into the Holy of Holies with His own blood. By Him exercising this rite, the Old Covenant had to pass away; and that it did. With the passing of the Old Covenant was also the passing of an *excellent ministry* which was to be replaced with *a more excellent ministry.* The ministry that was in association with Moses could only pertain to the earthly; the ministry that was in association with Christ pertained to that which was heavenly.

1. The New Covenant is marked by faith. (8:6-7)

Another thing that makes this covenant better is that it is marked by faith. The writer of Hebrews quotes Jeremiah 31:31-34 where the prophet used the words "new covenant" in describing this better covenant. Jeremiah prophetically made a contrast involving the Old and the New Covenant. The Old Covenant was conditional and was not of itself to be found with fault. The fault was in the people who failed to keep it. The Old Covenant showed the *righteous standards of God, but it also showed the absolute weakness of man.* With the additional passing of time, there was more evidence constantly being gathered that proved man was incapable of keeping the law.

The covenant of faith is going to be more than the observing of external laws; it will involve the obedience of God from the heart as the Spirit possesses the heart. Just as Jeremiah spoke of the Spirit being inside the believer, also Ezekiel said the same in Ezekiel 36:27: *"And I will put my spirit within you, and cause you to walk in my statutes, and ye shall keep my judgments, and do them."*

The message of the New Covenant is the Gospel of Christ. It has a much greater glory than did the Old Covenant. "The promises in the first covenant pertained mainly to the present life. They were promises of length of days; of increase of numbers; of seed time and harvest; of national privileges; and of extraordinary peace, abundance, and prosperity. That there was also the promise of eternal life it would be wrong to doubt; but this was not the main thing. In the new covenant however, the promises of spiritual blessings becomes the principle thing. The mind is directed to heaven; the heart is cheered with the hopes of immortal life; the favor of God and the anticipation of heaven are secured in the most ample and solemn manner." (Barnes).

The operation of faith as it pertains to this covenant requires that we go to the Father through the Son, Christ Jesus. He mediates on our behalf. He has the right to approach us as we do Him, on the basis of His humanity and He has the right to approach the Father on the basis of His deity. We must not dare or pretend to approach God the Father except through Christ Jesus. This is the reason that we pray in the name of Jesus. This better covenant was *established upon better promises*. The promises of the Old Covenant could not accomplish what the new could and this is by the design of the Lord. He gave the human family the opportunity of measuring how awful sin is and with that measure the human family found that man is incapable of obtaining by the zeal and the efforts of the flesh the righteousness of God. (Romans 10:1-2). We find that because of our inability through the weakness of the flesh, we too are unable to answer the demands of the law (Romans 8:3).

Even though the Old Covenant required exact and legal obedience, it offered no help to accomplish this. Man always came up pitifully short (Romans 3:23). But the covenant of grace, which we refer to as the New Covenant, is called a *ministration of the Spirit:* and under the Gospel of this covenant, we are said to not serve in the *oldness of the letter*, but in the *newness of the Spirit.* The fault of the Old Covenant lay in the fact that, in saving, it was defective. The law in its morality was blameless; man just could not meet its demanding requirements.

2. The Old Covenant is marked by failure. (8:8-9)

The fact that the Lord finds fault in the Old Covenant shows how temporal and inadequate it was. This does not at all suggest that the Lord misjudged neither the strength of the covenant nor the weakness of the people. When the Lord uses terms and expressions such as "for finding fault with them...", He is not saying that this fault was revealed to Him as a fault or failure would be revealed in human terms. The expression that the Lord used is to show or reveal to mankind that man was incapable of keeping a covenant that His Son could keep. Man's failure emphasizes the Lord's strength. It shows a contrast of how weak man is in not keeping the law and how strong the Lord is in keeping the same.

The expression that the Lord uses also shows that the Lord is willing, after exposing man's complete weakness in keeping the law, to establish another covenant based upon better promises and will also show how the Lord will be *"merciful to their unrighteousness"* and goes on to say, *"and their sins and their iniquities will I remember no more"* (V. 12). With this explanatory note may we further analyze "the covenant that will be marked by failure."

a. The fault that marked the Old Covenant. (8:8)

The covenant in the Old Testament and specifically the covenant delivered to and by Moses was for the purpose of emphasizing the moral elements of the people of God. They were given standards for all aspects of their living. This involved the marriages, their families, their jobs, their worship, the consideration of the weak and the poor, the care of the dumb animals, purity in the relations of life, and the spirit of brotherhood, etc. These laws gave the rules for one's practical and spiritual existence and one's conduct.

The word *fault* as used does not imply a weakness upon the part of God nor on the covenant, itself. Jeremiah said that the people broke the covenant. The New Covenant unlike the Old Covenant will be unconditional; its provisions will include (1) a change of heart, (2) fellowship with God, (3) knowledge of the Lord, and, (4) forgiveness of sin. All of this will be fulfilled for Israel when the Lord returns. (Romans 11:26-27). (Ryrie).

"Behold, the days come, saith the Lord," This expression denotes the prophetic significance of what will happen when the Old Covenant is replaced with the New Covenant. The word *behold* is a word that is used to emphasize the importance of the forthcoming announcement. The Lord is about to do something wonderful; at least in a relative sense, it is so. The New Covenant will be in association with the last days. The last of the "last days" will have the New Covenant fulfilled as God designed it. Israel will see or recognize "whom they pierced" and will have rejected the covenant of the Antichrist and will then accept the covenant of King Jesus and will enter into the Kingdom

Age. Different parts of the New Covenant, as it pertains to the Church and the Age of the Gentiles, are already in effect. We who are of the seed of Christ are already enjoying the benefits of the New Covenant.

b. The fault that marked the covenant breaker. (8:9)

The inability of man to keep the covenant showed clearly that the human family is incapable of living a sin-free existence. There was only one that could satisfy the holy demands and the holy requirements of the law. That One is the Lord Jesus Christ. This further demonstrates that we need a covenant of grace. Romans 8:2 tells us that, *"For the law of the Spirit of life in Christ Jesus hath made me free from the law of sin and death."* Also, we are told *"For as many as are led by the Spirit of God, they are the sons of God."* We have a relationship that is built upon the goodness of the New Covenant that allows us spiritual freedom and spiritual exercise in the things pertaining to God.

B. It is a Covenant for the Believer. (8:10-13)

The following will show the virtues of the New Covenant as opposed to the Old Covenant. May this compilation by David Guzik be helpful:

Differences Between the New Covenant and the Old

Covenant

1. They were instituted at different times. The Old Covenant around 1446 B.C., the New Covenant around 33 A.D.

2. They were instituted at different places. The Old Covenant at Mount Sinai, the New Covenant at Mount Zion.

3. They were spoken in different ways. The Old Covenant was thundered with fear and dread at Mount Sinai (Exodus 19:17-24). Jesus Christ, God the Son, declared the New Covenant with love and grace.

4. They are different in their mediators. Moses mediated the Old Covenant. Jesus is the Mediator of the New Covenant.

5. They are different in their subject matter. The Old Covenant *demanded* a covenant of works. The New Covenant *fulfills* the covenant of works through the completed work of Jesus.

6. They are different in how they were dedicated. The Old Covenant was dedicated with the blood of animals sprinkled on the people (Exodus 24:5-8). The New Covenant was dedicated with Jesus' blood spiritually applied to His people.

7. They are different in their priests. The Old Covenant is represented by the priesthood of the Law of Moses and high priests descended from Aaron. The New Covenant has a priesthood of all believers and a High Priest according to the order of Melchizedek.

8. They are different in their sacrifices. The Old Covenant demanded endless repetition of imperfect sacrifices. The New Covenant provides a once and for all, perfect sacrifice of the Son of God Himself.

9. They are different in how and where they were written. The Old Covenant was written by God on tablets of stone. The New Covenant is written by God on the hearts of His people.

10. They are different in their goals. The goal of the Old Covenant was to discover sin, to condemn it, and to set a "fence" around it. The goal of the New Covenant is to declare the love, grace, and mercy of God, and to give repentance, remission of sin, and eternal life.

11. They are different in their practical effect on living. The Old Covenant ends in bondage (through no fault of its own). The New Covenant provides true liberty.

12. They are different in their giving of the Holy Spirit. Under the Old Covenant, God did grant the Holy Spirit, but not in the same way and extent that He is given to believers under the New Covenant.

13. They are different in their idea of the Kingdom of God. Under the Old Covenant, it is mainly seen as the supreme rule of Israel over the nations. Under the New Covenant, it is both a present spiritual reality and a coming literal fact.

14. They are different in their substance. The Old Covenant has vivid shadows. The New Covenant has the reality.

15. They are different in the extent of their administration. The Old Covenant was confined to the descendants of Abraham through Isaac and Jacob according to the flesh. The New Covenant is extended to all nations and races under heaven.

16. They are different in what they actually accomplish. The Old Covenant made nothing perfect. The New Covenant can and will bring about the perfection of God's people.

17. They are different in their duration. The Old Covenant was designed to be removed. The New Covenant was designed to last forever.

Even as the old writer John Owens told us, we should faithfully execute the ministry of grace that is ours…"Let us observe from these things, that the state of the gospel, or of the Church under the New Testament, being accompanied by the highest privileges and advantages that it is capable of in this world, there is a great obligation on all believers unto holiness and fruitfulness in obedience, unto the glory of God; and the heinousness of their sin, by whom this covenant is neglected or despised, is abundantly manifested." (John Owen)

Chapter Eighteen

THE EARTHLY, THE ETERNAL AND THE ENDURING PRIESTHOOD (Part One)

Text: Hebrews 9:1-10

1 Then verily the first covenant had also ordinances of divine service, and a worldly sanctuary.
2 For there was a tabernacle made; the first, wherein was the candlestick, and the table, and the shewbread; which is called the sanctuary.
3 And after the second veil, the tabernacle which is called the Holiest of all;
4 Which had the golden censer, and the ark of the covenant overlaid round about with gold, wherein was the golden pot that had manna, and Aaron's rod that budded, and the tables of the covenant;
5 And over it the cherubims of glory shadowing the mercyseat; of which we cannot now speak particularly.
6 Now when these things were thus ordained, the priests went always into the first tabernacle, accomplishing the service of God.
7 But into the second went the high priest alone once every year, not without blood, which he offered for himself, and for the errors of the people:
8 The Holy Ghost this signifying, that the way into the holiest of all was not yet made manifest, while as the first tabernacle

was yet standing:
9 Which was a figure for the time then present, in which were offered both gifts and sacrifices, that could not make him that did the service perfect, as pertaining to the conscience;
10 Which stood only in meats and drinks, and divers washings, and carnal ordinances, imposed on them until the time of reformation

.

This great study in Hebrews allows the student to see many comparisons and many contrasts while revealing who Christ is in all of His superiority. He is the Superior One. This chapter examines the priesthood in three dimensions. First we will look at The Earthly Priesthood, then we will look at The Heavenly Priesthood, followed by The Enduring Priesthood. As we further examine the priesthood we will have even a clearer picture of who Christ is. This is the reason for all of the types, the shadows, the Levitical ceremonies and the first covenant. They all were wedded together to reveal different aspects of Christ. From this composite of truth, we gain a better understanding of the superior priesthood.

I. THE EARTHLY PRIESTHOOD. (9:1-10)

We shall examine the first covenant which had ordinances of divine service, and a worldly sanctuary according to the first verse of this chapter. The significance of each part given is to show us more about the Lord Jesus Christ through the ministry of the earthly priesthood and the first tabernacle. In the first tabernacle there are three objects mentioned. There is the candlestick, the table and the shewbread where the priests went at will. In the second tabernacle there is the golden censer and the Ark of the Covenant which contained the golden pot of manna, Aaron's rod that budded, and the tables of the covenant. The high priest, alone, went in once a year. The first tabernacle pictured the fellowship that is in Christ, whereas the second tabernacle pictured the fragrance that is in Christ. When we are referring to the tabernacle first and second, we are not doing so to describe two separate buildings, but instead it is showing two sections of the one overall tabernacle. The first was called the holy place in distinction from the holy of holies which was the second part of the tabernacle. The first was more common and available to be accessed, but the second was reserved for the high priest alone, on the Day of Atonement. It was separated by a veil. The earthly priesthood involved the entire order of Aaron and Melchesidec with all of the included rituals and ceremonies.

Everything that is being described in this section pertains and relates to the time of ministry and worship as it took place upon the earth. This is the worship that took place before the birth, the death and the resurrection of Christ. The Lord used the tabernacle with all of its fixtures to allow the exercising of worshipping the Lord and also teaching the Holiness of God. Though this worship was earthly in nature, it pictured that which was heavenly and eternal as it pertained to God. The first tabernacle pictured a place of sacred fellowship that ultimately will be found in Christ alone.

A. The First Tabernacle: Pictures A Place of Sacred Fellowship. (9:1-2)

There is no way to fully describe the fellowship that is found in Christ Jesus. In the first rectangular chamber that is being described here, we discover that access was more freely obtained as the priests would come in and out while doing their daily activities; whereas in the square chamber, only the high priest could enter once a year on the Day of Atonement. This first sanctuary had three mentioned items that speak of the fellowship already here alluded. This chamber of sacred fellowship speaks of what may be found in Christ Jesus alone. The fellowship that we enjoy with the Father is made possible through the Son. The fellowship that we have in the church is because of Christ. To remove the fellowship from the church would certainly have a crippling affect on our worship and communion. The first Epistle of John tells something of the fellowship that I am describing. In the economy of grace that we now live, we are privileged to have the fellowship made possible when Christ Jesus manifested Himself. I John 1:1-4 proves this statement: *"That which was from the beginning, which we have heard, which we have seen with our eyes, which we have looked upon, and our hands have handled, of the Word of life; (For the life was manifested, and we have seen it, and bear witness, and shew unto you that eternal life, which was with the Father, and was manifested unto us;) That which we have seen and heard declare we unto you, that ye also may have fellowship with us: and truly our fellowship is with the*

Father, and with his Son Jesus Christ. And these things write we unto you, that your joy may be full."

1. The candlestick shows how God is revealed. (9:2a)

The purpose of a candlestick is to produce light. The figure here is that Christ is that Light that the church so desperately needs. Every activity that the church is involved in needs Christ the Light for spiritual truth and spiritual things to be revealed. Without Him our churches would be covered in darkness. I John 1:5-7 further indicates this truth. *"This then is the message which we have heard of him, and declare unto you, that God is light, and in him is no darkness at all. If we say that we have fellowship with him, and walk in darkness, we lie, and do not the truth: But if we walk in the light, as he is in the light, we have fellowship one with another, and the blood of Jesus Christ his Son cleanseth us from all sin."*

If Christ is excluded from the church, then the church plunges into darkness. It cannot escape that darkness no matter how refined and how formal the church may be in its liturgy or worship. The triumphant church must have Christ as its light, for without Him the church has neither fellowship nor direction. Even the old puritan writer and theologian, John Gill, knew this to be true. Notice how he very eloquently described the role of the candlestick with its symbolism: "wherein was the candlestick; that this was in the tabernacle, and on the south side of it, and without the vail, where the apostle has placed it, is plain from Ex. 26:35. This was wanting in the second temple: it was a type of

Christ mystical, or the church; in the general use of it, to hold forth light, so the church holds forth the light of the Gospel, being put into it by Christ; in the matter of it, which was pure gold, denoting the purity, worth, splendour, glory, and duration of the church; in the parts of it, it had one shaft in the middle of it, in which all the parts met and cemented, typical of Christ the principal, and head of the church, whose situation is in the midst of the church, and who unites all together, and is but one: the six branches of it may intend all the members of the church, and especially the ministers of the word; the seven lamps with oil in them, may have a respect to the seven spirits of God, or the Spirit of God with his gifts and graces, and a profession of religion with grace along with it: and it was typical of the church in its ornaments and decorations; its bowls, knops, and flowers, may signify the various gifts of the Spirit, beautifying ministers, and fitting them for usefulness; and in the appurtenances of it, the tongs and snuff dishes may signify church discipline, censures, and excommunications." (John Gill).

2. The table shows how God relates. (9:2b)

The Word of God is very specific. Even the location of the candlestick and the table is given in Exodus 26:35. *"And thou shalt set the table without the vail, and the candlestick over against the table on the side of the tabernacle toward the south: and thou shalt put the table on the north side."* There is reason for the location to be given or else it would not be given. One great reason is that everything that the Lord does is to be done decently and in order. The table speaks of communion. It is indeed wonderful to be able to sit at the table of God's mercy and commune with Him. The Christian has the personal privilege of communing with Christ, but the church has that same given right and privilege. To commune speaks of intimacy. For there to be intimacy there needs to be closeness. Sin can take away the communion that we need to maintain that closeness. There is no greater privilege than sitting at the table with Jesus having that communion. The Lord relates to us not from a distance as it was in the old economy, but we may draw near to Him and abide with Him. In John 15:5 we are told, *"I am the vine, ye are the branches: He that abideth in me, and I in him, the same bringeth forth much fruit: for without me ye can do nothing."*

The table spoken of here was made of shittim wood covered with gold. The wood speaks of the humanity of Christ and the gold relates to His majesty and His royalty in association with His deity. As this table appeared in the Old Testament it was a preview of the way that communion was granted to the believer. The Lord came to the earth in human form to fellowship with us and also manifest Himself to us for the purpose of going to the cross. He went to the tomb, dying as man; He came forth in resurrection splendor as God! We see in the construction of the table both deity and humanity.

3. The shewbread shows how God refreshes. (9:2c)

While still considering the typical significance of the furnishings of the tabernacle, may we remind ourselves that our nourishment comes from Christ alone who is the Bread of Life. He is the only one who can sustain us and refresh us. He satisfies the hunger pains that plague us. Once we have tasted of Him, we may continue to feast off of Him for all eternity. As we continue to look at these furnishings typically, may we remind ourselves that each piece had practical significance as well. All the pieces were in the framework to reveal how the priests were to render worship back to the Lord. The shewbread also had its purpose.

With that being said, may we meditate on the refreshing aspects of God's Word. In Psalm one, the first verse tells us, *"Blessed is the man that walketh not in the counsel of the ungodly, nor standeth in the way of sinners, nor sitteth in the seat of the scornful."* Verse two says, *"But his delight is in the law of the LORD; and in his law doth he meditate day and night."* The refreshing aspects of God's Word lifts us from the "slough of despond" and puts a new song in our mouth. We are encouraged and refreshed to continue on our pilgrim journey. That kind of refreshment only comes from the Lord.

B. The Second Tabernacle Pictures the Place of Sweet Fragrance. (9:3-10)

The place of fragrance is where God is. The further that you remove yourself from Him, the less will be the fragrance. The second chamber was called the holiest of all. That is where the fragrance was; that is where God was relative to priestly worship. It was a good way, even then; it is a better way now. We can now come boldly to the throne of grace where the veil has been rent in twain. With Him being the Fragrance, would it be crude to say, "We should smell more like Him?" Of course not…. Yet, I am afraid that even the church may have more of the fragrance of the world than the fragrance of Christ. This happens when the church drifts further and further away from Him. The reason that I refer to this chamber as *the place of fragrance* is because this is where the censer was to be found. The censer was the place of burning. The burning yielded a smell that was in association with what was found burning on the altar. To the world, the smell may be repulsive; to the believer, it is a sweet smelling savor.

1. Golden censer – place of sacrifice.

The theologians may be divided as to whether the censer is the container which held the burning ashes and the incense or whether it was the altar itself. In either case the censer is used in association with sacrifice. By design, the atonement could in no way forever put away the wrath of God; it only pictured a greater place of offering and sacrifice where the ultimate Sacrifice was made. The sacrifice of Christ grants all who so desire a way of approach. When Christ shed His blood offering Himself, He gave a new way of grace that is available to all who will come by faith to Him. Once again, I would like to refer to the studies of John Gill as he describes the censer both historically and typically. "There were various censers used by the priests in the daily service, but this was a peculiar one, which was used by the high priest on the day of atonement; on other days he used a silver censer, but on that day a golden one, and with it he entered into the holy of holies; and though Moses does not call it a golden one, Lev.16:12 yet Josephus does; and so do the Jewish doctors in the place referred to, with whom the apostle agrees, and to this the allusion is in Rev. 8:3 but here a difficulty arises, how this can be said to have been in the holy of holies, and within the vail, when, according to Moses, it was without the vail, and was only carried within on the day of atonement; and so Philo the Jew places it in the other part of the tabernacle; and it seems as if it was to avoid this difficulty, that the Ethiopic version has removed it from this verse to verse the second, and put it among the things that were in the holy place; but there is no need of this, nor to say that the altar of incense is intended, for that is never so called, and, besides, was without the vail too. It should be observed, that the apostle does not say, that the golden censer was laid up in the holy of holies, and kept there, but that it "had" it; as it had it on the day of atonement, when it was carried in there by the high priest, who there made use of it; and it was for the use of it in that place, that it was peculiarly designed. What was done by it was this, burning coals were with it taken off from the altar before the Lord, and were brought in within the vail, where incense was put upon them, which covered the mercy seat, that so the high priest died not. The burning coals signify the very great sufferings of Christ, not only the sufferings of his body, which were very painful, but those of his soul, when the wrath and hot displeasure of God was poured out upon him; and those coals being taken off from the altar before the Lord, show that the sufferings of Christ were according to the will of God, were grateful to him, and always before him; and their being brought within the vail, does not denote that

Christ is now in a suffering state, though he is in the midst of the throne, as a lamb that had been slain; but the continued virtue and efficacy of his sufferings, and that our faith and hope, which enter within the vail, have to do with his blood and sacrifice thither carried. And the incense, which was carried in with those coals, typified the intercession of Christ in heaven, which is pure and holy, sweet, fragrant, and perpetual; and the priest having his hands full of it, expresses the fullness of Christ's intercession for all his elect, and for all things for them, and his fullness of merit to plead, which makes his intercession efficacious and prevalent; and hence, through his much incense, the prayers of his people become odorous and acceptable: and the incense being put upon the burning coals in the censer, shows that Christ's intercession proceeds upon the foot of his blood and sacrifice, his sufferings and death; and hence it becomes grateful, and has its influence; the smoke of it covers the mercy seat, or throne of grace, and makes that accessible; and as the priest, who offers it, never dies, so none of those for whom he intercedes."

2. Ark of the Covenant – pictures the work of sanctification (9:4)

I certainly hope that I am not bending the truth by saying that the ark with those articles contained therein pictures the Christian's work of sanctification. The physical ark was sanctified or set apart as being holy unto the Lord. What we do as Christians is not part secular and part sacred. We truly should not differentiate between the two. Instead, everything that we do should be sacred. Everything that we do should refer back to and issue forth from God. We will examine the three items listed in the ark and make spiritual application as we do.

a. The golden pot of manna – pictures the provisions of

God. (9:4c)

The preserved manna could have been so to remind a forgetful people of a remembering God. We may forget that He is more than able to supply us with all of our needs according to His riches in glory. But He has His ways of reminding us. The nation of Israel was so wonderfully cared for even while they were under the discipline of God for forty years. Their time spent in the wilderness was because of their sin of unbelief, yet God still sent them angel food. The manna that He sent them was sent faithfully, meeting their daily needs.

It may be that God wanted the priest to see that very pot of manna to remind the people that God provides. To be mentioned in the New Testament, is to call attention to the fact that as God cared for those earlier, He can provide for us later. For our service to God we need to be reminded that God owns everything and that He has given us something. Because He has given us something that makes us stewards. As stewards we need to further know that we are accountable for our stewardship. We must give account of how we serve God. The manna pictures the spiritual nourishment that we receive to do the ministry that God has given us. He gives us all of the gifts and the talents that we need to adequately serve Him.

Some believe that the manna is a type of Christ, as Gill observed: "The 'manna', in this pot, was typical of Christ; in the signification of its name, whether it comes from מנה, 'manah', which signifies to appoint, prepare, and distribute, Christ being appointed, prepared, and distributed, as food for his people; or from ' מן הו, man hu', what is it? the words said by the Israelites, when they first saw it, not knowing what it was; so Christ is unknown to his people until revealed to them, and remains unknown to all natural and unregenerate men:"

b. Aaron's rod that budded – pictures the power or authority of God. (9:4d)

Great care should be taken when explaining the truth of God's Word so as to not make an improper interpretation. This we are trying to do. In regards to Aaron's rod that budded, because we are not given a clear interpretation, I would rather make application truth than make interpretational truth. I suppose that this is really the way that we are treating each of these items, while understanding that the sacred writer did not explain the reason that the rod that budded or the other items were inside the ark. Yet, we do also know that we may arrive at a proper interpretation by comparing scripture with scripture. That is what we are doing here. In Numbers 17:8-10, we are given a clue as to why the rod was in the ark. We are told that the rod was *"to be kept for a token against the rebels; and thou shalt quite take their murmurings from me, that they die not."* We may determine from this text that the priesthood of Aaron is being confirmed, as the rod that had his name on it began to bloom, to blossom and bare fruit. There were those who were questioning the leadership of Moses and of Aaron and because of this, God showed supernaturally His will before those "rebels." (Numbers 17:10)

There were twelve rods that were laid down before the Lord and it was only Aaron's that budded. This was the way that the Lord chose to reveal from which tribe the priesthood would come. (Numbers 17:5)

c. The tables of God – pictures the purpose of God. (9:4e)

The law and the purpose of God are revealed in the giving of the law, beginning with the Ten Commandments. A thorough study of the Ten Commandments and the law that was given to Moses at Mount Sinai can say much about the purpose and will of God. Human government today borrows so much from the law that was given to Moses and yet at the same time takes the Ten Commandments out of the court houses.

It is God's will that we live in obedience, which strengthens our being sanctified or set apart to the doing of His will and purpose.

d. The ordination – pictures the procedures of God. (9:5-10)

Everything that the Lord did had decency and order attached to it. We are also instructed to do everything *decently* and in order (I Corinthians 14:40). The word decently means doing things in a serious manner and with purpose. The Lord's work is not to be done casually, nor did He lay out the sacrifices and the priesthood in a way that was void of order and of purpose. Notice these three aspects of the priesthood: 1. Notice first the way that the way work was ordained, 2. How the way was ordered, and 3. How the worship was offered.

1. How the work was ordained. (9:6a)

May it be understood that the entire legal system, including the priesthood and the offerings, was ordained by God and given to Moses at Mount Sinai. In human terms, "the law was given by Moses" in that the LORD chose him for that role (John 1:17).

2. How the way was ordered. (9:6b-7a)

The first tabernacle was available to the priests on an ongoing basis to do their priestly work. It was there that they accomplished "the service of God."

3. How the worship was offered. (9:7b-10)

The second tabernacle was used only on the Day of Atonement to put off the wrath of God for another year.

Even though this was only temporary in its effect, there still had to be the shedding of the blood which pictured the time that Christ was going to shed His own blood and forever put off the wrath of God for those who would believe. With Christ doing this, it is referred to as the time of reformation. Reformation means in this instance that what all the figures, types, and the symbols could not do, Christ did. The more we study the book of Hebrews, the more that we should be convinced that a better way has been provided through the Lord Jesus Christ.

The word *errors* in verse seven also applies to "sins of ignorance." I think this is a great picture of the way Christ's sacrifice covers *all* our sins. When we accept Jesus as Saviour, all of our sins are forgiven. If we are aware of a sin that we have committed and we do not repent of it, we will be chastised for it; but they are forgiven nonetheless.

There are probably times though, that we commit sins of which we are unaware. We are not perfect in knowledge and God is constantly teaching us more and more about how we should live according to His Word; so what about the sins that we commit in ignorance?

Consider the new convert. He or she has not learned yet how to live right and there will be many sins that he will commit, transgressing God's laws and commands, of which he is not even aware. That person's sins have to be forgiven though, or else he could not enter into Heaven. It is great to know that Jesus, our High Priest, covers all of our sins; even those of which we are not aware?

When a child of God commits a transgression in ignorance,

can't you just picture our Saviour turning to God the Father and saying something similar to the statement He made on the Cross, "Father forgive him, for he does not realize that he has transgressed." I think when we get to Heaven, we will find that many times Jesus pled our cause, and we did not even know we had done wrong. To Him be all glory!!

Chapter Nineteen

THE EARTHLY, THE ETERNAL AND THE ENDURING PRIESTHOOD (Part Two)

Text: Hebrews 9:11-28

11 But Christ being come an high priest of good things to come, by a greater and more perfect tabernacle, not made with hands, that is to say, not of this building;
12 Neither by the blood of goats and calves, but by his own blood he entered in once into the holy place, having obtained eternal redemption for us.
13 For if the blood of bulls and of goats, and the ashes of an heifer sprinkling the unclean, sanctifieth to the purifying of the flesh:
14 How much more shall the blood of Christ, who through the eternal Spirit offered himself without spot to God, purge your conscience from dead works to serve the living God?
15 And for this cause he is the mediator of the new testament, that by means of death, for the redemption of the transgressions that were under the first testament, they which are called might receive the promise of eternal inheritance.
16 For where a testament is, there must also of necessity be the death of the testator.
17 For a testament is of force after men are dead: otherwise it is of no strength at all while the testator liveth.

18 Whereupon neither the first testament was dedicated without blood.

19 For when Moses had spoken every precept to all the people according to the law, he took the blood of calves and of goats, with water, and scarlet wool, and hyssop, and sprinkled both the book, and all the people,

20 Saying, This is the blood of the testament which God hath enjoined unto you.

21 Moreover he sprinkled with blood both the tabernacle, and all the vessels of the ministry.

22 And almost all things are by the law purged with blood; and without shedding of blood is no remission.

23 It was therefore necessary that the patterns of things in the heavens should be purified with these; but the heavenly things themselves with better sacrifices than these.

24 For Christ is not entered into the holy places made with hands, which are the figures of the true; but into heaven itself, now to appear in the presence of God for us:

25 Nor yet that he should offer himself often, as the high priest entereth into the holy place every year with blood of others;

26 For then must he often have suffered since the foundation of the world: but now once in the end of the world hath he appeared to put away sin by the sacrifice of himself.

27 And as it is appointed unto men once to die, but after this the judgment:

28 So Christ was once offered to bear the sins of many; and unto them that look for him shall he appear the second time without sin unto salvation.

I. THE ETERNAL PRIESTHOOD. (9:11-14)

A. His Eternal Priesthood Has Omnipotence. (9:11)

The priesthood that is Christ's is certainly a better priesthood that is made perfect by the sacrifice of Christ offering both His blood and offering Himself. How much better is His priesthood. He brings into His priesthood all the attributes that describe Him as being God. His priesthood has *omnipotence* which guarantees the power necessary to perform the doing of that priesthood. There is no offering or need that will challenge His ability or His power. No one should think that his sin is too great for Him. One need not question or discuss whether His power is adequate to minister to the needs of the wicked sinner. Saying this reminds me of the Rolls-Royce salesman being questioned by a potential buyer. The salesman was asked, "How much horsepower does the Rolls-Royce have?" to which the salesman replied, "It is adequate." Such is so in regards to our High Priest. He can adequately take care of the needs of each and every sinner. He is all powerful. Colossians 2:9-10 tells us: *"For in him dwelleth all the fullness of the Godhead bodily. And ye are complete in him, which is the head of all principality and power."*

The strength of the offering is no stronger than the sacrifice being offered and the one who is doing the offering. With that being said, Christ first demonstrated His omnipotence during His creation work. Colossians further proves this truth in Colossians 1:16-19 when it tells us, *"For by him were all things created, that are in heaven, and that are in earth, visible and invisible, whether they be thrones, or dominions, or principalities, or powers: all things were created by him, and for him: And he is before all things, and by him all things consist. And he is the head of the body, the church: who is the beginning, the firstborn from the dead; that in all things he might have the preeminence. For it pleased the Father that in him should all fullness dwell;"*

He could not be the Priest that meets God's holy and righteous demands if He were not all powerful. Satan would be the foe who conquers if Christ were not more powerful than he. Satan also could destroy and corrupt the priesthood if Christ were not more powerful.

B. His Eternal Priesthood Has Omnipresence. (9:12-13)

Christ is not a part-time priest who only occasionally ministers to the priesthood. He took His own blood *"into the holy place, having obtained eternal redemption for us."* The blood of the bulls and of goats and even the ashes of a heifer could not do what Christ's priesthood could. Poole describes the work of the heifer in the earthly sacrificial system, *"And the ashes of an heifer sprinkling the unclean:* the rite of preparing it, read in Num. 19:1-10. A red heifer was by the people given to the priest; he was to bring her without the camp, and order her to be slain, and then take the blood with his finger, and sprinkle it towards the tabernacle seven times; after which she was to be wholly burnt in his sight, with cedar wood, hyssop, and scarlet, the ashes of which were reserved; when they used them, they took them in a vessel, and put running water to them, and then sprinkled them with a bunch of hyssop on persons legally unclean, Heb 9:18-20, and so they purified them from their ceremonial filth and pollution; but none of these could purify an unclean soul, that was left unholy and unclean still (Poole).

The earthly priesthood had no offerings that could purify an unclean soul and the atonement could only be offered on an annual basis, thus showing further the weakness of the earthly system. The priesthood of Aaron with such offerings was to end with the earthly priest and had to be replaced with another Priest. This is another reason that Christ's priesthood was superior. It was an everlasting priesthood and He was able to exercise His priesthood forever with omnipresence, for His priesthood has no ending. The earthly priests during the time of Moses until the time that Christ made His offering, did not enjoy the attribute of omnipresence. He, being a human priest, could only do as humans are capable of doing. He could only represent those with whom he had personal contact. The earthly priest was both time and space restricted. The Lord Jesus Christ has no restrictions. The Psalmist David knew this well in Psalm 139:7-10, *"Whither shall I go from thy spirit? Or whither shall I flee from thy presence? If I ascend up into heaven, thou art there: if I make my bed in hell, behold, thou art there. If I take the wings of the morning, and dwell in the uttermost parts of the sea; Even there shall thy hand lead me, and thy right hand shall hold me."*

With our Priest being omnipresent, He is able to immediately respond to our sin need. He can make intercession for us because He is always where we are. This does not mean that we have a free ticket to sin and then immediately find forgiveness. When we study Hebrews chapter ten, we will discover that when a person sins, there may be forgiveness but there will also be consequences for that sin. That is the reason Hebrews 10:26 says that, *"...if we sin willfully after that we have received the knowledge of the truth, there remaineth no more sacrifice for sins,"*

C. His Eternal Priesthood Has Omniscience. (9:14)

Omniscience is an attribute of God that only He has. Satan does not have this attribute and quality, nor did the earthly priests have it. David described this quality also in Psalm 139. *"O Lord thou hast searched me, and known me. Thou knowest my downsitting and mine uprising, thou understandest my thought afar off. Thou compassest my path and my lying down, and art acquainted with all my ways. For there is not a word in my tongue, but, lo, O LORD, thou knowest it altogether."*

Such describes only the Lord. There may be some of His subjects that belong to the family of the redeemed, who would not appreciate knowing that He knows all. This is only because they do not know the great value of such knowledge. It could be because such has something to hide. When we are doing evil, it may be thought that it would be better if even God did not know those things. Yet, it is this kind of knowledge that protects us from the ease of sinning; or at least it should serve that more noble purpose. It also should encourage our hearts just in knowing that He is constantly abiding. This abiding requires both His omniscience and His omnipresence at work.

In verse fourteen a great question is asked: *"How much more shall the blood of Christ who through the eternal Spirit offered himself without spot to God, purge your conscience from dead works to serve the living God?"* There is no way to measure or compare the work of Christ, when He gave His blood with the blessings and with the acceptance of God. His offering was without spot, meaning that there was nothing at all wrong with His perfect offering. It is this blood that is available to help every sinner wherever that sinner might be. The requirement to purge one's conscience recognizes that there is one who knows us in a very present tense *on location*, wherever we may be.

II. THE ENDURING PRIESTHOOD. (9:15-28)

These next closing verses of chapter nine show us the way the Lord fulfills His promises in a very enduring manner. Forever is a very long time. The priestly work will continue on forever without ending. Who Christ is and what Christ did is what makes His priesthood enduring. This is what the book of Hebrews proves. We shall look at some of the characteristics that mark His enduring.

A. The Promises Involving the Priesthood. (9:15)

Never would it have been enough for Christ to have only lived a perfect life upon this earth for the sin payment to have been made or redemption to have been purchased. His life upon this earth only witnessed the truth that He was a suitable sacrifice. It took His death upon the cross and the offering of His blood to secure our redemption. For Him to be a mediator of the New Testament there had to be the death of the testator. Colossians 1:18-22 shows the importance of both the blood being shed and the body being offered as a sacrifice: *"And he is the head of the body, the church: who is the beginning, the firstborn from the dead; that in all things he might have the preeminence. For it pleased the father that in him should all fullness dwell; And, having made peace through the blood of his cross, by him to reconcile all things unto himself; by him, I say, whether they be things in earth, or things in heaven. And you, that were sometime alienated and enemies in your mind by wicked works, yet now hath he reconciled In the body of his flesh through death, to present you holy and unblameable and unreproveable in his sight:"* The requirements of God demand that there be an adequate sacrifice to satisfy His holy standard of righteousness. The death of Christ was far reaching in that it not only met the needs of those who were living at the time of His crucifixion, but reached all the way back to Adam and to the last man who shall be born coming to Christ by faith. John Gill has a wonderful way of wording and giving commentary on this verse: "Christ became the Mediator of the New Testament, and assumed human nature that he might die, and by dying might obtain redemption for his people; not only for those that were then in the world, or should be in it, but also for all those that had been in it." The first testament is the first dispensation of the covenant of grace, reaching from the first promulgation of it to Adam after the fall, to the death of Christ; "the transgressions" that were under it are the sins of the saints who lived under that dispensation, from Adam to Moses, and from Moses to Christ, and takes in all their iniquities of every kind: and the "redemption" of these, or from these, by Christ, at and through his death, does not suppose that there was no remission of sins, or justification from them, under that dispensation; or that the Old Testament saints did not go to heaven, but were detained in a prison, till redeemed by the death of Christ; or that their sins were only redeemed, not their persons; for transgressions may stand for transgressors; and so the Syriac version renders it, "that by his death he might be a redemption for them who transgressed the first testament"; so the Jews say, that the Messiah must die לפדות את אבות "to redeem the fathers "(b): but the sense is, that though legal sacrifices could not atone for sin, nor ceremonial ablutions cleanse from them; yet the sins of Old Testament saints were expiated, their iniquities pardoned, and they justified and saved, through the blood of Christ, the Lamb slain from the foundation of the world; whose death is a redemption from transgressions past, present, and to come; whose blood is the ransom price for them, and was shed for the remission of them, even of sins that are past through the forbearance of God; who took the surety's word for the performance of all this, which in the fulness of time he strictly fulfilled, to the satisfaction of law and justice;" (Gill).

The first testament in this verse refers to all that pertained to the Law of Moses up until the time of Christ when the New Testament was given. The first testament was the law and was a covenant that tied back to the Law that was given at Mount Sinai. The New Testament is that which refers to the birth, the death and the resurrection of the Lord Jesus Christ.

B. The Provisions Involving the Priesthood. (9:16-22)

Beginning in verse 16, it says: *"For where a testament is, there must also of necessity be the death of the testator.*

For a testament is of force after men are dead: otherwise it is of no strength at all while the testator liveth." May we understand this as it would relate to a person who predisposes of his property in a will, but it does not go into effect until the writer and the one who signs the will dies. The will is only read with value and purpose after the death of the person who gave the will. Until the death takes place, the will has no value. The New Testament could never have taken effect in regards to redemption until the death of the "Testator." This proves to be one of the great provisions of the priesthood and must be understood to be appreciated.

Every blood offering that involved the blood of calves and of goats was only picturing a better way. Including with these animals being offered was water, scarlet wool, and hyssop. Water pictures cleansing; scarlet wool pictures sin or the sinner (which could relate to the truth that He became sin for us) and the hyssop is a picture of applied suffering. As the offering was made, those who offered and were offered for were mindful that there was only a temporary effect to these offerings. They knew that the Day of Atonement was only putting off the wrath of God. As we look back with the full canon of Truth, we are clearly able to see the purpose of the Old Testament offerings and understand why there had to be a better way.

C. The Patterns Involving the Priesthood. (9:23-27)

Great respect was to be given for those things in Heaven by the offerings that were made. God accepted these offerings to purify the "things in the heavens" but He also shows us from our text that there were "better sacrifices than these". Hebrews shows us that the Lord did not enter into *"the holy places made with hands, which are the figures of the true; but into heaven itself, now to appear in the presence of God for us:"* Every good and perfect gift comes from above, including the Gospel of Christ. The salvation that we now enjoy came from Heaven and the pattern that pictured "so great salvation" was all pictured in the earthly offerings. We call these patterns "pictures and types." As much as these offerings pictured the greater Offering, they could have never done any more than that. It was for this reason that there had to be the death of the Testator so that the new and better way could come into effect. The yearly offering was to be replaced by Christ Himself making the offering that satisfied: *"For then must he often have suffered since the foundation of the world: but now once in the end of the world hath he appeared to put away sin by the sacrifice of himself."* When He did this He served the role of the Testator by the sacrifice of Himself (V. 26).

This offering that took place and only had to be done once, contradicts the papists who offer His body every time they offer up mass. Their practice of transubstantiation goes contrary to biblical truth as clearly defined in our text. There is no need or reason for any priestly activity to be performed again, for He satisfied the requirements of God with His one-time offering.

D. The *Parousia* Involving the Priesthood. (9:28)

This last verse in this chapter states that the Priest who

satisfied God's requirements will return and is alive to do so. We who are looking for Him have the promise that He will *"appear the second time without sin unto salvation."* This will indeed be a glorious day in which we look forward to with great anticipation. Though He had to die as the Testator, He now lives as the Saviour.

Chapter Twenty

NO PLEASURE

Text: Hebrews 10:1-18

1 For the law having a shadow of good things to come, and not the very image of the things, can never with those sacrifices which they offered year by year continually make the comers thereunto perfect.
2 For then would they not have ceased to be offered? because that the worshippers once purged should have had no more conscience of sins.
3 But in those sacrifices there is a remembrance again made of sins every year.
4 For it is not possible that the blood of bulls and of goats should take away sins.
5 Wherefore when he cometh into the world, he saith, Sacrifice and offering thou wouldest not, but a body hast thou prepared me:
6 In burnt offerings and sacrifices for sin thou hast had no pleasure.
7 Then said I, Lo, I come (in the volume of the book it is written of me,) to do thy will, O God.
8 Above when he said, Sacrifice and offering and burnt offerings and offering for sin thou wouldest not, neither hadst pleasure therein; which are offered by the law;
9 Then said he, Lo, I come to do thy will, O God. He taketh

away the first, that he may establish the second.
10 By the which will we are sanctified through the offering of the body of Jesus Christ once for all.
11 And every priest standeth daily ministering and offering oftentimes the same sacrifices, which can never take away sins:
12 But this man, after he had offered one sacrifice for sins for ever, sat down on the right hand of God;
13 From henceforth expecting till his enemies be made his footstool.
14 For by one offering he hath perfected for ever them that are sanctified.
15 Whereof the Holy Ghost also is a witness to us: for after that he had said before,
16 This is the covenant that I will make with them after those days, saith the Lord, I will put my laws into their hearts, and in their minds will I write them;
17 And their sins and iniquities will I remember no more.
18 Now where remission of these is, there is no more offering for sin.

In Christian service, there is no greater motive for serving God than doing those things which would be pleasing to Him and that would also bring pleasure to Him. We are told in this chapter that the Lord found no pleasure in burnt offerings and sacrifices. We must understand that it was God who ordained the legal system when He gave the law to Moses. We also must understand that there is nothing wrong with the law. The offerings that were given which pertained to the law were not capable of satisfying the holy demands of God; these weak sacrifices could only put off the wrath of God for a little while. In an absolute and also in a relative sense, the Lord could not find pleasure in the offering of the "burnt offerings and sacrifices for sin" (Vv. 6-7). When the offerings are compared to the offering of His Son, they proved to be entirely inadequate. When these burnt offerings and sacrifices are seen by the Lord they absolutely do not measure up, thus He finds no pleasure in them.

One might ask, if these offerings were not suitable to put off forever the wrath and anger of God, then why did He ordain the legal system? Galatians 3:19-25 answers this concern when it tells us that the law "was our schoolmaster to bring us unto Christ" (V. 24). We also are instructed that the law was "added because of transgressions, till the seed should come to whom the promise was made; and it was ordained by angels in the hand of a mediator" (V. 19). This verse shows us that the offerings served a very temporary purpose until the "seed should come," and that seed was the Lord Jesus Christ.

We will examine: I. God's Displeasure Revealed Concerning the Old Offering (Vv. 1-8); II. God's Pleasure Recognized Concerning the New Offering (Vv. 9-18).

I. GOD'S DISPLEASURE REVEALED CONCERNING

THE OLD OFFERING (10:1-8)

From time to time, I will pull out a certain old video

which was made over twenty years ago. When I do, it brings me joy to watch and hear my parents, who are deceased, once again speak. The image is of them and the voice is theirs, but it is only a shadow of what was. The "law having a shadow of good things to come" is only a shadow of Him who is. In regards to my parent's shadow, if I could I would trade the shadow for them. The shadow follows them. In regards to Him, I will not trade Him for the shadow. In His case the shadow came first. The law is that shadow. With Him being the substance which the shadow represented, we now have a better offering.

A. The Offerings Were Insufficient to Satisfy God's Requirements. (10:1-3)

The offerings that were prescribed by the law had to be offered over and over again. There was an insufficiency that marked these offerings as they were identified with the sin-cursed earth. Each of the offerings left a "remembrance again made of sins every year." The offerings were made on the Day of Atonement to put off the wrath of God until Christ Jesus would come and forever put off God's anger. God's anger is a holy anger that demonstrated God's disposition to both the sin and the sinner. He certainly is angry with sin and His anger extends to the sinner, but thank God so also does His mercy. There is mercy and peace for the time of need. *"But God, who is rich in mercy, for his great love wherewith he loved us, Even when we were dead in sins, hath quickened us together with Christ, (by grace ye are saved;)"*

(Ephesians 2:4-5).

Everything which lies underneath the curse will be insufficient in meeting God's holy requirements. God's standard is way above man's and any offering that he is capable of offering apart from that of faith and obedience will only be a "Cain-like" offering in which God will have no respect (Genesis 4:5). The entire creation is underneath the sin curse and thus is so affected that nothing eternally satisfying can be extracted as an offering from it. Though the offering made according to the law was inefficient and insufficient in and of itself, the Lord honored it, because when it was being offered, the person offering it demonstrated a faithful obedience to the Lord. They were exercising a faith that was anticipating the better offering of Christ, Himself. They in doing so may not have understood all of the theology that was involved, but they obeyed anyway while making their offerings unto the Lord. The Lord was not saying that the offering was sufficient at this time, only the exercising of faith was sufficient in anticipation of the Offering that was perfect.

B. The Offerings Were Inferior in Supplying God's Requirements. (10:4-8)

Verse four says, *"For it is not possible that the blood of bulls and of goats should take away sins."* We immediately understand that His blood is superior to animal blood. His blood is superior to all blood. Animal sacrifice under the Old Covenant could only *cover* sin. The Hebrew word for *atonement* is *kophar*, which literally means "to cover." But animal sacrifice could never *take away sins*. Only Jesus, the Perfect Sacrifice of the New Covenant, takes sins *away*.

The sacrifices of the old economy had a prophetic significance. They were offered not only to *protect*, but also to *project* an object lesson pertaining to the greater offering of Jesus. The greater offering was in every way superior to the lesser offering. Thank God that He is the altogether Lovely One. This is demonstrated in the fact that God found pleasure in Him. He was pleased with His Son as indicated at both the baptism of Jesus and also the transfiguration of Jesus. Notice these scriptures. *"And lo a voice from heaven, saying, This is my beloved Son, in whom I am well pleased."* (Matthew 3:17). This voice came at the baptism of Jesus and it was the voice of the Father declaring that His Son pleased Him. Then the same occurrence of the voice took place at the transfiguration giving the same declaration: *"While he yet spake, behold, a bright cloud overshadowed them: and behold a voice out of the cloud, which said, This is my beloved Son, in whom I am well pleased; hear ye him"* (Matthew 17:5). These are two major public events that let something take place that had never happened before, when the Lord publicly placed His acceptance and satisfaction on His Son.

Once again, under the inspiration of the Holy Ghost, Peter restated the fact that the Father was satisfied with His Son as they witnessed from the holy mount the voice of God. *"For he received from God the Father honour and glory, when there came such a voice to him from the excellent glory, This is my beloved Son, in whom I am well pleased. And this voice which came from heaven we heard, when we were with him in the holy mount"* (II Peter 1:17-18). These events took place indicating the superiority of the Son of God as being One uniquely set apart from all others in being able to please God.

Verse five says, *"Wherefore when he cometh into the world, he saith, Sacrifice and offering thou wouldest not, but a body hast thou prepared me:"* The incarnation of the Son yielded a body that was acceptable to the Father as a Superior Sacrifice. As the Lamb of God, Jesus walked upon this earth to be watched and observed for all to see. The writers of the Scriptures testify to this. John thus indicated that Christ was observed in I John 1:1-2: *"That which was from the beginning, which we have heard, which we have seen with our eyes, which we have looked upon, and our hands have handled, of the Word of life; (For the life was manifested, and we have seen it, and bear witness, and shew unto you that eternal life, which was with the Father, and was manifested unto us;)"*

The burnt offerings and sacrifices for sin brought no pleasure to the Lord and thus were inferior according to His lofty and holy requirements. The coming of Christ Jesus was to satisfy the will of the Father: *"Then said I, Lo, I come (in the volume of the book it is written of me,) to do thy will, O God"* (V. 7). When we begin to have a proper grasp on why Jesus came, then we will have an understanding of the sacerdotal (priestly) system as God intended it. We will then begin to understand that God is the Superior Priest who offered Himself as a Superior Sacrifice. What other priest could both be the one who offers and the offering itself? By serving as He did as the High Priest, he has put away the need for an earthly priesthood. He has made the better offering that once and for all satisfies God the Father.

Verse eight restates what we have been saying as we make a comparison of the offerings that were acceptable and those which were not. *"Above when he said, Sacrifice and offering and burnt offerings and offering for sin thou wouldest not, neither hadst pleasure therein; which are offered by the law;"*

II. GOD'S PLEASURE RECOGNIZED CONCERNING

THE NEW OFFERING. (10:9-18)

The writer of the book of Hebrews, under the inspiration of the Holy Spirit, understood that Christ came in obedience to the will of God. Verse nine says, *"Then said he, Lo, I come to do thy will, O God. He taketh away the first, that he may establish the second."* "He taketh away" seems to be an expression which shows that the Lord is removing the Old Testament means of atonement, which involved the earthly priesthood with its many offerings, and replacing it with His Son Jesus who offers up Himself once and for all. It was only the offering up of the Lord Jesus that would bring satisfaction and pleasure to the Lord.

A. The Sufficiency of the Offering. (10:9-10)

The tenth verse in our text shows that *"we are sanctified through the offering of the body of Jesus Christ once for all."* How wonderful it is to know that God's offering of His Son was absolutely sufficient in meeting the requirements of the Father. There is nothing that need be or can be offered to increase the sufficiency of the offering. The purity of the offering means that it was in no way defiled. The lambs that were offered, according to the Levitical offerings, had to be without blemish, which pictured the Lamb of God being without blemish. Whereas the lamb could only be without blemish in a purely earthly sense, the Lamb of God was without blemish in an eternal sense. Our sanctification required the once for all offering of the body of Jesus Christ. He laid Himself down as an offering that was sufficient to bring about our sanctification. The word *sanctification* is a word that is used in conjunction with the word holiness. It speaks of setting apart from that which is vain and unholy. The Lord provided for our sanctification by first setting Himself apart as the Sanctified One.

Colossians 1:19-22 helps us to understand this truth when it says, *"For it pleased the Father that in him should all fulness dwell; And, having made peace through the blood of his cross, by him to reconcile all things unto himself; by him, I say, whether they be things in earth, or things in heaven. And you, that were sometime alienated and enemies in your mind by wicked works, yet now hath he reconciled In the body of his flesh through death, to present you holy and unblameable and unreproveable in his sight:"* The word *reconcile* means that enmity can be replaced with friendship. The word reconciliation means to "become friends again." What a Friend we have in Jesus!

In our study we keep noticing the emphasis that is being given to Christ offering His *body* as a sacrifice. This is no accident that the emphasis is given in this way. All of the Levitical offerings required the bodies of animals. His offering is also an offering of a body, but it is of a different kind of body. It is His very own body that was born of the virgin Mary so that He could fulfill the requirements of making an acceptable sacrifice. He did this by offering up *His body* which required His sacrificial death upon the cross. His offering was sufficient in every way. When Christ Jesus offered Himself, he took on the form of a servant... *"Let this mind be in you, which was also in Christ Jesus: Who, being in the form of God, thought it not robbery to be equal with God: But made himself of no reputation, and took upon him the form of a servant, and was made in the likeness of men: And being found in fashion as a man, he humbled himself, and became obedient unto death, even the death of the cross"* (Philippians 2:5-8).

B. The Satisfaction of the Offering. (10:11-18)

Several things had to happen for the Lord to be satisfied with the offering of Christ Jesus on the cross. There had to be an offering that was capable of taking away sins in a satisfactory manner. He was both the Man and the Sacrifice that was acceptable and able to do such. *"But this man, after he had offered one sacrifice for sins for ever, sat down on the right hand of God; From henceforth expecting till his enemies be made his footstool. For by one offering he hath perfected for ever them that are sanctified"* (Vv. 12-14). When He sat down, He indicated by doing so that His priesthood had met all the requirements that was expected of Him.

This is a very strong verse indicating one's security as a believer. There is nothing further that is required of Christ. We have shown from our text, the completion of the work and the covenant pertaining to that work. The law will no longer be just words on a stone, but will be engraved instead on the heart. Within the covenant of Grace, when we enjoy a sensitive heart to the things of God, we find that the law becomes a part of us and we find ourselves performing the law out of a heart of gratitude to the one who offered Himself as a ransom for all. The offering should be an offering of *delight* rather than an offering of *duty*.

The Lord goes on to say, *"And their sins and iniquities will I remember no more."* What a great and comforting promise when we are told that the Lord will remember our sins and iniquities no more. This verse was a favorite to my daddy as long as he lived upon this earth as a saved man. Even up until the time that he was nearly 90 years of age he would talk about this verse and how it spoke of his freedom in Jesus and his forgiveness that he had in the Lord. All who are in Christ Jesus can rest in Him just as my father did, because of the work that Christ performed when He offered up His body upon the cross as a payment for our sins.

Chapter Twenty-one

LET US DRAW NEAR WITH A TRUE HEART

Text: Hebrews 10:19-39

19 Having therefore, brethren, boldness to enter into the holiest by the blood of Jesus,
20 By a new and living way, which he hath consecrated for us, through the veil, that is to say, his flesh;
21 And having an high priest over the house of God;
22 Let us draw near with a true heart in full assurance of faith, having our hearts sprinkled from an evil conscience, and our bodies washed with pure water.
23 Let us hold fast the profession of our faith without wavering; (for he is faithful that promised;)
24 And let us consider one another to provoke unto love and to good works:
25 Not forsaking the assembling of ourselves together, as the manner of some is; but exhorting one another: and so much the more, as ye see the day approaching.
26 For if we sin wilfully after that we have received the knowledge of the truth, there remaineth no more sacrifice for sins,
27 But a certain fearful looking for of judgment and fiery indignation, which shall devour the adversaries.
28 He that despised Moses' law died without mercy under two or three witnesses:

29 Of how much sorer punishment, suppose ye, shall he be thought worthy, who hath trodden under foot the Son of God, and hath counted the blood of the covenant, wherewith he was sanctified, an unholy thing, and hath done despite unto the Spirit of grace?
30 For we know him that hath said, Vengeance belongeth unto me, I will recompense, saith the Lord. And again, The Lord shall judge his people.
31 It is a fearful thing to fall into the hands of the living God.
32 But call to remembrance the former days, in which, after ye were illuminated, ye endured a great fight of afflictions;
33 Partly, whilst ye were made a gazingstock both by reproaches and afflictions; and partly, whilst ye became companions of them that were so used.
34 For ye had compassion of me in my bonds, and took joyfully the spoiling of your goods, knowing in yourselves that ye have in heaven a better and an enduring substance.
35 Cast not away therefore your confidence, which hath great recompence of reward.
36 For ye have need of patience, that, after ye have done the will of God, ye might receive the promise.
37 For yet a little while, and he that shall come will come, and will not tarry.
38 Now the just shall live by faith: but if any man draw back, my soul shall have no pleasure in him.
39 But we are not of them who draw back unto perdition; but of them that believe to the saving of the soul.

At this juncture, we are leaving the theological and going on to the teachings that involve the practical. Most of what has been considered up to this point has been for the purpose of defining the theology of the priesthood as it pertains to the Levitical system and also to the *better* system that is found in Christ Jesus. A very smooth transition is being made from one discipline of study to this one as indicated by the use of the words, *"Having therefore, brethren, boldness to enter into the holiest by the blood of Jesus."* This is a tremendous summary statement that tells both what we should do in this new economy and how it is made possible. The payment that permits this boldness for the believer is the blood of Jesus. The emphasis for this section of study will be on the boldness that the believer should have in approaching the Lord for both salvation and for service.

I. THE WAY THAT ONE'S BOLDNESS IS REVEALED. (10:19-31)

You can determine either one's timidity or boldness in worship by the way that person approaches God. The Hebrews were confused as they attempted to reconcile the old economy to the new. It was with that fear and trepidation that they approached the Lord thinking that they still had to go through and earthly priest. It was this reverting back that insisted upon the writing of the book of Hebrews. Just as there was a warning not to revert back into the old economy based upon the Levitical system, there is also a warning for the believer not to mix law and grace which will bring intimidation to his worship. God wants no such fear and intimidation; He wants us to come with a holy boldness because of what was accomplished by His Son.

A. Boldness Should Be Revealed By Ones Approach. (10:19-21)

There is a commanded obedience as to how one should approach and enter the *holiest*. It is by the blood of Jesus that we are granted the right of approach. The veil was unlike the

Old Testament veil that concealed worship. This veil was His flesh that revealed or granted access to worship. Until the veil was rent, no man but the high priest could have the right of approach. Even he had to meet 146 external requirements to have that right. It was a very fearful thing on the Day of Atonement for both the priest and the people as he entered into the holy place. There was great concern as to whether the priest would be accepted or refused. There was relief only after God's wrath had been put off for one more year after the offering had been accepted. This holy dread continued until the Lord Jesus Christ came and made the one offering that ended all other offerings and with that being so, we are now permitted to come with boldness.

Verse 20 tells us that this is a new and living way: *"By a new and living way, which he hath consecrated for us, through the veil, that is to say, his flesh."* In the old economy, after the offerings had been made there were only the dead ashes of life that once was. But with Christ, there was an offering that was totally consumed by God's wrath, but once the body was placed in the garden tomb something wonderful happened on that resurrection morning! The Lord came forth as our forever living High Priest who had absolutely satisfied the holy requirements of God. He ever lives and makes intercession on our behalf, Praise God!.

B. A Boldness Should Be Revealed By Ones Assurance. (10:22-23)

The Levitical system was incapable of offering lasting assurance. The system had no lasting security that it could offer because of its weakness. There is no such plea for one to come boldly and with assurance, as it applied to the Levitical system, that is found anywhere in the Scriptures. Such is not the case with the offering of Christ. We who are under the blood can come with much assurance. While we are in our sinful bodies, we are capable of sinning. With this being so, we absolutely must have someone interceding on our behalf. The fact that Christ continues to intercede for us grants us the assurance that we need. The Lord intercedes on our behalf to help us pray: *"Likewise the Spirit also helpeth our infirmities: for we know not what we should pray for as we ought: but the Spirit itself maketh intercession for us with groanings which cannot be uttered. And he that searcheth the hearts knoweth what [is] the mind of the Spirit, because he maketh intercession for the saints according to [the will of] God."* (Romans 8:26-27).

Christ intercedes for us while seated upon the throne next to the Father. *"Who [is] he that condemneth? [It is] Christ that died, yea rather, that is risen again, who is even at the right hand of God, who also maketh intercession for us."* (Romans 8:34). This certainly should give us boldness in knowing that Christ is seated at the Father's right hand. The right hand speaks both of authority and also of strength. He is the Strong One who endured the cross and is seated at the Father's right hand. (Hebrews 12:2).

Another reason for having assurance is that the Lord saves us to the uttermost: *"Wherefore he is able also to save them to the uttermost that come unto God by him, seeing he ever liveth to make intercession for them."* (Hebrews 7:25). Though He saves us to the uttermost, there is the personal requirement of spiritual cleanliness. We are to have "our hearts sprinkled from an evil conscience, and our bodies washed with pure water." Having our hearts sprinkled from an evil conscience is to have the forgiveness of God upon us as we approach Him. We should be always mindful that it is He who forgives and grants us access into His presence. We should reverently approach Him and have our conduct with an awareness that we are in His presence by way of His omniscience. Spiritually, even while we walk upon this dusty earth, we are at the same time seated in the heavenlies.

C. A Boldness Should Be Revealed By Ones Attitude.

(10:24-31)

Our attitude towards others and our attitude toward ourselves should be different because of our new relationship made possible by the putting away of the old and the bringing in of the new economy. We should be willing to share our blessings with others even as they were shared with us. *"And let us consider one another to provoke unto love and to good works:"* (V. 24). What is more Christian than that? How can we be Christian and at the same time selfishly have our own existence. Everything that we do should be done as ambassadors to others. We should, as we walk in the faith, encourage others to do the same.

Everything that we accomplish spiritually should be on the basis of "love and to good works." Love is not a wimpy word as some would have you to believe. It is as though some would have you to think that *love* challenges one's toughness. Is there not such a thing as "tough love"? God demonstrated just how strong and how enduring true love is when He went to the cross. He died shedding His own precious blood. This is the spirit in which we should serve the Lord while at the same time provoking others to good service. The word *provoke* (paroxysmos) means to incite in a passionate way. The root meaning carries the idea of doing it in close proximity. If I am to provoke one to good service, I must develop a spiritual intimacy with that person, even as Christ shares an intimacy with us. As we assemble together as a church, we should strive to have a kindred spirit with those who surround us and those who make up our local assembly. This spirit should be marked by unity. Christ should be seen in our every activity as we worship and serve Him. This should be the spirit which causes us to provoke or encourage others to do well.

In the new economy of grace, we should exercise our Godly provocation within the discipline of the local church. By interpretation, within the immediate text the Hebrew was being addressed; by application the church is now being addressed. For this reason, we are exhorted to be in faithful attendance to our church. *"Not forsaking the assembling of ourselves together, as the manner of some is; but exhorting one another and so much the more, as ye see the day approaching."* (Hebrews 10:25). There seems to be a trend to slack off from the church rather than intensify the opportunity of assembling together. This goes contrary to Truth.

Verses 26 through 29 show the severity of doing "despite unto the Spirit of grace." *"For if we sin willfully after that we have received the knowledge of the truth, there remaineth no more sacrifice for sins, But a certain fearful looking for of judgment and fiery indignation, which shall devour the adversaries. He that despised Moses' law died without mercy under two or three witnesses: Of how much sorer punishment, suppose ye, shall he be thought worthy, who hath trodden under foot the Son of God, and hath counted the blood of the covenant, wherewith he was sanctified, an unholy thing, and hath done despite unto the Spirit of grace?"*

Just because we can come boldly into the presence of God does not mean we can come casually. It is a serious thing even in the economy of grace to commit willful sin. One who sins the sin of presumption, or the willful sin spoken of in our text, while thinking that he will not be required to face the consequences of that sin, is being greatly deceived. There will always be consequences to sinning. So many today are lacking the reverential fear and the respect that they should have as they commit their willful sins, thinking that there is no penalty to be paid. There will be a "fearful looking for of judgment and fiery indignation." We also are told that "It is a fearful thing to fall into the hands of the living God."

II. THE WAY ONE'S BOLDNESS IS REWARDED (10:32-39).

God wants us to approach Him with confidence. He does not want us to cast away our confidence any more than He did the converted Jews who were made a *gazingstock* **(Theatrizo)** (V. 33). The Greek word *theatrizo* is the Greek word from which we get our word theater. The word gazingstock means to put on a stage or to set forth as a spectacle. It also means to expose to contempt. The Jews had to suffer much when they began to embrace Christ and His teachings. Even the Apostles, who were there for their example, had to suffer much persecution. Peter and John were arrested for healing a lame man in Jesus' name. Stephen was stoned to death; James was beheaded; Peter was imprisoned and tradition tells us that he was hanged upside down. Paul was executed by Nero. In church history at the beginning of the Church Age many precious souls were martyred. Even though there was much persecution going on, that was being directed against the Christian, there were still those who were faithful to follow Christ as this verse indicates. *"For ye had compassion of me in my bonds, and took joyfully the spoiling of your goods, knowing in yourselves that ye have in heaven a better and an enduring* *substance"* (V. 34).

A. One's Boldness Rewarded by the Promises Given by Him. (10:32-36).

The Word of God is a promise Book that is so rich in those promises which serves to encourage us while we are on our earthly pilgrimage. God's Word tells us that these promises are exceeding great and precious promises. *"Whereby are given unto us exceeding great and precious promises: that by these ye might be partakers of the divine nature, having escaped the corruption that is in the world through lust."* (2 Peter 1:4). I am so grateful to the Lord that I personally can cling by faith to the many wonderful promises that is outlined and given in God's Word, the Bible. The promises of God were what were used to sustain the early pilgrims as they went into the arena of faith. Many of these Christian martyrs would hold their hands upward as they were looking towards heaven in faithful anticipation of soon being with the Father. In chapter 11 we will be looking at those who were faithful to the Lord even if it meant being "sawn asunder" or if it meant being "slain with the sword" (V. 37). They were those who did not cast away their confidence. They were those who endured "seeing him who is invisible."

In this section the reader is told that he has need of patience. The patience that is spoken of means the temper that does not easily succumb under suffering and also means a patient enduring, sustaining and perseverance. Satan has so many tricks to introduce great tribulation and suffering in the course of one's Christian existence to cause that one to succumb. The weight of such can cause discouragement and also bring about that person's defeat if the Christian casts away his confidence. Psalm 27:1 tells us that, *"The LORD [is] my light and my salvation; whom shall I fear? the LORD [is] the strength of my life; of whom shall I be afraid?"* Verses like this should be a promise that the Lord will strengthen us for all that befalls us.

B. One's Boldness Is Rewarded by the Payment Given by Him. (10:37).

The coming of the Lord will be reward enough. When a believer exercises faithfulness towards the Lord, he can additionally expect the rewards or the crowns for his faithfulness to the Lord. Paul knew this to be so when he wrote young Timothy. Paul said, "I have fought a good fight, I have finished my course, I have kept the faith: Henceforth there is laid up for me a crown of righteousness, which the Lord, the righteous judge, shall give me at that day: and not to me only, but unto all them also that love his appearing." Not falling out of the race has great rewards. In chapter number 12 a warning and an encouragement is to be given that we should stay in the race, "looking unto Jesus." When one attempts to live for Christ there will be obstacles and hurdles that are before us to discourage us. We need to focus on the fact that God is not forgetful to remember our labour of love. Once we cross the finish line there will be a crown waiting!

C. One's Boldness Is Rewarded by the Pleasure Received

by Him. (10:38-39).

The Lord finds pleasure with those who operate by faith. An entire chapter is devoted to this truth in the book of Hebrews (Chapter 11). This chapter introduces those who were rewarded and listed in what has been commonly referred to as "Faith's Hall of Fame." There are those who did not cast away their confidence and they brought much pleasure to the Lord. The Scriptures are given to us as the complete and comforting Word of God. When we read about those who faithfully endured, we will notice that many did not even have a name listed; yet God knows who they are. You may think that you are serving the Lord as an unknown because you never receive any recognition. Be assured that God knows you and He is keeping record and that should inspire us to never cast away our confidence. Even as I present this study, I am gleaning from these truths and being encouraged as I do.

It encourages me to know that I can bring pleasure to the Lord by faithfully serving Him. May God cause us that stay in the race to "stay in the race."

Chapter Twenty-two

FAITH'S HALL OF FAME

Text: Hebrews 11

1 Now faith is the substance of things hoped for, the evidence of things not seen.
2 For by it the elders obtained a good report.
3 Through faith we understand that the worlds were framed by the word of God, so that things which are seen were not made of things which do appear.
4 By faith Abel offered unto God a more excellent sacrifice than Cain, by which he obtained witness that he was righteous, God testifying of his gifts: and by it he being dead yet speaketh.
5 By faith Enoch was translated that he should not see death; and was not found, because God had translated him: for before his translation he had this testimony, that he pleased God.
6 But without faith it is impossible to please him: for he that cometh to God must believe that he is, and that he is a rewarder of them that diligently seek him.
7 By faith Noah, being warned of God of things not seen as yet, moved with fear, prepared an ark to the saving of his house; by the which he condemned the world, and became heir of the righteousness which is by faith.
8 By faith Abraham, when he was called to go out into a

place which he should after receive for an inheritance, obeyed; and he went out, not knowing whither he went.
9 By faith he sojourned in the land of promise, as in a strange country, dwelling in tabernacles with Isaac and Jacob, the heirs with him of the same promise:
10 For he looked for a city which hath foundations, whose builder and maker is God.
11 Through faith also Sara herself received strength to conceive seed, and was delivered of a child when she was past age, because she judged him faithful who had promised.
12 Therefore sprang there even of one, and him as good as dead, so many as the stars of the sky in multitude, and as the sand which is by the sea shore innumerable.
13 These all died in faith, not having received the promises, but having seen them afar off, and were persuaded of them, and embraced them, and confessed that they were strangers and pilgrims on the earth.
14 For they that say such things declare plainly that they seek a country.
15 And truly, if they had been mindful of that country from whence they came out, they might have had opportunity to have returned.
16 But now they desire a better country, that is, an heavenly: wherefore God is not ashamed to be called their God: for he hath prepared for them a city.
17 By faith Abraham, when he was tried, offered up Isaac: and he that had received the promises offered up his only begotten son,
18 Of whom it was said, That in Isaac shall thy seed be called:
19 Accounting that God was able to raise him up, even from the dead; from whence also he received him in a figure.

20 By faith Isaac blessed Jacob and Esau concerning things to come.
21 By faith Jacob, when he was a dying, blessed both the sons of Joseph; and worshipped, leaning upon the top of his staff.
22 By faith Joseph, when he died, made mention of the departing of the children of Israel; and gave commandment concerning his bones.
23 By faith Moses, when he was born, was hid three months of his parents, because they saw he was a proper child; and they were not afraid of the king's commandment.
24 By faith Moses, when he was come to years, refused to be called the son of Pharaoh's daughter;
25 Choosing rather to suffer affliction with the people of God, than to enjoy the pleasures of sin for a season;
26 Esteeming the reproach of Christ greater riches than the treasures in Egypt: for he had respect unto the recompence of the reward.
27 By faith he forsook Egypt, not fearing the wrath of the king: for he endured, as seeing him who is invisible.
28 Through faith he kept the passover, and the sprinkling of blood, lest he that destroyed the firstborn should touch them.
29 By faith they passed through the Red sea as by dry land: which the Egyptians assaying to do were drowned.
30 By faith the walls of Jericho fell down, after they were compassed about seven days.
31 By faith the harlot Rahab perished not with them that believed not, when she had received the spies with peace.
32 And what shall I more say? for the time would fail me to tell of Gedeon, and of Barak, and of Samson, and of Jephthae; of David also, and Samuel, and of the prophets:
33 Who through faith subdued kingdoms, wrought

righteousness, obtained promises, stopped the mouths of lions,

34 Quenched the violence of fire, escaped the edge of the sword, out of weakness were made strong, waxed valiant in fight, turned to flight the armies of the aliens.

35 Women received their dead raised to life again: and others were tortured, not accepting deliverance; that they might obtain a better resurrection:

36 And others had trial of cruel mockings and scourgings, yea, moreover of bonds and imprisonment:

37 They were stoned, they were sawn asunder, were tempted, were slain with the sword: they wandered about in sheepskins and goatskins; being destitute, afflicted, tormented;

38 (Of whom the world was not worthy:) they wandered in deserts, and in mountains, and in dens and caves of the earth.

39 And these all, having obtained a good report through faith, received not the promise:

40 God having provided some better thing for us, that they without us should not be made perfect.

The classic chapter in the Bible that deals with faith practically is Hebrews 11. Volumes have been written as it pertains to this chapter. Men of all ages and races have been inspired and encouraged by the great example of those who lived before us-"so great a cloud of witnesses." It is my thrill to address this chapter knowing that I can only touch the *hem of the garment.* May we study this giant pearl with the greatest of respect.

I. THE DEFINING OF FAITH. (11: 1-3)

"Now faith is." How much more can be given, in such few words, the meaning of faith than by just simply stating that "faith is"? We are destined for spiritual ruin when we live as though *faith is not*. Strong's said this about faith as it is used in this first verse: "conviction of the truth of anything, belief; in the NT of a conviction or belief respecting man's relationship to God and divine things, generally with the included idea of trust and holy fervour born of faith and joined with it." We shall build upon that definition, complementing as we do the Holy Scriptures definition of faith. "Now faith is the substance of things hoped for, the evidence of things not seen."(V.1). We could just as accurately say that "faith is actuality" or perhaps, we could say that "faith is reality." We can say this because faith is real. It is not real in the sense that it can be tested or proven in a laboratory. It is real in the sense that it is something that God can detect and recognize. He approves when one has it and does not approve when one does not have it. (V.6). As we explore this foundational word "faith," I wish to bring in other definitions as it pertains to this word:

Easton's 1897 Bible Dictionary, excerpts;

Faith is in general the persuasion of the mind that a certain statement is true (Phil. 1:27; 2 Thes. 2:13). *Its primary idea is trust. A thing is true, and therefore worthy of trust. It admits of many degrees up to full assurance of faith, in accordance with the evidence on which it rests.*

Faith is the result of teaching (Romans 10:14-17). Knowledge is an essential element in all faith, and is sometimes spoken of as an equivalent to faith (John 10:38; 1 John 2:3). Yet the two are distinguished in this respect, that faith includes in it assent, which is an act of the will in addition to the act of the understanding. *Assent to the truth is of the essence of faith, and the ultimate ground on which our assent to any revealed truth rests is the veracity (truthfulness or accuracy) of God.*

Faith in Christ secures for the believer freedom from condemnation, or justification before God; a participation in the life that is in Christ, the divine life (John 14:19; Romans 6:4-10; Ephesians 4:15-16); "peace with God" (Romans 5:1); and sanctification (Acts 26:18; Galatians 5:6; Acts 15:9).

Davis Dictionary of the Bible, excerpts;

As far as a difference exists between belief and faith, belief is assent to testimony, and faith is assent to testimony, united with trust. Faith is an active principle; it is an act both of the understanding and the will. The distinction between belief and faith is that between "believe me" and "believe on me." *In the Bible faith of belief is confidence in the absolute truthfulness of every statement which comes from God* (Mark 11:22 & Rom. 4:3-5).

Unger's Bible Dictionary, excerpts;

Viewed more particularly with reference to its intellectual aspect, *faith is properly defined as the conviction of the reality of the truths and facts which God has revealed; such conviction resting solely upon the testimony of God.*

There is an element that is intellectual; also an element, of even deeper importance, that is moral. *Faith is not simply the assent of the intellect to revealed truth; it is the practical submission of the entire man to the guidance and control of such truth,* "The devils believe and tremble." Thus in its beginning and completion faith is part of the fruit of the Spirit (Gal. 5:22).

When regarding the Biblical definition of faith, we must understand what is being stated in verse two as it applies to faith. *"For by it the elders obtained a good report."* The elders who are being referred to are all those mentioned by name and then some who were not mentioned by name who were able to please God by the exercising of their faith. They received a good report based upon the fact that they pleased God. The Jewish Christians who were struggling to maintain their faithful fidelity needed to hear the testimony of those who were mentioned in our text. Those of us who continue to live today need the same support by reading the story of how these early elders pleased God by living faithful lives.

The main reason that these people are worthy of mention in this great chapter is because they demonstrated faith and were recognized by God for doing so.

"Through faith we understand that the worlds were framed by the word of God, so that things which are seen were not made of things which do appear." (V. 3). The Hebrew mindset allowed the Jews to accept the fact that God is the creator God. This belief was inherent to the Hebrew, whereas with the Greek it was a different story. The Greek had to be convinced that God is the Creator. Most who live in our culture today will have a Greek mindset, rejecting that God created everything that exists from that which previously did not exist. As we approach these kinds of people, we need to have the understanding that we may need

to give them the apologetics having to do with God being the Creator.

It takes faith to believe that God created everything that is *from that which previously did not exist.* Creation is entirely an act of God and as you approach these people who have been taught that there is no creation by God, they must be first introduced to the Bible and then be given an opportunity to believe what the Bible teaches. That means that faith requires knowledge as Romans teaches us in chapter 10, *"So then faith cometh by hearing, and hearing by the word of God."* (Romans 10:17). This verse indicates the source of faith. Faith has as its source the precious Word of God. Biblical faith cannot be derived from any source other than the Word of God and still be Biblical faith. That is the reason that we must embrace without compromise the entire Word of God and resist those who wish to tamper with it either by *refuting it, polluting it or diluting it.*

II. THE DISPLAYING OF FAITH. (11:4-40)

This next section of study in chapter 11 is for the purpose of observing and commenting on how the Lord listed and also displayed these elders from the past who lived lives of faith. These who are listed are not listed for never having *failure* in their lives; for they did. They are listed, instead for having *faith* in their lives. Some are mentioned by name, not because they are more important, but perhaps because they are more familiar to us. The ones who are not mentioned by name are just as preferred by the Lord as those who are not, because God is no respecter of persons. He is honoring them for their faith. While doing this study, we may not consider each person listed. If we do not, that does not mean that we are attaching a lesser value on the ones not mentioned in this study. As I mentioned earlier, volumes could have and have been written on this chapter.

A. Abel: The Man Who Witnessed for God. (11:4)

Abel is very appropriately listed in "Faith's Hall of Fame." He was the very first martyr mentioned in the Scriptures. He obediently offered the sacrifice that was pleasing to God. He exercised faithful obedience to the Lord upon making his offering, whereas his brother Cain did not. In Cain's jealous rage in finding that God had respect for Abel's offering and did not have respect for his, he murdered Abel and was guilty of the first murder in the Bible. This was also the first fratricide mentioned in the Bible. (Genesis 4:1-17).

B. Enoch: The Man Who Walked With God. (11:5-6)

In Genesis 5:22, 24 we are told that Enoch walked with God. Enoch is a type of those who will not be required to go through the tribulation, but will be caught up in the rapture. One of the things that stand out from our text in Hebrews concerning Enoch is that he had the testimony of pleasing God. He pleased God because he in some manner exercised faith. The sixth verse tells us that without faith it is impossible to please God. Verse five tells us that Enoch had the testimony of pleasing God. It will be most interesting when we arrive in Heaven to find what it was that Enoch did that pleased God in this manner. We can only speculate, but I believe that he pleased God in his manner of conduct while living in a very wicked world leading up to the flood. The flood was God's judgment upon the world just as the Great Tribulation will be judgment upon the world after the rapture of the saints.

C. Noah: The Man Who Was Warned by God. (11:7)

People are exercising faith when they take the Word of God seriously. Such was the case with Noah when he was warned of God that something was going to happen that no one had ever witnessed before. He had no prior evidence upon which to build his faith. He simply trusted God at His Word. How important this is in both serving faith and in saving faith. Had Noah not heeded the warnings of God, he and his family would have been destroyed and so would the human race. We may think that it is not that important to take God seriously by not taking seriously God's Word. I often encounter people who boast of being a Christian but never take seriously the warnings that are given to us in the Bible. We learned in chapter 10:31 that *"It is a fearful thing to fall into the hands of the living God."* This statement is true whether one chooses to believe it or not. About belief and faith, Billy Sunday once said that you may not believe that there is a literal hell; you also may not believe that oranges are orange, but that does not change the fact.

Noah worked up to 120 years building an ark, I am sure with much challenging ridicule, yet he built on. That is what characterizes the work of faith. People trust God enough to do what may be neither popular nor politically correct.

D. Abraham: The Man Who *Went* For God. (11:8-19)

"By faith Abraham, when he was called to go out into a place which he should after receive for an inheritance, obeyed; and he went out, not knowing whither he went." He *"went out*, not knowing whither he went." This marked his faith. He did not need to know; he simply trusted God. Many repeated times since then there have been countless missionaries and pastors who go out not knowing where they go. They trust God as did Abraham. Abraham went to a place while sojourning in the "land of promise, as in a strange country, dwelling in tabernacles with Isaac and Jacob, the heirs with him of the same promise."

Abraham's pilgrimage was more than just an earthly one; it involved the heavenly. He looked for a "city which hath foundations, whose builder and maker is God." He also was able to enjoy the promised blessing of having the son of promise born to him and Sarah when they were beyond the age of having children. He received the benefits of the Abrahamic Covenant.

With all of the benefits and the blessings that accompany one's faith, there was also the testings that came to him when he was called to offer up *"his only begotten son, Of whom it was said, That in Isaac shall thy seed be called: Accounting that God was able to raise him up, even from the dead; from whence also he received him in a figure"* (Vv. 17-19). As we encounter the many trials that come to us as we walk in the faith, we must remember that the way we handle these trials determines our testimony. The Lord is also pleased when we trust God as we exercise our faith.

E. Jacob: The Man Who Worshiped God. (11:21)

Jacob may not have started out right, but he certainly ended right. Isaac blessed Jacob and Jacob passed this blessing on to his children and his grandchildren. David Guzik explains how faith enters into the picture when one does not start out right but later embraces faith. "By faith Isaac blessed Jacob: Isaac was really in the *flesh*, not in faith, when he first intended to bless Jacob and Esau. He wanted to bless Esau with the birthright for carnal reasons (he liked him as a more "manly" man, and he liked the wild game he brought home), instead of blessing Jacob, whom God had chosen.

Yet Isaac came to the place of faith when he discovered that he had actually blessed Jacob instead of Esau, Genesis 27:33 says *Isaac trembled exceedingly*. When *Isaac trembled exceedingly*, what was he troubled about? He was troubled because he knew that he had tried to box God in, to defeat God's plan, and that God had beaten him. He realized that he would always be defeated when he tried to resist God's will, even when he didn't like it. And he came to learn that despite his arrogance against God's will, God's will was glorious.

So, where is the faith in Isaac's blessing? After Isaac's attempt to thwart the will of God had been destroyed, when he said of Jacob, *and he shall be blessed* (Genesis 27:33). He knew that God had defeated his puny attempt to box God in, and he responded in the faith that says, "O.K. God, You win. Let Isaac be blessed with the birthright, and let Esau be blessed after him in his own way." (Guzik)

F. Moses: The Man Who Withstood for God. (11:23-29)

Moses was a man who could have chosen temporal blessings and then missed out on the eternal. He could have enjoyed the benefits and the blessings of being called the son of Pharaoh's daughter. He also chose "rather to suffer affliction with the people of God, than to enjoy the pleasures of sin for a season." He put aside in his heart the treasures of Egypt and forsook Egypt, not fearing the king. The Word of God tells us in verse 27 that he "endured, as seeing him who is invisible." For one to endure as seeing him who is invisible, he must be looking through the eye of faith.

It certainly takes faith to continue and endure in the Lord's work when there seems to be no clear sign or signal to usher one on. This is the reason that we should learn the importance of following and trusting the Lord in all that we do. We should trust Him when there is no visible sign. We like to see "fleece," but we may just have to see Him who is invisible, instead. This is the way that we develop our faith; by simply acting upon the Word.

Moses also partook of the Passover, and "the sprinkling of the blood, lest he that destroyed the firstborn should touch them" (V. 28). With the Egyptian army in pursuit, Moses led the nation of Israel, to the Egyptian's destruction. All of these events were listed in "Faith's Hall of Fame" to show forth the faith of these ancient elders, thus receiving a good report.

G. The Many Others: Those Others Who Witnessed For

God. (11:30-40)

These others who are listed either by name or deed only make up a small list of who is to be included in "Faith's Hall of Fame." The writer of Hebrews said "the time would fail me to tell of all who were faithful to the Lord. There are those today that would like for you to believe that there is such a small number who are faithful to the Lord's work. This is simply not so. God is keeping His record and these that He has referred to should serve the purpose of causing us who are in the faith to "Look Unto Jesus."

Chapter Twenty-three

LOOKING UNTO JESUS

Text: Hebrews 12:1-17

1 Wherefore seeing we also are compassed about with so great a cloud of witnesses, let us lay aside every weight, and the sin which doth so easily beset us, and let us run with patience the race that is set before us,
2 Looking unto Jesus the author and finisher of our faith; who for the joy that was set before him endured the cross, despising the shame, and is set down at the right hand of the throne of God.
3 For consider him that endured such contradiction of sinners against himself, lest ye be wearied and faint in your minds.
4 Ye have not yet resisted unto blood, striving against sin.
5 And ye have forgotten the exhortation which speaketh unto you as unto children, My son, despise not thou the chastening of the Lord, nor faint when thou art rebuked of him:
6 For whom the Lord loveth he chasteneth, and scourgeth every son whom he receiveth.
7 If ye endure chastening, God dealeth with you as with sons; for what son is he whom the father chasteneth not?
8 But if ye be without chastisement, whereof all are partakers, then are ye bastards, and not sons.

9 Furthermore we have had fathers of our flesh which corrected us, and we gave them reverence: shall we not much rather be in subjection unto the Father of spirits, and live?

10 For they verily for a few days chastened us after their own pleasure; but he for our profit, that we might be partakers of his holiness.

11 Now no chastening for the present seemeth to be joyous, but grievous: nevertheless afterward it yieldeth the peaceable fruit of righteousness unto them which are exercised thereby.

12 Wherefore lift up the hands which hang down, and the feeble knees;

13 And make straight paths for your feet, lest that which is lame be turned out of the way; but let it rather be healed.

14 Follow peace with all men, and holiness, without which no man shall see the Lord:

15 Looking diligently lest any man fail of the grace of God; lest any root of bitterness springing up trouble you, and thereby many be defiled;

16 Lest there be any fornicator, or profane person, as Esau, who for one morsel of meat sold his birthright.

17 For ye know how that afterward, when he would have inherited the blessing, he was rejected: for he found no place of repentance, though he sought it carefully with tears.

This chapter is introduced with the transitional word, "Wherefore" which strongly connects back to the eleventh chapter which is known for its treatment of the subject of faith. In hermeneutics, one may recognize a principle that is called, "The full mention principle" being employed in chapter eleven as the subject of faith is being considered. The "full mention principle" states that when everything is fully given in a chapter or passage as it pertains to a particular truth, where nothing else need be said to make it more complete than that which has been already stated, then "The full mention principle" has been exercised. Another way of saying it is: "God declares his full mind upon any subject vital to our spiritual life."

Such is the case with the eleventh chapter of Hebrews. In this chapter both the definition and the application of faith are given. Beginning in chapter twelve, we find ourselves entering into a section of Hebrews that gives great practical insight as to the way that the believer is to conduct himself and how he is to be encouraged in his own spiritual journey. This twelfth chapter likens the believer's journey to a race. There is the encouragement to remove anything that would impede or hinder the race. The analogy is being made to a conditioned runner who is outfitting himself to win the race while at the same time keeping his eyes glued on the goal.

While running our spiritual races, we should make sure that we avoid the awful pitfall of taking our eyes off of Jesus. We will discover that the "sin which doth so easily beset us" is taking our eyes off of Jesus. We will learn some of the ways that God helps us to keep our eyes focused upon Him and also what happens when we do take our eyes off of Him.

I. THE WAY HIS SAINTS ARE INSTRUCTED.
(12:1-3)

The first word of this chapter is the word "wherefore" as we have already noted. This word is a transitional word that connects by example the previous chapter to this chapter, thereby giving us a strong reason to run our race well. All those who are mentioned in chapter eleven are there for our examples to encourage us to be faithful by their faithfulness. They have lived and then died, save the one who was translated that he should not see death, and they all left behind a great example of how each of us should proceed in the faith.

A. By The Cloud That Surrounds Us. (12:1a)

The great cloud is a metaphor that describes the great number of people that made up the faithful believers. These who made up the cloud of witnesses were great in that they pleased God. We have learned from our previous study that it is impossible to please God without faith. These patriots of the faith certainly pleased God. If we constantly examined and studied their lives we would have much by way of example to encourage us. When we are given instructions to go forth in the Lord, we may observe Abraham as an example, who left his land and people and trusted God as he journeyed. While he was in the land of promise, there were times that his faith suffered a lapse, yet God graciously helped him return to where he needed to be.

As we observe this cloud of witnesses to be our example, we may also observe it to be our challenge; a good example should also challenge. The writer of Hebrews, under the inspiration of the Spirit, gave us an encouraging challenge as he gave us these good examples. They were given to us as witnesses. They all witnessed their faith in a very admirable way, even those who were "sawn asunder" (Hebrews 11:37). Those who make up "so great a cloud of witnesses" are those whom the Lord especially honored. He thought them worthy to be put on display as examples because of the faithful exercising of their faith. The expression "great cloud of witnesses" indicates a most worthy number of witnesses; it represents a far reaching number. When one observes a great cloud, he does so recognizing that it covers a great span of space. The space that has been covered by those mentioned in chapter eleven and referred back to in chapter twelve covers many years. This shows that the Lord has had, and still has, those who faithfully worship Him across a great period of time.

B. By the Command That Strengthens Us. (12:1b)

We notice the expression that is given in verse one, "let us lay aside every weight, and the sin which doth so easily beset us." We recognize that this command is given in two parts with the second command saying, "let us run with patience the race that is set before us." This command involves *removing* and *running.* The metaphor is given of a runner in a race. Those who were to run in the race did not always free themselves from those things which could have hindered their race. Such things were capable of impeding or hindering their race to the extent that they could not claim the prize for finishing well.

In a practical sense, anything that was capable of weighing down or slowing down the runner was to be avoided. This meant that the runner was to carefully examine himself and determine just what it was that could hinder him from running his very best.

Spiritually, we are all challenged as the runner to remove anything that would be a hindrance to running the "race of faith." It certainly should be obvious that we should "lay aside every weight." These weights would be any sin that would hinder one's race of faith. It could be habits that are sinful, it could be the neglecting of Bible time, not praying, not being faithful to church, lying, stealing, watching anything or listening to anything that would be defiling and anything that violates the Scriptures.

Then there is "the sin which doth so easily beset us." I have read much commentary on just what that besetting sin may be, but I believe that a careful study of our context tells us exactly what that sin is. It is the sin of *taking our eyes off of Jesus.* One of the easiest sins for the believer to commit is when he takes his eyes off of Jesus.

C. By the Challenge That Sends Us. (12:2-3)

What greater challenge do we have than the challenge to look "unto Jesus the author and finisher of our faith." This section considers within its context the importance of keeping one's eyes on Jesus. It also shows the way that the Lord chastens one to help that one keep his eyes upon the Lord. The Lord Jesus Christ is our example, and in our "faith race" He is our Goal. In this section of study, we will also be observing some of the awful consequences of taking our eyes off of Him. As we are looking at Jesus, it should be comforting just in knowing that He is the Author and the Originator of our faith. It all rests upon Him. He is the one who "endured the cross, despising the shame, and is set down at the right hand of the throne of God." The same power that allowed Him to conquer the cross is available to us as we exercise our practical faith. We only get in trouble spiritually when we take our eyes off of Jesus.

Can you imagine what it is like to be running in a race knowing that there are those in the grandstands who had run previously? They are there not only to *observe* you as you run, but they are there also to *inspire* you as you run. Then the greatest inspiration of all is in seeing the One who outran them all and is now standing at the "finish line" encouraging you to faithfully run. We see Him through the eye of faith. That is exactly what is taking place as we read and study our text. There is One who ran before us for our example. This tells us that Christ is not only a witness, but a *better* witness.

II. THE WAY THE SAINTS ARE CORRECTED. (12:4-11) (through chastening)

Even as a father corrects his children, so also does the Heavenly Father correct us. These next several verses give us tremendous insight as to the purpose of chastisement.

A. The Receivers of Chastening. (12:4-8)

According to our text, one should never despise the chastening that comes from the Lord. The chastening should also not cause one to faint or be discouraged, knowing that it comes from the Lord and is exercised towards those whom He loves and those who are His dear children. These verses show us that he deals with His children in the faith as a father would deal with his own children. A good father uses discipline and correction in the form of chastisement to correct his children because he loves them. Can anything less than that be said about our Heavenly Father chastening His own children whom He loves?

The important thing that should be observed from our text is that when a person does not receive any chastisement, then that person is not a son. That should be a very scary thought for the "pretender." Though you may think that all is well and at the same time live in violation of the Scriptures and see no evidence of chastisement, you best make your calling and election sure. The Scriptures are clear on this; those who do not receive correction are not His children (V. 8).

B. The Reason for Chastening. (12:9-10)

The Lord chastens us for our profit. This is a word that is used to impress upon the one that is being chastening that there are benefits to being corrected. The Lord wisely applies the chastening to bring us to a higher level of spiritual maturity. The Lord knows just what is needed. Whether this chastening is in the form of a rod or in the form of the Word spoken, He is doing it for our profit. When we are non-responsive to the Word spoken, then He finds it necessary to apply the "rod of correction." Chastening involves a *parental* interest in His children. He chastens us with better consistency than an earthly father could ever chasten his own children. We mean well as earthly parents, but like the children we are chastening, we always come up short. But He does not, for He is always consistent. He knows when and He knows just how much chastening to apply.

The Lord also has a *providential* interest in His children. He always knows where we are and He knows what is going on with us, wherever we might be. He knows what we are doing before we even do it. We might also say that He has a *personal* interest in what we are doing. This is so because we are His own and His beloved. He not only knows us, but He is jealous of His own name. We who are members of His family reflect who He is by the manner of our living. We should very carefully carry the family name. We should do all that we can to live our lives out of respect of who He is and who we are because of Him.

C. The Results of Chastening. (12:11)

This verse indicates that chastening, though it may not be joyous but grievous, yields *the peaceful fruit of righteousness.* The Lord chastens us so that we will be more like Him. To be more like Him, we must fix our eyes upon Him. By fixing our eyes upon Him and being chastened when we do not, we will develop more *Christ-likeness* and gain the peaceful fruit of righteousness. Romans 8:28 and 29 tells us the extent of His purpose in chastening us. *"And we know that all things work together for good to them that love God, to them who are the called according to his purpose. For whom he did foreknow, he also did predestinate to be conformed to the image of his Son, that he might be the firstborn among many brethren."* When it is necessary, He applies chastening to bring about the conforming that is necessary for our spiritual growth and maturity. He knows just how much correction that we need and how much chastening to apply to bring forth *the peaceful fruit of righteousness.*

III. THE WAY THE SAINTS ARE PROTECTED. (12:12-17) (By keeping our eyes upon Jesus).

In verse two, we are instructed to look unto Jesus. In verse three we are told to *consider him*. This means that we are not to look at Him with a passing glance, but to fix our eyes upon Him. In 1 John 1:1 the verse reads: *"That which was from the beginning, which we have heard, which we have seen with our eyes, which we have looked upon, and our hands have handled, of the Word of life:"* The phrase, "which we have looked upon" means to look intently as you would be watching a public show. The word *theater* comes from the same word *looked*. Notice Strong's definition of this word *looked*. To behold, look upon, view attentively, contemplate (often used of public shows). In the same way, we should consider Him. We should fix our eyes upon Him to gain all that we can about Him. We do this by looking at Him through God's Word. Unless you fix your eyes upon the Word of God, you cannot see Him. He is invisible except through the eye of faith.

We are told to look at Him and to consider Him; we are also told to look diligently at Him. When we look diligently, we look carefully and intently. Again, this is not just a casual glance, it is looking with purpose. The way that we *focus* on Him will determine how we become like Him. Now we shall look at what happens when one takes his eyes off of Jesus.

A. Taking Your Eyes Off of Jesus Will Affect Your Journey. (12:12-14a).

The runner is encouraged to go on while facing spiritual fatigue. The believer's race is not just a 100 yard dash; it is a marathon. Just like the Boston Marathon's *Heartbreak Hill*, there are also some hills which seem impossible in the Christian race. Yet, we must run and *make straight paths for our feet* and *follow peace with all men and holiness*. When we take our eyes off of Jesus, it will affect the believer's journey. The Christian race is to be run with courage and determination. There is enough grace for the entire course. To fail of the grace of God is to fail to appropriate all of the grace that God has for the journey. I liken the grace of God to being a coupon book that the runner can clip while running his race. I heard the imaginary story once of how someone died and went to heaven. Upon his arrival, he was given a tour that led him to a large room with many shelves. The person asked, "What is all the stuff in this room and why are some of the shelves empty?" He was answered in this way, "The shelves are where those things that you had need of while you were living were stored. Every time that you asked the Lord to provide you with something, you clipped a coupon of faith from this coupon book." Then the person who had just arrived in Heaven asked, "Why so much stuff still on the shelves and why are there so many coupons still in the book?" To which he received this answer: "The articles still on the shelves are what you could have had if you had clipped all of the coupons."

This is an illustration that shows that God has all of the grace that we need for the journey. When we take our eyes off of him and began focusing on the problems, we forget that we have a "Problem Solver." He certainly has all that we need to continue the journey and to finish the journey.

B. Taking Your Eyes Off of Jesus Will Affect Your Joy. (12:14b.)

This part of the verse indicates how it is for a root of bitterness to spring up in one's life and then affect others. It is common to find bitterness both in the church and also in people in general. Much of the bitterness that I have experienced has affected not only me but also affects others. An experiment was once conducted in a sociology class where the professor staged a situation that involved a school class that was enjoying a spirit of frivolity because of something that the professor had said to them. While they were experiencing much joy and jubilation, a student came into the room that had been prepared to come in to show the emotion of anger and pretend also to have a foul mood. It was not long after his arrival that the entire class was taking on this same personality. The professor then told the class that everything had been staged and that the entire class was negatively affected by the one student. They saw how one person could affect them all.

This shows how one person can allow a root of bitterness to spring up within himself and it then begins to take its toll on many. Churches are especially vulnerable to this happening. One disgruntled member suffering from bitterness can cause hurt to come to the entire body. While running in the race, one's eyes should be fixed straight ahead and not looking on to the surrounding problems. One's problems will cause bitterness, and bitterness will hinder the journey and may even stop the race.

C. Taking Your Eyes Off of Jesus Will Affect Your Judgment. (12:15-17)

Just as Esau took his eyes off of the covenant promises of God, so does the believer when he takes his eyes off of Jesus. It is a terrible event in one's life when he gets to the place that he no longer gives attention to the Word of God and begins to do that which is right in his own eyes. When the fear of God is gone, it is a fearful thing to fall in the hands of an angry God. During this time, those who have taken their eyes off of Jesus, will make judgments or decisions that will hurt them for the remainder of their lives. If during this time no chastening or correction comes, then that is a clear indication that the person is not even saved. It is not a light sin, the sin of taking one's eyes off of Jesus. It is a very serious sin and as our text has already indicated, it is the sin that "doth so easily beset us". We must strive to stay in the race, because our adversary the Devil would love to destroy us by knocking us out of the race.

Chapter Twenty-four

THE TWO MOUNTAINS

Text: Hebrews 12:18-29

18 For ye are not come unto the mount that might be touched, and that burned with fire, nor unto blackness, and darkness, and tempest,
19 And the sound of a trumpet, and the voice of words; which voice they that heard intreated that the word should not be spoken to them any more:
20 (For they could not endure that which was commanded, And if so much as a beast touch the mountain, it shall be stoned, or thrust through with a dart:
21 And so terrible was the sight, that Moses said, I exceedingly fear and quake:)
22 But ye are come unto mount Sion, and unto the city of the living God, the heavenly Jerusalem, and to an innumerable company of angels,
23 To the general assembly and church of the firstborn, which are written in heaven, and to God the Judge of all, and to the spirits of just men made perfect,
24 And to Jesus the mediator of the new covenant, and to the blood of sprinkling, that speaketh better things than that of Abel.
25 See that ye refuse not him that speaketh. For if they escaped not who refused him that spake on earth, much more

shall not we escape, if we turn away from him that speaketh from heaven:
26 Whose voice then shook the earth: but now he hath promised, saying, Yet once more I shake not the earth only, but also heaven.
27 And this word, Yet once more, signifieth the removing of those things that are shaken, as of things that are made, that those things which cannot be shaken may remain.
28 Wherefore we receiving a kingdom which cannot be moved, let us have grace, whereby we may serve God acceptably with reverence and godly fear:
29 For our God is a consuming fire.

    As we look at these two mountains we are reminded of the contrasting differences of law and grace. What took place at these two mountains serves as a summary statement of the way law and grace operates in its respective dispensation. The book of Hebrews was placed in the canon of Scriptures to show God's way of communicating His riches that we now enjoy in the economy of Grace as opposed to the legal economy that first existed. As the book of Hebrews is being concluded, we are strongly reminded in this great chapter of two things that is required of the Lord. We are required to keep our eyes fixed upon the Lord Jesus Christ and we are to carefully listen to what He has to say. In both instances, it is required that we do this by receiving the Word of God. There is nothing mystical about seeing and hearing the Lord.

    By this, we do not look for dreams and visions, nor do we look for voices. There are so many who get caught up in their charismatic confusion who are continually looking for, or listening for, something new. With all due respect, we have all that we need in God's sacred, precious Word. It is from the Word of God that I am able to see Him. It is His Word that allows me to hear what He has to say. The warning to listen to Him was given in Hebrews chapter 1, beginning with the very first verse: *"God, who at sundry times and in divers manners spake in time past unto the fathers by the prophets, Hath in these last days spoken unto us by his Son, whom he hath appointed heir of all things, by whom also he made the worlds; Who being the brightness of his glory, and the express image of his person, and upholding all things by the word of his power, when he had by himself purged our sins, sat down on the right hand of the Majesty on high;"* (Hebrews 1:1-3).

In Barnes' notes, when he was giving an analysis of the first chapter of Hebrews, he showed that the book was written to discourage a drift back into Judaism. Notice the way that he worded the purpose of Hebrews chapter one: "The main object of the epistle is to commend the Christian religion to those who were addressed in it, in such a way as to prevent defection from it. This is done, principally, by showing its superiority to the Mosaic system. The great danger of Christians in Palestine was of relapsing into the Jewish system. The imposing nature of its rites; the public sentiment in its favour; the fact of its antiquity, and its undisputed Divine origin, would all tend to that. To counteract this, the writer of this epistle shows that the gospel had higher claims on their attention, and that, if that were rejected, ruin was inevitable. In doing this, he begins, in this chapter, by showing the superiority of the Author of Christianity to prophets, and to the angels; that is, that he had a rank that entitled him to the profoundest regard. The drift of this chapter, therefore, is to show the dignity and exalted nature of the Author of the Christian system—the Son of God." (Barnes' Notes on the New Testament).

What Barnes said clearly demonstrates the intent of the writer under the inspiration of the Holy Spirit to give us Hebrews as he did. It is for this purpose that the Lord concludes the study of Hebrews with such a graphic display of the contrasting nature of the old system with the new. Thus, we will examine these two mountains to further emphasize this difference.

I. THE MOUNT THAT SPEAKS OF TERROR.

(12:18-21)

"For ye are not come unto the mount that might be touched, and that burned with fire, nor unto blackness, and darkness, and tempest." So begins the verse that describes the terror of this mountain. The phrase, "that might be touched" speaks of this mountain as being an actual mountain that was chosen to convey the spirit of the dispensation of law. Though it was a mountain that could be touched as its realness is being described, it could not be touched as the law required. To touch it by human or beast would mean certain death. Again, quoting from Barnes we see how clearly he understood this truth: "The mount that might be touched. Mount Sinai. The meaning here is, that that mountain was palpable, material, touchable-in

contradistinction from the Mount Zion to which the church had now come, which is above the reach of the external senses, Hebrews 12:22. The apostle does not mean that it was permitted to the Israelites to touch Mount Sinai-for this was strictly forbidden, Exodus 19:12; but he evidently alludes to that prohibition, and means to say that a command forbidding them to "touch" the mountain, implied that it was a material or palpable object. The sense of the passage is, that every circumstance that occurred there was fitted to fill the soul with terror. Everything accompanying the giving of the law, the setting of bounds around the mountain which they might not pass, and the darkness and tempest on the mountain itself, was adapted to overawe the soul. The phrase, "the touchable mountain"-if such a phrase is proper—would express the meaning of the apostle here. The "Mount Zion" to which the church now has come, is of a different character. It is not thus visible and palpable. It is not enveloped in smoke and flame, and the thunders of the Almighty do not roll and re-echo among its lofty peaks as at Horeb; yet it presents stronger motives to perseverance in the service of God." (*Barnes' Notes on the New Testament*).

A. Notice the Awful Sight of It. (12:18)

When viewing the awfulness of this mountain, we do not view it as being unnecessary in its awfulness. The terror of this mountain is not an evil terror, but a necessary terror that describes the strength of the law. The law was not evil but good, but it was absolutely demanding and because of man's inability to keep it, it may have appeared to be evil. To illustrate this, when I was disobedient to my parents' instructions, my father had a strap that I feared and I also feared him when he held it and put it on me. When he was correcting me this way, he for that moment of time appeared as an awful sight, but he certainly was not evil – he just appeared that way. The strap that my Dad held in his hand pictured his law. When he applied it, it was because I had broken his law.

The ancient commentator Gill wrote of the terror of the sight and that which was associated by it and meant by it: "and that burned with fire; as Mount Sinai did, Exodus 19:18. Deuteronomy 4:11 which set forth the majesty of God, when upon it, at whose feet went forth burning coals; and also the wrath of God, as an avenging lawgiver and Judge; and the terror of that law, which strikes the minds of the transgressors of it with an expectation of fiery indignation; and so points out the end of such transgressors, which is, to be burnt: nor unto blackness and darkness; which covered the mount when God was upon it, Exodus19:16, and which also may express the majesty of God, round about whom are clouds and darkness; and also the horror of the legal dispensation, and the obscurity of it; little being known by the Jews of the spirituality of the law, of the strict justice of God, and of the righteousness which the law requires, and of the end and use of it; and especially of the way of salvation by Christ; and so dark were they at last, as to prefer their own traditions before this law: it is added, and tempest; there being thunderings and lightnings, which were very terrible, Exodus19:16 and though there is no express mention made of a tempest by Moses, yet Josephus speaks not only of very terrible thunderings and lightnings, but of violent storms of wind, which produced exceeding great rains: and the Septuagint on Deuteronomy 4:11 use the same words as the apostle does here, "blackness, darkness, and tempest". This also may denote the majesty of God, who was then present; the terror of that dispensation; the horrible curses of the law; and the great confusion and disquietude raised by it in the conscience of a sinner."

As this ancient writer carefully understood, there is a pressure and a fear which is in association with the law, but in a very wonderful way that pressure now brings about the necessary conviction upon the soul of the poor lost sinner that is required for his conversion. It is only with such conviction that the sinner can truly recognize the majesty of God. The law is now a schoolmaster that brings us to Christ Jesus.

B. Notice the Awful Sound of It. (12:19)

"And the sound of a trumpet, and the voice of words; which voice they that heard intreated that the word should not be spoken to them any more:" The sound that was described coming from the trumpet was a sound that evoked terror upon the poor soul who heard it. The sound that was heard would increase in intensity like a siren warning the person that would carelessly approach the mountain that it was not to be done. One's beast was not even permitted to touch this mountain at Sinai. There was a fear that became more intense as the Voice spoke invisibly from the midst of the described scene. Those there were so afraid of the voice of deity that they began to prefer the voice of Moses rather than the voice of the Lord as the following scriptures indicate: *"And all the people saw the thunderings, and the lightnings, and the noise of the trumpet, and the mountain smoking: and when the people saw it, they removed, and stood afar off. And they said unto Moses, Speak thou with us, and we will hear: but let not God speak with us, lest we die. And Moses said unto the people, Fear not: for God is come to prove you, and that his fear may be before your faces, that*

ye sin not. And the people stood afar off, and Moses drew near unto the thick darkness where God was." (Ex 20:18-21)

C. Notice the Awful Strength of It. (12:20-21)

The descriptive narrative of this section shows the strength of God's anger in respect to the broken law. His strength is also demonstrated by the activities that were taking place at Mount Sinai. For the law to be valid it had to be backed up by strength that is greater than itself. God, who is the Giver of the law, is also the Enforcer of the law. It was for this reason that Moses admitted fear in Deuteronomy 9:19 when he came down from the mount and broke the Decalogue, or the two tablets that comprised the Ten Commandments. *"For I was afraid of the anger and hot displeasure, wherewith the LORD was wroth against you to destroy you"* (Deuteronomy 9:19a).

Moses' fear was based upon a reverential respect and awe that He had for God. We see the contrasting differences of these two mountains and we recognize that within the historical context of why we are shown these two mountains is to understand that God wanted to move the converted Hebrews away from that which they were converted. He wanted to draw their affections to the new economy of which they were now a part. This does not mean that the old economy was to be despised for its failure to serve a purpose, for it did serve a noble purpose in showing how unable the human family was in keeping the law. It not only is hard, it is impossible for mankind to keep the law. The dispensation of law with all of its requirements only proved this to be so.

Yet the demands of God had to be met and there was only One who was capable of such. That was our better

Priest— the Lord Jesus Christ. He, as the Scriptures have already proven, kept the law as demanded by God. With the law being kept, there was no more necessity for one to keep it and for this reason the contrasting differences of the law was shown with no one but Christ being of strength to keep and conquer the law. The first mount is referred to as being unapproachable and the arrow of direction is now pointed to a new mount that can be approached and enjoyed by the redeemed; this is the mount that speaks of triumph.

II. THE MOUNT THAT SPEAKS OF TRIUMPH. (12:22-24)

Verse 22 opens with such wonderful encouragement. Several new things are mentioned that characterizes the new economy. This new economy is symbolized by the mention of Mount Sion. Though Mount Sion is the place where the city of Jerusalem is built, it tells not in this instance of an earthly city, but of a heavenly city – a New Jerusalem. The New Jerusalem is being identified by the language that is being used. Notice how this is indicated in verses 22-24: *"But ye are come unto mount Sion, and unto the city of the living God, the heavenly Jerusalem, and to an innumerable company of angels, To the general assembly and church of the firstborn, which are written in heaven, and to God the Judge of all, and to the spirits of just men made perfect, And to Jesus the mediator of the new covenant, and to the blood of sprinkling, that speaketh better things than that of Abel."* (Hebrews 12:22-24)

A. Notice The Wonder of the Place of Triumph. (12:22-23)

The first notable mention of this city is that it is the city of the Living God. The law and the previous economy are so closely connected to death. The priest in the earlier system had to die. His time on earth and time to serve was for only an abbreviated time. Yet in contrast to the earthly priest and the system that he was a part of, this new economy was marked by the city of the Living God. Also populating this city is an innumerable company of angels. There is absolutely no way that the human mind can comprehend such truth that involves this better and new economy of Grace. In our pictures and also in our imagination, we may plug in a few angels, relatively speaking, but this verse tells us that the number of angels cannot even be numbered. Certainly in heaven we will have such knowledge, but in human terms I am thinking that what is meant by this statement is that a person could not live long enough to number the angels. This would be like someone counting one dollar bill at a time while counting up the national debt. So much is owed that a person could not count that many dollar bills in a lifetime.

Also mentioned in this New Jerusalem is the general assembly and church of the firstborn. It is my belief that this is a reference to all of those who have been assembled out of the churches that make up the Bride of Christ. Whereas on earth there are many churches or local assemblies, in Heaven they are all molded into one. Included in this verse is a reference to the spirits of just men made perfect. This may refer to all of the redeemed who were not members of the church, including the Old Testament saints as well. I will not comment much on this section, because I am sure that I have much to learn and may even stand to be corrected. Even as I study and write this commentary, I am doing it as a student who still has much to learn. The primary purpose of a study like this for me is to place myself under a personal discipline of study causing me to give more attention to the Scriptures than I normally would. I have learned that "Reading makes a learned man and writing makes an exact man." To write something in regards to truth places a heavy responsibility upon the writer to be exact. For this reason, I felt it necessary to remind the reader that there is so much yet to be learned by this writer and if you see mistakes in my interpretation, I certainly will not be surprised.

B. Notice the Wonderfulness of the Person of Triumph.

(12:24)

Barnes noted how much better this new economy is by Jesus being the crowning Excellence of the redeems' affection. "And to Jesus the mediator of the new covenant. This was the crowning excellence of the new dispensation, in contradistinction from the old. They had been made acquainted with the true Messiah; they were united to him by faith; they had been sprinkled with his blood. Hebrews 7:22, and Hebrews 8:6. The highest consideration which can be urged to induce any one to persevere in a life of piety is the fact that the Son of God has come into the world and died to save sinners." (Barnes' Notes on the New Testament)

The Lord Jesus Christ is what makes this new economy so wonderful and so possible. Everything that had been written in Hebrews was written to establish this fact. All the shadows of the Old Testament were only a prelude to the splendor that is found in the Christ of the New Testament. A new covenant was established to guarantee this to be so.

Everything that this covenant says and defines can be counted as being true. For God said it!

III. THE MOUNT THAT ALSO SPEAKS OF TRUTH.

(12:25-28)

Lest we forget that the new economy of God still retains God's holy hatred of sin, we are reminded that we must not refuse Him that speaketh. Though the new economy is lacking the burning with fire, the blackness, the darkness and the tempest, it does still have God's same attitude towards sin. With the completed Canon of Truth, we have the Voice of Him that speaketh. We are to listen to what He says and if we refuse to listen, there will be sure judgment. For the unbeliever, there will be an eternal judgment for refusing to hear. There will also be an awful tribulation that will bring about a shaking like creation has never before seen. The Lord will shake both the earth and the heaven. This indicates how the Lord will forever purge His creation of its sin to His own satisfaction.

A. The Truth Speaks of His Power. (12:25-26)

When thinking of power as it pertains to the Lord God Almighty, we immediately must recognize that it pertains to power in every sense of the word. We know that God has all power as it pertains to government and order. Structurally, within the chain of command, He is always at the head. He is the Head of all government and principality. He also is the Source of all power as it pertains to creation. By Him all things consist. He is the nuclear energy for all existing matter. This power is found and comes forth from His Word. When God said, "Let there be Light," there was light. When God spoke before, it shook the earth; and, He warns that when He speaks again, it will shake the heaven also.

B. The Truth Speaks of His Permanence. (12:27-28)

The Lord will totally tear away the shroud of religion and also remove the governments that oppose Him when He brings tribulation and judgment upon the earth. He will shake the pretenses which make up our worldly system and bring total destruction causing all opposing empires to crumble, but those who make up the family of the redeemed will survive the shaking. Just as verse 28 tells us, we will receive a kingdom that cannot be moved. With this being so, we should serve God acceptably with reverence and godly fear.

C. The Truth Speaks of His Purging. (12:29)

Fire is a tool that is used for purging and purifying. For

the unbeliever it will burn in a consuming manner, but for the believer the fire will burn in a purifying manner. Job knew the meaning of this truth when he said that he will come forth as gold. This last verse should be seriously considered by the saved and the lost alike. The lost should be warned to hear the Voice of mercy while there is yet hope. The saved should be warned to hear the Voice of the Lord and also to keep their eyes upon the Lord. Barnes seem to understand the meaning of this verse as we look at his comments: "For our God is a consuming fire. This is a further reason why we should serve God with profound reverence and unwavering fidelity. The quotation is made from Deuteronomy 4:24: "For the Lord thy God is a consuming fire, even a jealous God." The object of the apostle here seems to be, to show that there was the same reason for fearing the displeasure of God under the new dispensation which there was under the old. It was the same God who was served. There had been no change in his attributes, or in the principles of his government. He was no more the friend of sin now than he was then; and the same perfections of his nature which would then lead him to punish transgression would also lead him to do it now. His anger was really as terrible, and as much to be dreaded, as it was at Mount Sinai; and the destruction which he would inflict on his foes would be as terrible now as it was then. The fearfulness with which he would come forth to destroy the wicked might be compared to a fire that consumed all before it. Mark 9:44-46. The image here is a most fearful one, and is in accordance with all the representations of God in the Bible, and with all that we see in the Divine dealings with wicked men, that punishment, as inflicted by him, is awful and overwhelming. So it was on the old world; on the cities of the plain; on the hosts of Sennacherib; and on Jerusalem;-and so it has been in the calamities of pestilence, war, flood, and famine, with which God has visited guilty men. By all these tender and solemn considerations, therefore, the apostle urges the friends of God to perseverance and fidelity in his service. His goodness and mercy; the gift of a Saviour to redeem us; the revelation of a glorious world; the assurance that all may soon be united in fellowship with the angels and the redeemed; the certainty that the kingdom of the Saviour is established on a permanent basis, and the apprehension of the dreadful wrath of God against the guilty, all should lead us to persevere in the duties of our Christian calling, and to avoid those things which would place in jeopardy the eternal interests of our souls." (*Barnes' Notes on the New Testament*)

Chapter Twenty-five

A FINAL CHALLENGE TO HOLY LIVING

Text: Hebrews 13

1 Let brotherly love continue.
2 Be not forgetful to entertain strangers: for thereby some have entertained angels unawares.
3 Remember them that are in bonds, as bound with them; and them which suffer adversity, as being yourselves also in the body.
4 Marriage is honourable in all, and the bed undefiled: but whoremongers and adulterers God will judge.
5 Let your conversation be without covetousness; and be content with such things as ye have: for he hath said, I will never leave thee, nor forsake thee.
6 So that we may boldly say, The Lord is my helper, and I will not fear what man shall do unto me.
7 Remember them which have the rule over you, who have spoken unto you the word of God: whose faith follow, considering the end of their conversation.
8 Jesus Christ the same yesterday, and to day, and for ever.
9 Be not carried about with divers and strange doctrines. For it is a good thing that the heart be established with grace; not with meats, which have not profited them that have been occupied therein.
10 We have an altar, whereof they have no right to eat which

serve the tabernacle.

11 For the bodies of those beasts, whose blood is brought into the sanctuary by the high priest for sin, are burned without the camp.

12 Wherefore Jesus also, that he might sanctify the people with his own blood, suffered without the gate.

13 Let us go forth therefore unto him without the camp, bearing his reproach.

14 For here have we no continuing city, but we seek one to come.

15 By him therefore let us offer the sacrifice of praise to God continually, that is, the fruit of our lips giving thanks to his name.

16 But to do good and to communicate forget not: for with such sacrifices God is well pleased.

17 Obey them that have the rule over you, and submit yourselves: for they watch for your souls, as they that must give account, that they may do it with joy, and not with grief: for that is unprofitable for you.

18 Pray for us: for we trust we have a good conscience, in all things willing to live honestly.

19 But I beseech you the rather to do this, that I may be restored to you the sooner.

20 Now the God of peace, that brought again from the dead our Lord Jesus, that great shepherd of the sheep, through the blood of the everlasting covenant,

21 Make you perfect in every good work to do his will, working in you that which is wellpleasing in his sight, through Jesus Christ; to whom be glory for ever and ever. Amen.

22 And I beseech you, brethren, suffer the word of exhortation: for I have written a letter unto you in few

words.
23 Know ye that our brother Timothy is set at liberty; with whom, if he come shortly, I will see you.
24 Salute all them that have the rule over you, and all the saints. They of Italy salute you.
25 Grace be with you all. Amen.

The world," said Alexander Malaren, "takes its notion of God most of all from those who say they belong to God's family. They read us a great deal more than they read the Bible. They see us; they only hear about Jesus Christ." This statement is a reason that chapter 13 is given to us in the manner that it is. Most of Hebrews is given for the purpose of doctrine with the last two chapters emphasizing the duty of the believer in his practical existence. It certainly is not enough to only know the truth without obeying the truth. Like a laser beam of truth, this last chapter is beaming with exhortation challenging us to let our light so shine. Weeks of study would produce a great benefit to the student who would outline and examine all of the instructions that are given in this thirteenth chapter. I will group this final challenge in three parts as I give an exposition of these last words of the book of Hebrews.

I. THE IMPORTANCE OF MAINTAINING ONE'S PERSONAL CONDUCT. (13:1-6)

There are a number of different areas mentioned in this last chapter that pertain to the believer's conduct. Here is a list of those things that are mentioned: brotherly love, Hebrews 13:1; hospitality, Hebrews 13:2; sympathy with those in bonds, Hebrews 13:3; fidelity in the marriage relation, Hebrews 13:4; contentment, Hebrews 13:5-6; submission to those in authority, Hebrews 13:7-8; stability in the doctrines of religion, Hebrews 13:9-15; benevolence, Hebrews 13:16; obedience to those entrusted with office, Hebrews 13:17; and special prayer for him who wrote this epistle, Hebrews 13:18-19. The epistle then closes with a beautiful and impressive benediction that should serve to challenge each of us to a personal commitment to the Lord in regards to our personal conduct, Hebrews 13:20-21.

A. Maintaining a Personal Conduct as It Involves Others. (13:1-3)

Verse one begins with "Let brotherly love continue" as though to say let this be an ongoing virtue that marked these early believers. The phrase *brotherly love* describes an attitude that should mark the church. There should be a family love that even marks the church family. Tenderness and caring one for another should be that which marks us. The word *brotherly* gives a clue as to the kind of love that should mark us and also a study of the word love as it is defined in the Greek gives a further indication of the atmosphere of love that should characterize the church family. Notice what Guzik says regarding the use of the

Greek words for our English word love: "In the ancient Greek language the New Testament was written in, there were four words at hand that we might translate love. *Eros* was one word for love. It described, as we might guess from the word itself, erotic love. It refers to sexual love. *Storge* was a second word for love. It refers to family love, the kind of love there is between a parent and child or between family members in general. *Agape* is another word for love. It is the most powerful word for love in the New Testament, and is often used to describe God's love towards us. It is a love that loves without changing. It is a self-giving love that gives without demanding or expecting re-payment. It is love so great that it can be given to the unlovable or unappealing. It is love that loves even when it is rejected. Agape love gives and loves because it wants to; it does not demand or expect repayment from the love given - it gives because it loves, it does not love in order to receive. Agape love is not about feelings, it is about decisions. But the word for love used in Hebrews 13:1 is *philadelphia*, coming from the root *philia*. This ancient Greek word speaks of a brotherly friendship and affection. It is the love of deep friendship and partnership. There should always be plenty of this kind of love among Christians, and it should continue."

In verse two we are told, *"Be not forgetful to entertain strangers: for thereby some have entertained angels unawares."* In Bible history we know how both Abraham and Lot were called on to entertain angels. The meaning of having a spirit of hospitality is not for the purpose of entertaining angels, as they did, but doing so realizing that according to God's providence, He may have someone to come your way that He has sent which you can be a benefit to in ways that will have eternal value. This kind of hospitality should certainly mark the believer and also his church. When a missionary drops by or calls on the church, we should have a kind and benevolent spirit towards that one realizing that he is a messenger (angel) from God. The word *angel* means "messenger."

When we invite friends over and especially the Lord's servants into our homes, their presence and their influence will have tremendous and long term value. I recall many pastors and missionaries who stayed in my home and the great positive influence that it made on me. That may have strongly contributed to my now being a minister of the Gospel.

Verse three reminds us to remember those who are in bonds and who are suffering adversity. We need to be very careful not to only think of ourselves. There could be those who are suffering for having done right and either are, or have been, imprisoned for such. There will be more and more religious persecution for just doing right as the days proceed. Just this week I received word that a Christian organization is going to be under investigation. The man that is involved in this seems to be a man of real character. Whatever he is being accused of could be very innocent unless a liberal judge interprets otherwise. Then, likewise, we need to pray for any who are going through adversity. Churches are so openly vulnerable to Satan's attack as well as individuals who make up the church. We certainly need to pray for and encourage one another in this area.

B. Maintaining a Personal Conduct as It Involves Oneself. (Vv. 4-6)

In verse four, we are challenged to acknowledge and to maintain the sanctity of marriage. In recent years, marriage has been greatly cheapened. There is a frontal attack on marriage by the devil, the world, and the flesh. If we lessen in our own minds the value and the true meaning and purpose of marriage, we will open our own marriages to "marriage failure." There are many who so slowly are allowing marriage plaque to build up on the heart of their marriage, not realizing that they are preparing themselves for a marriage thrombosis. When the marriage is compromised by unfaithfulness, you are inviting the fiery wrath of God to fall upon you. This kind of judgment should be avoided by every believer in preference to guarding and maintaining a wonderful and a holy relationship to the marriage partner that God has given us. Each of us should remind ourselves from the text: *"Marriage is honourable in all, and the bed undefiled: but whoremongers and adulterers God will judge."* There is no way to escape the warning that is given in our text, when a violation has taken place…

In verse four we are told to have the right attitude towards our marriage partner and in verse five, we are told to have the right attitude towards our material possessions. We should never have a spirit of covetousness. We should remind ourselves that everything we have or own comes from the Lord. Then, when that is so as verse six indicates, we will realize that our help truly comes from the Lord. One of the greatest weaknesses we can encounter in our lifetime is a failure to recognize that the Lord is our Strength and our Substance. Without Him, we have nothing and we can do nothing. We are totally helpless.

II. THE IMPORTANCE OF MAINTAINING ONE'S PRACTICAL CHRISTIANITY. (Vv. 7-19)

We have been given heroes in the faith who have gone before as chapter 11 tells us; we also are being given guides to help us keep our eyes and our ears upon Jesus. Any distraction that we have in life comes from losing our focus and taking our eyes off the Lord Jesus Christ and from not listening to what He has to say. In the span of our lifetime God has given us guides and instructors to help us who have given us a life and testimony to follow. I personally am indebted to so many who have given me good instructions to help me advance in the faith. This is the meaning of verse seven which says, *"Remember them which have the rule over you, who have spoken unto you the word of God: whose faith follow, considering the end of their conversation."* God has appointed within my lifetime and yours, those who are there to give you encouragement to help you stay in the will and the purpose of God. They do not give such instructions for selfish reasons; they do it to share the benefits and the blessings that have constituted their lives. For such reason, we should consider the end or the end results of what they are telling us. We should be careful to have the right attitude towards such.

A. By One's Attitude Towards the Truth. (Vv. 7-14)

Our Christian heritage is given to us to sustain us with reminders from the past. These reminders show us how those before us were able to stay in the race and continue in the faith. We are not only to remember those who went on before us and what they had to say, but we also are not to be "carried about with divers and strange doctrines," because we have One: "Jesus Christ the same yesterday, and to day, and for ever." Barnes understood how valuable this knowledge is for challenging and comforting our hearts when he wrote the following: "The evident design of this independent proposition here is, to encourage them to persevere by showing that their Saviour was always the same; that he who had sustained his people in former times was the same still, and would be the same for ever. The argument here, therefore, for perseverance is founded on the immutability of the Redeemer. If he were fickle, vacillating, changing in his character and plans; if to-day he aids his people, and to-morrow will forsake them; if at one time he loves the virtuous, and at another equally loves the vicious; if he formed a plan yesterday which he has abandoned today; or if he is ever to be a different being from what he is now, there would be no encouragement to effort. Who would know what to depend on? Who would know what to expect tomorrow? For who could have any certainty that he could ever please a capricious or a vacillating being? Who could know how to shape his conduct if the principles of the Divine administration were not always the same? At the same time, also, that this passage furnishes the strongest argument for fidelity and perseverance, it is an irrefragable proof of the divinity of the Saviour. It asserts immutability-sameness in the past, the present, and to all eternity—but of whom can this be affirmed but God? It would not be possible to conceive of a declaration which would more strongly assert immutability than this." (Barnes' Notes on the New Testament)

These next several verses show the way that the Lord Jesus went outside of the gate of religious customs and traditions to the place of offerings and the place of sacrifice. We too, are to identify with Christ by leaving all false religions and false worshipping to worship only Jesus and to be identified with only Christ Jesus. He alone is worthy of such worship and such worship in kind. We identify by faith knowing that we do not have a continuing city here, but we certainly do on the other side.

B. By One's Acceptance of Truth. (Vv. 15-16)

One proves his acceptance of truth by the sacrifice of his lips and by doing well and maintaining a spirit of sharing. This is what the word communicate means. The Greek word means, having in common with others. The meaning is, that they were to show liberality to those who were in want, and were to make a special effort not to forget this sacred duty. This same spirit is seen throughout the First Epistle of John. As born again believers, we should show that we have accepted truth by the applying of truth. Truth should mark us in all of our doings. What we do should be done in a very unselfish manner; we are by nature selfish and must resist the tendency to act so selfishly. This was the problem with Ananias and Sapphira. They were selfishly thinking of themselves. Because of their selfishness the Lord judged them harshly.

C. By One's Acting Upon Truth. (Vv. 17-19)

The first admonition involving the obeying of truth involved mostly those who have already died while leaving behind words of truth that we are to recall to our remembrances. This next admonition involves obeying those who are presently our guides. These are our religious leaders who speak the truth to us in a very unselfish manner knowing that they have both an obligation and also accountability back to the Lord for instructing us in the ways of the Lord. We should give heed to what they say so that it will not be unprofitable to those who refuse to obey the truth.

III. THE IMPORTANCE OF MAINTAINING ONE'S

PERSONAL COMMITMENT. (Vv. 20-25)

Just knowing that we have One who has given us a better Priesthood and with that a better economy, we can be challenged by knowing that He will make us "perfect in every good work to do his will, working in you that which is well pleasing in his sight, through Jesus Christ; to whom be glory for ever and ever." These last few verses are a concluding benediction to some particularly mentioned in the text and also to the readers of the book of Hebrews. As this book closes, the reader who is the believer can keep his eyes upon Jesus as he goes on to perfection.

The Lord does not affirm that the reader is perfect or that he will be perfect in this life, but it carries the idea of being perfected in an eternal sense with God giving the graces that is necessary for being perfected. The meaning of the word perfect as used here means that Paul prayed that God would fully endow them with whatever grace that was necessary for the believer to do His will and to keep His commandments. This is the purpose of Hebrews being written; that as believers we can clearly see that we have much better things, as we LOOK UNTO JESUS!

Bibliography

Barnes, Albert. *Barnes' Notes on the New Testament*. Baker Pub Group, June, 1990.

Cloud, David. *Bible History and Geography*. Way of Life Literature, 2002.

Gill, John. *Exposition of the Old and New Testaments*. Mathews & Leigh-London, 1810.

Henry, Matthew. *The Matthew Henry Commentary*. Zondervan Publishing House, 1961.

Murray, Andrew. *The Holiest of All, An Exposition of the Epistle to the Hebrews*. Whitaker House Publishers, 2004.

Murray, Andrew. *Jesus Christ: Prophet Priest*. Mass Market Paperback.

Made in the USA
Columbia, SC
31 July 2024

33fad0d6-563a-430a-9ecd-df91ab9e2477R01